Alexis De Vos

Reversible Computing

Related Titles

Weidemüller, M., Zimmermann, C. (eds.)

Cold Atoms and Molecules
Concepts, Experiments and Applications to Fundamental Physics

2009
ISBN: 978-3-527-40750-7

Wolf, E. L.

Quantum Nanoelectronics
An Introduction to Electronic Nanotechnology and Quantum Computing

2009
ISBN: 978-3-527-40749-1

Morsch, O.

Quantum Bits and Quantum Secrets
How Quantum Physics is Revolutionizing Codes and Computers

2008
ISBN: 978-3-527-40710-1

Stolze, J., Suter, D.

Quantum Computing
A Short Course from Theory to Experiment

2008
ISBN: 978-3-527-40787-3

Imre, S., Balazs, F.

Quantum Computing and Communications
An Engineering Approach

2004
ISBN: 978-0-470-86902-4

Alexis De Vos

Reversible Computing

Fundamentals, Quantum Computing, and Applications

WILEY-VCH

WILEY-VCH Verlag GmbH & Co. KGaA

The Author

Prof. Dr. Alexis De Vos
Universiteit Gent
elektronika en informatiesystemen
Sint Pietersnieuwstraat 41
9000 Gent
Belgium

All books published by Wiley-VCH are carefully produced. Nevertheless, authors, editors, and publisher do not warrant the information contained in these books, including this book, to be free of errors. Readers are advised to keep in mind that statements, data, illustrations, procedural details or other items may inadvertently be inaccurate.

Library of Congress Card No.: applied for

British Library Cataloguing-in-Publication Data:
A catalogue record for this book is available from the British Library.

Bibliographic information published by the Deutsche Nationalbibliothek
The Deutsche Nationalbibliothek lists this publication in the Deutsche Nationalbibliografie; detailed bibliographic data are available on the Internet at http://dnb.d-nb.de.

© 2010 WILEY-VCH Verlag GmbH & Co. KGaA, Weinheim

Typesetting   le-tex publishing services GmbH, Leipzig
Printing and Binding   Fabulous Printers Pte Ltd, Singapore
Cover Design   Formgeber, Eppelheim

Printed in Singapore
Printed on acid-free paper

ISBN 978-3-527-40992-1

Contents

Reversible Computing. Alexis De Vos
Copyright © 2010 WILEY-VCH Verlag GmbH & Co. KGaA, Weinheim
ISBN: 978-3-527-40992-1

Preface

The present book is dedicated to Dr. Rolf Landauer, whose early work on the subject of reversible computing inspired me to begin more than 15 years of research in this special corner of computer science. Twice I had the privilege to meet him personally: once in West Berlin (1992) and once in Boston (1996). Twice he encouraged me to continue my investigations. My research became a fascinating journey, exploring the various aspects of reversible computing. The present book aims to illustrate how the subject is interwoven with many different sections of mathematics, physics, electronics, and informatics. Reversible computers are related to low-power computing, digital electronics, analog and neural computing, quantum mechanics, as well as Boolean algebra, group theory, Lie groups and many more.

I wish to thank the three people whose support has been fruitful for many years, and without whom the book would never have been written:

- Prof. Herman Pauwels,
- Prof. Marc Vanwormhoudt,
- Prof. Andreas De Leenheer,

all three from the Universiteit Gent. I especially wish to thank people whose detailed comments, contributions and suggestions have been a continuing inspiration and encouragement:

- Prof. Leo Storme of the Universiteit Gent,
- Dr Stijn De Baerdemacker and Dr Jan De Beule of the Universiteit Gent,
- Prof. Paweł Kerntopf of the Politechnika Warszawskiego,
- Prof. Robert Glück of the Københavns Universitet, and
- Prof. Bernd Steinbach of the Bergakademie Freiberg.

The following institutions gave invaluable support:

- the *v.z.w.* Imec (i.e., the Flemish Interuniversity Microelectronics Center), and
- the Universiteit Gent.

Reversible Computing. Alexis De Vos
Copyright © 2010 WILEY-VCH Verlag GmbH & Co. KGaA, Weinheim
ISBN: 978-3-527-40992-1

In particular,

- the *Invomec* division of *v.z.w.* Imec, and
- the *Eurochip* and *Europractice* consortia

gave invaluable aid with the realization of prototype chips at *Alcatel Microelectronics* (Oudenaarde, Belgium), *Austria Mikro Systeme* (Unterpremstätten, Austria), and *AMI Semiconductor* (Oudenaarde, Belgium). Finally, the following people are thanked for their direct help with the accomplishment of the book:

- Ph.D. students Bart Desoete, Filip Beunis, and Yvan Van Rentergem for their precious scientific contributions,
- Jean Bekaert for drawing all figures (the scientific and technical diagrams as well as the artist's impressions and the cover),
- Michael Thomsen for carefully checking the text of Chapter 8, and
- the staff of Wiley-VCH Verlag for their valuable help in editing the book.

Gent, 28 June 2010   *Alexis De Vos*

Introduction

We are living in a world with an ever-increasing hunger for energy. Human energy consumption continues to grow. This evolution is not without problems, such as fuel depletion, waste disposal and climate change. Therefore, huge efforts are being made to appease our hunger for energy in a manner that generates as little damage to our environment as possible. We try to harvest renewable energy sources. We try to convert one kind of energy into another as smoothly as possible. We try to transport energy as efficiently as possible. When searching for ideal equipment to do this, engineers often refer to the Carnot engine (named after the young but visionary French engineer Sadi Carnot) as the ideal standard. This engine constitutes the ideal limit of a heat engine that converts heat into work, and attains the ultimate efficiency, known as the Carnot efficiency. Such an engine, which in the real world can only be approximated by a real engine, has the peculiar property of being reversible. This means that it runs so slowly and gently, that, at any moment, we may, by an infinitesimally small intervention, decide to reverse its sense of operation. By making an infinitely small change to an external parameter, all inside velocities, revolutions, heat flows, work flows, and so on are reversed. Produced power becomes consumed power; heat engine becomes heat pump; clockwise becomes counterclockwise; forward becomes backward.

While reversible heat engines have long been conceived (and approximated in technology), this is also true of reversible chemical engines. Conventional motors are based on the internal combustion of fuel. In the combustion chamber, a chemical reaction occurs in the form of a deflagration. Once the combustion has been initiated (by either a spark or compression), little control over it is possible, and it is very difficult to stop or reverse the burning reaction. In contrast, when it is performed in a so-called fuel cell, the same chemical reaction (oxidation) occurs in a reversible way. By applying an appropriate (external) electric voltage, we can control the direction (forward or reverse) of a chemical reaction and how swiftly it occurs. In the case of an ideal fuel cell, an infinitely small change in the external voltage is sufficient to change the direction of the chemical reaction: associations between atoms become dissociations of molecules; oxidation becomes reduction. It is no surprise that fuel cells display a much higher efficiency than internal combustion engines.

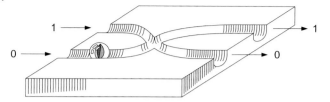

Figure 1 The simplest possible reversible computer.

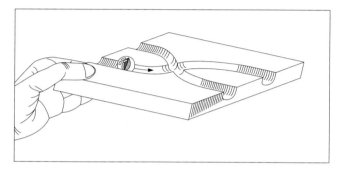

Figure 2 Computation.

Besides an ever-increasing hunger for energy, our society also displays an ever-increasing hunger for information. People are constantly harvesting, transporting and processing information. Little attention has been paid to the efficiency of these processes. Little effort has been expended to make these processes reversible. A loudspeaker converts electrical information into acoustic signals. For the inverse operation, we use another device: a microphone. However, the laws of physics allow the construction of devices that perform both conversions, according to an outside signal that we can influence. Current computer hardware and software are designed to perform computations in a definite direction, from input information to output information, from *questions* to *answers*. However, we can also conceive systems that can compute in either direction (forward or backward), and where the direction of computation can be chosen by the user. Indeed, at any moment (e.g., in the middle of a calculation), the user could change his or her mind and decide to alter the direction of computation. Such reversible computing models allow us to explore the fundamentals of computation, independent of any particular choice of computer hardware and computer language.

An example is shown in Figure 1, which depicts the simplest possible reversible computer. This is a mechanical computer that computes with one bit. It computes the inverse of an input number, which either is 0 or 1. In the former case (see Figure 2), the result is NOT(0) = 1; in the latter case, the result is NOT(1) = 0. The computation is triggered by gently raising the hand so that the bit (i.e., the marble) slowly descends from the input side (left) to the output side (right).

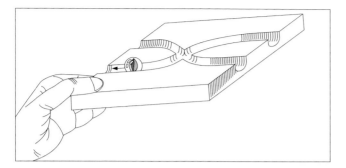

Figure 3 Decomputation.

After the marble arrives, we can change the direction of the slope in order to 'undo' the calculation and reproduce the original starting situation. Moreover, if we apply a very shallow slope, we can reverse this slope at any moment (e.g., in the middle of a computation) by exerting an infinitesimally small mechanical effort, resulting in a decomputation (see Figure 3).

Reversible energy conversion and reversible information conversion are not independent subjects. In our example, the gradient in the gravitational potential energy dictates the direction of computing. On the other hand, it is important to realize that about 10% of the world's electricity consumption is dissipated in computers. If we also consider audio and video equipment to be information processing systems, more than 20% of all electrical power is consumed in information transport and information manipulation (the rest is used for lighting, cooking, . . .).

The toy computer in the above figures demonstrates that bit manipulation happens through the manipulation of physical objects. In the words of Landauer, "information is physical". There is no such thing as a 'bare' information particle (informaton). Bits piggyback on material objects (marbles, electrons, ions, photons, . . .). The reversible manipulation of information and the reversible manipulation of information carriers cannot be separated. It is thus no surprise that the key to energy-efficient computing is reversible computing.

We can therefore state that the study of reversible computing leads to two benefits: on the one hand, it leads to an understanding of the basic principles; on the other hand, it leads to recipes for efficient implementations. We should not forget that Carnot's 1824 book *Réflexions sur la puissance motrice du feu et sur les machines propres à développer cette puissance*[1] was the foundation for both a new science (thermodynamics) and a new technology (steam power).

---

1) Reflections on the Motive Power of Fire and on the Machines Fitted to Develop this Power.

1
Boolean Algebra

The vast majority of computers are digital computers; that is, computers based on a set of two numbers: $\mathbb{B} = \{0, 1\}$. We call the mathematics based on these two numbers Boolean algebra (named after the Irish mathematician George Boole). A Boolean variable or bit can thus take only two different values: either 0 or 1. We call $f(A_1, A_2, \ldots, A_n)$ a Boolean function of n independent Boolean variables A_1, $A_2, \ldots, A_{n-1}$, and A_n. It takes either the value 0 or the value 1, depending on the values of its arguments $A_1, A_2, \ldots, A_n$. This dependency is fully described using a truth table, which tells us which value f takes for each of the 2^n different values of the (Boolean) vector $(A_1, A_2, \ldots, A_n)$.

In the present chapter, we will survey some properties of Boolean functions, which will allow us to gain a good understanding of binary reversible logic circuits. First, we will take a close look at Boolean functions $f(A)$ of a single variable, then at Boolean functions $f(A_1, A_2)$ of two variables, before we discuss Boolean functions $f(A_1, A_2, \ldots, A_n)$ of an arbitrary number of Boolean variables. Besides recording a Boolean function unambiguously by writing down its truth table, we can also fully define a Boolean function by means of a (Boolean) formula. There are many ways to write down such a formula. We will discuss some standard ways: the minterm expansion, the maxterm expansion, the Reed–Muller expansion, and the minimal ESOP expansion. Finally, we will define a few special classes of Boolean functions: true functions and balanced functions, linear functions, affine linear functions, and monotonic functions.

1.1
Boolean Functions of One Variable

There are only four Boolean functions $f(A)$ of a single Boolean variable A. Table 1.1 shows the four corresponding truth tables. However, two of these functions are not really dependent on A; they are constants:

$$f(A) = 0 \quad \text{(Table 1.1a)}$$
$$f(A) = 1 \quad \text{(Table 1.1b)} .$$

Reversible Computing. Alexis De Vos
Copyright © 2010 WILEY-VCH Verlag GmbH & Co. KGaA, Weinheim
ISBN: 978-3-527-40992-1

Table 1.1 Truth table of the four Boolean functions $f(A)$: (a) the constant function 0, (b) the constant function 1, (c) the identity function, and (d) the NOT function.

A	f
0	0
1	0

(a)

A	f
0	1
1	1

(b)

A	f
0	0
1	1

(c)

A	f
0	1
1	0

(d)

We thus have only two true functions (or proper functions) of A:

$$f(A) = A \quad \text{(Table 1.1c)}$$
$$f(A) = \overline{A} \quad \text{(Table 1.1d)} \;.$$

Here, we have introduced the following shorthand notation for the inverting function or NOT function:

$$\overline{X} = \text{NOT } X \;.$$

1.2
Boolean Functions of Two Variables

There are $2^4 = 16$ different Boolean functions of two variables[2]. Table 1.2 shows them all. However, some of these functions $f(A, B)$ are not actually functions of A and B; two functions are independent of both A and B. They are constants:

$$f_0(A, B) = 0$$
$$f_{15}(A, B) = 1 \;.$$

Another four functions are in fact functions of a single variable; f_3 and f_{12} are independent of B, whereas both f_5 and f_{10} are independent of A:

$$f_3(A, B) = A$$
$$f_5(A, B) = B$$
$$f_{10}(A, B) = \overline{B}$$
$$f_{12}(A, B) = \overline{A} \;.$$

This leaves only $16 - 2 - 4 = 10$ functions that are truely dependent on both A and B. We call them *true functions* of A and B.

2) Besides using the notation $A_1, A_2, \ldots, A_n$ for the variables, we will also use the letters $A, B, C, \ldots$ whenever this is more convenient.

Table 1.2 Truth table of all sixteen Boolean functions $f_i(A, B)$.

AB	f_0	f_1	f_2	f_3	f_4	f_5	f_6	f_7	f_8	f_9	f_{10}	f_{11}	f_{12}	f_{13}	f_{14}	f_{15}
0 0	0	0	0	0	0	0	0	0	1	1	1	1	1	1	1	1
0 1	0	0	0	0	1	1	1	1	0	0	0	0	1	1	1	1
1 0	0	0	1	1	0	0	1	1	0	0	1	1	0	0	1	1
1 1	0	1	0	1	0	1	0	1	0	1	0	1	0	1	0	1

Table 1.3 Truth tables of three basic Boolean functions: (a) the AND function, (b) the OR function, and (c) the XOR function.

AB	f
0 0	0
0 1	0
1 0	0
1 1	1

(a)

AB	f
0 0	0
0 1	1
1 0	1
1 1	1

(b)

AB	f
0 0	0
0 1	1
1 0	1
1 1	0

(c)

Three out of the ten true functions of two variables (i.e., f_1, f_7, and f_6) are well known: the AND function, the OR function, and the XOR function (also known as the EXCLUSIVE OR). Table 1.3 gives the corresponding truth tables. We will use the following shorthand notations for these basic Boolean functions:

$$X Y = X \text{ AND } Y$$
$$X + Y = X \text{ OR } Y$$
$$X \oplus Y = X \text{ XOR } Y \, .$$

The remaining $10 - 3 = 7$ functions are considered a combination of the NOT, AND, OR, and XOR functions. For example,

$$f_2(A, B) = A \text{ AND } (\text{NOT } B) = A\overline{B} \, .$$

For convenience, the NOT of an AND is called a NAND, the NOT of an OR is called a NOR, and the NOT of a XOR is called a NXOR. For example,

$$f_8(A, B) = \text{NOT } (A \text{ OR } B) = \overline{A + B} = A \text{ NOR } B \, .$$

NXOR is also called XAND, with the shorthand notation $X \odot Y$.

We observe that all six functions AND, OR, XOR, NAND, NOR, and NXOR are commutative:

$$X \text{ AND } Y = Y \text{ AND } X \, ,$$

and there are similar identities for the other five functions. This is not the case for any function $f(X, Y)$. For example, the function f_2 is not commutative:

$$f_2(X, Y) \neq f_2(Y, X) \quad \text{but} \quad f_2(X, Y) = f_4(Y, X) .$$

We end this section by stressing that there is no fundamental difference between the functions AND, OR, NAND, and NOR. They all are true functions that have either one 0 and three 1s or three 0s and one 1 in their truth tables. The functions XOR and NXOR are fundamentally different: they display two 0s and two 1s in their truth tables. This important distinction between AND, OR, NAND, and NOR on the one hand and XOR and NXOR on the other was stressed by Yokoyama *et al.* [1]. The function A XOR B is *injective* in its first argument, as is NXOR. This means that, for each value of B, the equality A XOR $B = A'$ XOR B necessarily implies $A = A'$. The reader can easily verify that this is not the case with the AND function for example: A AND $0 = A'$ AND 0 does not imply $A = A'$ (as we could have $A = 0$ and $A' = 1$). These facts will have far-reaching consequences.

1.3
Boolean Functions of *n* Variables

There are 2^{2^n} different Boolean functions of n variables. Each is represented by a truth table consisting of $n + 1$ columns and 2^n rows. Table 1.4 gives an example for $n = 3$. This function is just one of the $2^8 = 256$ possible for $n = 3$. Among these, only 218 are true functions of the three variables A, B, and C. Among the 256 functions for $n = 3$, seventy are so-called balanced functions; that is, functions that have an equal number of 1s and 0s in the output column. The function shown in Table 1.4 is both true and balanced.

It is important to use the expressions *true* and *balanced* carefully. For example, the function $A\overline{B}$ is a true function of A and B, but is an untrue function of A, B,

Table 1.4 Truth table of a function $f(A, B, C)$ of three variables.

$A\,B\,C$	f
0 0 0	0
0 0 1	1
0 1 0	1
0 1 1	0
1 0 0	1
1 0 1	0
1 1 0	1
1 1 1	0

and *C*. It is not a balanced function of *A* and *B*, but it is a balanced function of the three variables *A*, *B*, and *C*. The reader may also notice the following property: all untrue functions are balanced.

A truth table can be summarized by a single Boolean formula. However, there are multiple ways to write a given table as a Boolean expression [2]. We will now discuss a few of them.

1.3.1
The Minterm Expansion

Using the truth table, it is immediately possible to deduce the Boolean formula called the *minterm expansion*. For example, Table 1.4 yields:

$$f(A, B, C) = \overline{A}\,\overline{B}C + \overline{A}B\overline{C} + A\overline{B}\,\overline{C} + AB\overline{C} \,.$$

This consists of the OR of different terms. There are between 0 and 2^n different terms present. Each term is called a minterm and consists of the AND of exactly *n* literals. Here a literal is a letter, either inverted or not; thus, whereas *X* is called a letter, both *X* and $\overline{X}$ are called literals.

The algorithm for translating the truth table in the minterm expansion is straightforward: each row of the truth table with a 1 in the column furthest to the right yields one minterm. The latter consists of an AND of all input letters; an overlining is used if a 0 appears in the corresponding column, but not if a 1 appears in the corresponding column.

In the literature, such an expansion is sometimes referred to as a *sum of products*, because an OR resembles a sum in a way, while an AND resembles a product to some extext. The abbreviation SOP is also often used.

1.3.2
The Maxterm Expansion

As there is no fundamental difference between OR and AND, it is no surprise that there is a function expansion that is like the minterm expansion but has the roles of OR and AND interchanged. Such an expansion is an AND of ORs, and is called a *maxterm expansion*. In our example (Table 1.4), we have

$$f(A, B, C) = (A + B + C)(A + \overline{B} + \overline{C})(\overline{A} + B + C)(\overline{A} + \overline{B} + \overline{C}) \,.$$

The algorithm for translating the truth table into the maxterm expansion is completely analogous to the minterm algorithm: each row of the truth table with a 0 in the column furthest to the right yields one maxterm; the latter consists of an OR of all input letters, with a bar if a 1 appears in the corresponding column, and not if a 0 appears in the corresponding column. The maxterm expansion is an example of a POS or *product of sums*.

1.3.3
The Reed–Muller Expansion

A fundamentally different expansion is obtained as follows. We apply to the minterm expansion the two identities

$$\overline{X} = 1 \oplus X$$
$$X + Y = X \oplus Y \oplus XY . \tag{1.1}$$

This leads to an XOR of ANDs. The result is subsequently simplified by applying the identities

$$X \oplus X = 0$$
$$0 \oplus X = X .$$

In our example (Table 1.4), we obtain

$$f(A, B, C) = A \oplus B \oplus C \oplus AB . \tag{1.2}$$

A Reed–Muller expansion (named after the American mathematicians Irving Reed and David Muller) is an example of an ESOP expansion; that is, an 'EXCLUSIVE-OR sum of products'. Thus, just like the OR, the XOR function is considered a kind of sum. We note that the Reed–Muller expansion is fundamentally different from the minterm and maxterm expansions because of the *injectivity* of the XOR operation.

In many respects, a Reed–Muller expansion of a Boolean function resembles the well-known Taylor expansion of ordinary calculus. Let us assume a function f of the real numbers x, y, and z. Then, the Taylor expansion around the point $(x, y, z) = (0, 0, 0)$ looks like

$$\begin{aligned} f(x, y, z) = {} & c_{000} + c_{100}x + c_{010}y + c_{001}z \\ & + c_{110}xy + c_{101}xz + c_{011}yz + c_{200}x^2 + c_{020}y^2 + c_{002}z^2 \\ & + c_{111}xyz + c_{210}x^2y + \dots . \end{aligned}$$

The Reed–Muller expansion of a function f of the Boolean numbers A, B, and C looks like

$$\begin{aligned} f(A, B, C) = {} & c_{000} \oplus c_{100}A \oplus c_{010}B \oplus c_{001}C \\ & \oplus c_{110}AB \oplus c_{101}AC \oplus c_{011}BC \oplus c_{111}ABC . \end{aligned}$$

There are three main differences:

- The Reed–Muller coefficients c_{ijk} can only be either 0 or 1.
- Each of the exponents i, j, and k in the monomial (also known as the 'piterm') $A^i B^j C^k$ can only be either 0 or 1; as a result:
- There are only a finite number (i.e., a maximum of 2^n) of Reed–Muller terms.

Once again, we must stress that there is no fundamental difference between AND and OR, or between XOR and XAND. As the Reed–Muller expansion is an XOR of ANDs, there is a similar (dual) expansion that is an XAND of ORs [3, 4]. For example, expansion (1.2) can be rewritten as

$$f(A, B, C) = A \odot C \odot (A + C) \odot (B + C) .$$

Unfortunately, such expressions are paid little attention in the literature.

We end this section by noting that (at least for $n > 1$), the Reed–Muller expansion of a balanced function lacks the highest-degree term $A_1 A_2 \ldots A_n$. In other words, the Reed–Muller coefficient $c_{11\ldots1}$ of a balanced function is zero.

1.3.4
The Minimal ESOP Expansion

In the Reed–Muller expansion, NOT functions are not allowed.[3] If we do allow NOT operations, the 'XOR of ANDs' expansion can be shortened. The shortest expansion (i.e., the one with the fewest literals) is called the minimal ESOP expansion.

The minimal ESOP expansion is quite different from the three above expansions (i.e., the minterm expansion, the maxterm expansion, and the Reed–Muller expansion) in two respects:

- It is not unique: two or even more minimal ESOP expansions of the same Boolean function may exist, and
- There is no straightforward algorithm for finding the minimal ESOP expansion(s) (except, of course, for an exhaustive search).

The last fact explains why minimal ESOPs are only known for Boolean functions with $n = 6$ or less [5, 6].
Our example function (Table 1.4) has two different minimal ESOPs:

$$\begin{aligned} f(A, B, C) &= A \oplus C \oplus \overline{A} B \\ &= B \oplus C \oplus A \overline{B} . \end{aligned}$$

Whereas the Reed–Muller expansion (1.2) needs five literals, these minimal ESOPs contain only four literals.

1.4
Linear Functions

A function $f(A_1, A_2, \ldots, A_n)$ is linear iff ('iff' means 'if and only if') its Reed–Muller expansion only contains terms with one letter:

$$f(A_1, A_2, \ldots, A_n) = c_1 A_1 \oplus c_2 A_2 \oplus \cdots \oplus c_n A_n .$$

---

3) In the present book we limit ourselves to so-called 'positive-polarity Reed–Muller expansions'. We thus ignore 'negative-polarity Reed–Muller expansions' and 'mixed-polarity Reed–Muller expansions' [2].

Table 1.5 Truth tables for (a) a linear function, (b) an affine linear function, and (c) a monotonic function.

ABC	f
0 0 0	0
0 0 1	1
0 1 0	0
0 1 1	1
1 0 0	1
1 0 1	0
1 1 0	1
1 1 1	0

(a)

ABC	f
0 0 0	1
0 0 1	1
0 1 0	0
0 1 1	0
1 0 0	0
1 0 1	0
1 1 0	1
1 1 1	1

(b)

ABC	f
0 0 0	0
0 0 1	1
0 1 0	0
0 1 1	1
1 0 0	1
1 0 1	1
1 1 0	1
1 1 1	1

(c)

Because each of the n Reed–Muller coefficients c_j can take one of two values ($c_j \in \{0, 1\}$), the reader can easily verify that there are 2^n different linear functions with n arguments. It is clear that the function defined by Table 1.4 is not linear: its Reed–Muller expansion (1.2) contains a second-degree term AB. In contrast, the function defined by Table 1.5a is linear, as it equals $A \oplus C$.

1.5
Affine Linear Functions

A function $f(A_1, A_2, \ldots, A_n)$ is *affine linear*[4] iff its Reed–Muller expansion contains only terms with either zero or one letter:

$$f(A_1, A_2, \ldots, A_n) = c_0 \oplus c_1 A_1 \oplus c_2 A_2 \oplus \cdots \oplus c_n A_n \,.$$

Because each of the $n + 1$ Reed–Muller coefficients c_j can take one of two values, there are 2^{n+1} different affine linear functions of n arguments. Among these, 2^n are linear. The function defined by Table 1.5b is an example of an affine linear function, as it equals $1 \oplus A \oplus B$.

---

4) There seems to be some confusion about the meaning of the word 'linear'. Let us consider the ordinary functions $f(x)$ of a real variable x. Sometimes all of the functions $f(x) = ax + b$ are said to be 'linear'; sometimes only the functions $f(x) = ax$ are considered 'linear'. In the present book, we follow the latter convention, so that the functions $ax + b$ are said to be 'affine linear'.

1.6
Monotonic Functions

We consider a function of n binary variables A_i. We use the different values of the vector $(A_1, A_2, \ldots, A_n)$ as the coordinates of an n-dimensional hypercube. We can represent a Boolean function by giving each corner of the hypercube a label $f(A_1, A_2, \ldots, A_n)$. We call a path that travels from the point $(0, 0, \ldots, 0)$ to the point $(1, 1, \ldots, 1)$ via consecutive steps that each increase a single coordinate A_i from 0 to 1 a *climbing path*. Such a path necessarily contains n steps, with each being an edge of the hypercube. Note that:

- There are n possible choices for the first step,
- There are $n - 1$ possible choices for the second step,
- ...
- There are $n - j + 1$ possible choices for the jth step.

This means that there are $n!$ different climbing paths.

A Boolean function $f(A_1, A_2, \ldots, A_n)$ is *monotonic* (or monotone or unate) iff its value increases along each climbing path: $f(A'_1, A'_2, \ldots, A'_n) \geq f(A''_1, A''_2, \ldots, A''_n)$ as soon as $A'_i \geq A''_i$ for all i satisfying $1 \leq i \leq n$. There is no closed formula for the number of monotonic functions [7]. Neither Table 1.4 nor Table 1.5a nor Table 1.5b is a truth table of a monotonic function. Indeed, for each of these three functions, vertex $(0, 0, 1)$ of the hypercube has a label of 1, whereas vertex $(1, 0, 1)$ of the hypercube has a label of 0, such that f does not increase along the climbing path $(0, 0, 0)$–$(0, 0, 1)$–$(1, 0, 1)$–$(1, 1, 1)$. In contrast, the function defined by Table 1.5c is monotonic.

1.7
Boolean Derivative

Besides Boolean algebra, there is also Boolean calculus, which describes time-dependencies for example. At this point, it is sufficient to mention the three so-called subfunctions of a Boolean function $f(A_1, A_2, \ldots, A_{j-1}, A_j, A_{j+1}, \ldots, A_n)$:

$$f'(A_1, A_2, \ldots, A_{j-1}, A_j, A_{j+1}, \ldots, A_n) = \\ f(A_1, A_2, \ldots, A_{j-1}, 0, A_{j+1}, \ldots, A_n)$$
$$f''(A_1, A_2, \ldots, A_{j-1}, A_j, A_{j+1}, \ldots, A_n) = \\ f(A_1, A_2, \ldots, A_{j-1}, 1, A_{j+1}, \ldots, A_n)$$
$$f'''(A_1, A_2, \ldots, A_{j-1}, A_j, A_{j+1}, \ldots, A_n) = f' \oplus f'' .$$

All three functions are independent of A_j, and are thus untrue functions of $A_1, A_2, \ldots, A_n$. Sometimes [8, 9] f''' is called the partial derivative of f with respect to A_j, and it is then denoted $\frac{\partial f}{\partial A_j}$. The reason for this name may be made

Table 1.6 Truth tables of the three subfunctions f', f'', and f''' of the function $f(A, B, C)$ of Table 1.4.

$B\,C$	f'
0 0	0
0 1	1
1 0	1
1 1	0

(a)

$B\,C$	f''
0 0	1
0 1	0
1 0	1
1 1	0

(b)

$B\,C$	f'''
0 0	1
0 1	1
1 0	0
1 1	0

(c)

clearer by

$$\frac{\partial f}{\partial A_j} = \frac{f(A_j = 1) \oplus f(A_j = 0)}{1 \oplus 0},$$

which is a Boolean variant of the ordinary derivative of a real function $f(x_1, x_2, \ldots, x_n)$:

$$\frac{\partial f}{\partial x_j} = \lim_{a \to 0} \frac{f(x_j = a) - f(x_j = 0)}{a - 0}.$$

We apply the above to the example function $f(A, B, C)$ of Table 1.4 by choosing A_j to be equal to A. The subfunctions f' and f'' are found by merely slicing Table 1.4 into two halves, yielding Table 1.6a and Table 1.6b, respectively. The subfunction f''' is subsequently constructed by XORing the columns f' and f'', yielding Table 1.6c.

1.8
Boolean Decompositions

Subfunctions are particularly useful when implementing a Boolean function. Assume that we want to build a hardware circuit that realizes a function f of n variables. We have the following identities:

$$\begin{aligned}
f &= f' \overline{A_j} + f'' A_j \\
&= f' \oplus f''' A_j.
\end{aligned} \tag{1.3}$$

The former expression is called the Shannon decomposition (named after the American engineer Claude Shannon); the latter expression is known as the Davio decomposition (after the Belgian engineer Marc Davio).[5] As the subfunctions f',

5) We limit ourselves here to the so-called 'positive Davio decomposition'. We thus ignore the 'negative Davio decomposition' $f'' \oplus f''' \overline{A_j}$.

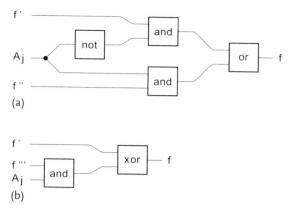

(a)

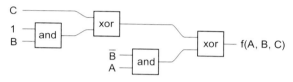

(b)

Figure 1.1 Circuit decompositions: (a) Shannon decomposition, (b) Davio decomposition.

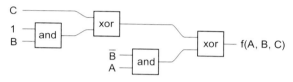

Figure 1.2 Davio decomposition.

f'', and f''' are functions of only $n - 1$ variables, both identities allow us to reduce the original design problem to two smaller design problems. Applying such a decomposition over and over again (each time with another variable A_j) eventually allows the synthesis problem to be reduced to trivial functions (i.e., literals or constants). Figure 1.1 shows the two circuit decompositions.

Figure 1.2 shows the result of applying the Davio decomposition to the example function (Table 1.4) twice: once with $A_j = A$ (right side of the figure), and then with $A_j = B$ (left side).

1.9
Exercises for Chapter 1

Exercise 1.1
XOR and XAND are injective in the first argument; OR, NOR, AND, and NAND are non-injective in the first argument. Verify that the same properties hold in the second argument (why is this the case?).

Exercise 1.2
Which of the 16 functions $f(A, B)$ is both injective in the first argument and non-injective in the second argument?

Exercise 1.3
Prove the second identity in (1.1). Demonstrate that, if X and Y represent different minterms, then this simplifies to

$$X + Y = X \oplus Y \, .$$

Exercise 1.4
Apply (1.1) in order to obtain (1.2).

Exercise 1.5
Verify the dual identities of (1.1):

$$\overline{X} = 0 \odot X$$
$$X Y = X \odot Y \odot (X + Y) \, .$$

Exercise 1.6
A Boolean function is said to be 'even' if it has an even number of 1s (and thus also an even number of 0s) in its truth table. Otherwise, it is said to be 'odd'. In other words, an even function has an even number of terms in its minterm expansion, while an odd function has an odd number of terms in its minterm expansion. Demonstrate the following properties:

- If both f and g are even, then $f \oplus g$ is even.
- If both f and g are odd, then $f \oplus g$ is even.
- If f is even and g is odd, then $f \oplus g$ is odd.

Exercise 1.7
Prove the property mentioned at the end of Section 1.3.3: that all balanced functions lack the highest-degree term $A_1 A_2 \ldots A_n$ in their Reed–Muller expansions. Demonstrate (with the help of a counterexample) that the inverse theorem (i.e., that all functions lacking the highest-degree Reed–Muller term are balanced) is false.

Exercise 1.8
Find the minterm expansion, the maxterm expansion, the Reed–Muller expansion, and the minimum ESOP expansions of the function $f_2(A, B)$ of Table 1.2.

Exercise 1.9
Check (1.3).

2
Group Theory

2.1
Introduction

One very important mathematical tool for investigating reversible circuits and computers is the group. For mathematicians, a group **G** is a combination of two things:

- A set $S = \{a, b, c, \ldots\}$, and
- An operation Ω (involving two elements of the set).

However, the set and operation must fulfil four conditions. Applying the infix notation for the bivariate function Ω, these conditions are:

- S must be closed:
  $a \, \Omega \, b \in S$.
- Ω must be associative:
  $(a \, \Omega \, b) \, \Omega \, c = a \, \Omega \, (b \, \Omega \, c)$.
- S must have an identity element i:
  $a \, \Omega \, i = a$.
- Each element of S must have an inverse in S:
  $a \, \Omega \, a^{-1} = i$.

The number of elements in the set is called the order of the group.

We start with an example. The set of all 2^{2^n} Boolean functions of n variables (Section 1.3) forms a group with respect to the operation XOR (and thus with $\Omega = \text{XOR}$). All four conditions are fulfilled:

- If f_1 and f_2 are Boolean functions, then $f_1 \oplus f_2$ is too.
- If f_1, f_2, and f_3 are Boolean functions, then $(f_1 \oplus f_2) \oplus f_3$ equals $f_1 \oplus (f_2 \oplus f_3)$. Therefore, we simply write $f_1 \oplus f_2 \oplus f_3$.
- There is an identity element i: the zero function 0. Indeed, if f is an arbitrary function, then $f \oplus 0 = 0 \oplus f = f$.
- If f is an arbitrary function, f is its own inverse, as $f \oplus f = 0$.

Reversible Computing. Alexis De Vos
Copyright © 2010 WILEY-VCH Verlag GmbH & Co. KGaA, Weinheim
ISBN: 978-3-527-40992-1

A counterexample is obtained by combining the same set with the OR operation. We have:

- If f_1 and f_2 are Boolean functions, then $f_1 + f_2$ is too.
- If f_1, f_2, and f_3 are Boolean functions, then $(f_1 + f_2) + f_3$ equals $f_1 + (f_2 + f_3)$.
- There is an identity element $i = 0$. If f is an arbitrary function, then $f + 0 = 0 + f = f$.

However, if f is an arbitrary function that is different from the zero function (and thus there is at least one 1 in the output column of the truth table), then there is no function g such that $f + g = 0$. Thus, the last group condition (existence of an inverse) is not fulfilled. This once again illustrates the fundamental difference between the XOR and NXOR operations on the one side, and the OR, NOR, AND, and NAND operations on the other hand.

We now give a second example of a group. The set S contains only two elements: the zero function 0 and one particular Boolean function f of n variables, with only one 1 in the truth table's output column. In other words, the minterm expansion of f consists of a single minterm. Therefore, we call it a minterm function. For a group, besides the set $S = \{0, f\}$, we also need a bivariate operation. The operation Ω is again the XOR function. The reader is invited to verify that all group conditions are fulfilled, such as the first group condition (in other words, that $0 \oplus 0$, $0 \oplus f$, $f \oplus 0$, and $f \oplus f$ are in $\{0, f\}$). We may call the group a *minterm group*. The order of the group is 2. Mathematicians call this group the 'symmetric group of degree 2', which is denoted $\mathbf{S}_2$. In general, the symmetric group of degree n consists of all possible permutations of n objects. It is denoted $\mathbf{S}_n$ and is of order $n!$ (i.e., the factorial of n). This will occupy center stage in the present book.

Below, we will drop the explicit rendering of the symbol Ω by writing ab instead of $a\Omega b$. We also will call ab the product of a and b, even in cases where Ω is not a multiplication. Note that ab is often not the same as ba. Groups where $ab = ba$ for all couples $\{a, b\}$ are called *commutative* or *Abelian* groups (after the young Norwegian mathematician Niels Abel, pioneer of the theory of finite groups). Most of the groups we encounter in the present book are *not* Abelian. The group $\mathbf{S}_2$ is Abelian; the groups $\mathbf{S}_n$ with $n > 2$ are not Abelian.

Two groups, $\mathbf{G}$ and $\mathbf{H}$, are said to be *isomorphic* if they have the same order and there is a one-to-one relationship $g \leftrightarrow h$ between the elements g of $\mathbf{G}$ and the elements h of $\mathbf{H}$, such that $g_1 \leftrightarrow h_1$ and $g_2 \leftrightarrow h_2$ automatically implies $g_1 g_2 \leftrightarrow h_1 h_2$. In other words, the two groups have the same 'product table' (or 'Cayley table', after the British mathematician Arthur Cayley).

We make a distinction between three kinds of groups according to group order. There are:

- Finite groups (i.e., groups with a finite order), and
- Groups of infinite order, where we must distinguish between
  - Groups with a denumerable (or countable) infinity of elements, and
  - Groups with a nondenumerable (or uncountable) infinity of elements.

Groups with a finite order or an order of denumerable infinity are called *discrete groups*. Uncountably infinite groups are known as *Lie groups* (named after another Norwegian mathematician, Sophus Lie, pioneer of the theory of infinite groups). The order of an infinite discrete group equals the cardinality of the natural numbers $\mathbb{N} = \{0, 1, 2, \ldots\}$, and will be denoted $\aleph_0$, the aleph-null convention introduced by the German mathematician Georg Cantor. The order of a Lie group equals the cardinality of the real numbers $\mathbb{R}$, and will be denoted either ∞ or ∞^m, where m is the dimension of the group space.

The three kinds of groups behave quite differently. In the present book we will mainly focus on finite groups. We will only encounter infinite groups in Chapters 5 and 7. To learn more about finite groups in general and symmetric groups in particular, the reader is referred to appropriate textbooks [10–12]. For more on Lie groups, the reader can consult some other textbooks [13–15]. Books on denumerably infinite groups are rare. Some aspects of the subject are discussed by Kaplansky [16].

We end this section by giving two examples of an infinite group. The first example is a discrete group: the set S consists of all rational numbers of the form 2^k (where k is an arbitrary integer number), so $S = \{\ldots, \frac{1}{4}, \frac{1}{2}, 1, 2, 4, 8, \ldots\}$, together with the operation of ordinary multiplication. This group is isomorphic to the infinite cyclic group $\mathbf{Z}$. Its order is $\aleph_0$.

The second example is a Lie group: the set consists of all matrices of the form

$$\begin{pmatrix} 1 & 0 \\ 0 & \exp(i\theta) \end{pmatrix}$$

(where i is the imaginary unit and θ is an arbitrary real number), together with the operation of matrix multiplication. This particular group is isomorphic to the Lie group U(1), i.e., the so-called unitary group of degree 1. Its order is ∞^1.

2.2
Permutation Groups

The study of permutation groups is interesting because any finite group is isomorphic to some permutation group. A permutation group consists of a set of permutations together with the operation of cascading. Tables 2.1a and 2.1b show two different permutations of the eight objects 1, 2, 3, 4, 5, 6, 7, and 8. Table 2.1c gives the permutation resulting from the cascading of the previous two permutations. In order to deduce Table 2.1c from Tables 2.1a and 2.1b, we proceed as follows. The first row of Table 2.1a indicates that '1 is mapped to 2', whereas the second row of Table 2.1b shows that '2 is mapped to 3'. Together, this says that '1 is mapped to 3' (to be filled in) in the first row of Table 2.1c. We can equally well say that, according to Table 2.1a, '2 is the image of 1', whereas, according to Table 2.1b, '3 is the image of 2'. Taken together, these indicate that '3 is the image of the image of 1' (to be filled in) in the first row of Table 2.1c. Proceeding in this manner for all eight rows of Table 2.1a yields the full Table 2.1c.

The correspondence table notation is usually considered too cumbersome for permutations, and is therefore replaced by the cycle notation. The latter consists of a product of disjoint cycles. An example of a cycle is $(1,2,3)$, meaning that 1 is mapped to 2, 2 is mapped to 3, and 3 is mapped to 1. Table 2.1a is written as $(1,2,3)(5,6)$, whereas Table 2.1b is written as $(2,3)(4,8)(5,6)$, and Table 2.1c as $(1,3)(4,8)$. Cascading is represented by a multiplication symbol, such as *. Thus we have the equality:

$$(1,2,3)(5,6)*(2,3)(4,8)(5,6) = (1,3)(4,8) . \tag{2.1}$$

Permutations can also be represented by permutation matrices; that is, square matrices where all entries are either 0 or 1 and the entries on each line sum to 1. By definition, a line sum is either a row sum or a column sum. Permutations of n objects are represented by $n \times n$ permutation matrices. For example, (2.1) can be rewritten as a matrix equation:

$$
\begin{pmatrix}
0 & 1 & 0 & 0 & 0 & 0 & 0 & 0 \\
0 & 0 & 1 & 0 & 0 & 0 & 0 & 0 \\
1 & 0 & 0 & 0 & 0 & 0 & 0 & 0 \\
0 & 0 & 0 & 1 & 0 & 0 & 0 & 0 \\
0 & 0 & 0 & 0 & 0 & 1 & 0 & 0 \\
0 & 0 & 0 & 0 & 1 & 0 & 0 & 0 \\
0 & 0 & 0 & 0 & 0 & 0 & 1 & 0 \\
0 & 0 & 0 & 0 & 0 & 0 & 0 & 1
\end{pmatrix}
\begin{pmatrix}
1 & 0 & 0 & 0 & 0 & 0 & 0 & 0 \\
0 & 0 & 1 & 0 & 0 & 0 & 0 & 0 \\
0 & 1 & 0 & 0 & 0 & 0 & 0 & 0 \\
0 & 0 & 0 & 0 & 0 & 0 & 0 & 1 \\
0 & 0 & 0 & 0 & 0 & 1 & 0 & 0 \\
0 & 0 & 0 & 0 & 1 & 0 & 0 & 0 \\
0 & 0 & 0 & 0 & 0 & 0 & 1 & 0 \\
0 & 0 & 0 & 1 & 0 & 0 & 0 & 0
\end{pmatrix}
=
$$

$$
\begin{pmatrix}
0 & 0 & 1 & 0 & 0 & 0 & 0 & 0 \\
0 & 1 & 0 & 0 & 0 & 0 & 0 & 0 \\
1 & 0 & 0 & 0 & 0 & 0 & 0 & 0 \\
0 & 0 & 0 & 0 & 0 & 0 & 0 & 1 \\
0 & 0 & 0 & 0 & 1 & 0 & 0 & 0 \\
0 & 0 & 0 & 0 & 0 & 1 & 0 & 0 \\
0 & 0 & 0 & 0 & 0 & 0 & 1 & 0 \\
0 & 0 & 0 & 1 & 0 & 0 & 0 & 0
\end{pmatrix} .
$$

As an example of a permutation group, we consider the group of all permutations of three objects 1, 2, and 3. This is of order $3! = 6$. Its six elements are the six permutations $()$, $(1,2)$, $(1,3)$, $(2,3)$, $(1,2,3)$, and $(1,3,2)$. It is the symmetric group of degree 3, denoted $\mathbf{S}_3$. Note that the element $()$ is the trivial permutation that maps each object to itself. In other words: no object is 'moved' by $()$. This element is the identity element i of the permutation group. Its matrix representation is a diagonal matrix, with 1s exclusively on the diagonal.

Table 2.1 Correspondence tables for three permutations of eight objects.

A	P
1	2
2	3
3	1
4	4
5	6
6	5
7	7
8	8

(a)

A	P
1	1
2	3
3	2
4	8
5	6
6	5
7	7
8	4

(b)

A	P
1	3
2	2
3	1
4	8
5	5
6	6
7	7
8	4

(c)

2.3
Matrix Groups

The study of matrix groups is also of interest, because any finite group is isomorphic to some matrix group and many infinite groups too. A matrix group consists of a set of square matrices together with the operation of matrix multiplication. The reader is invited to check that the following six 2×2 matrices form a group:

$$\begin{pmatrix} 1 & 0 \\ 0 & 1 \end{pmatrix}, \quad \begin{pmatrix} 1/2 & -\sqrt{3}/2 \\ -\sqrt{3}/2 & -1/2 \end{pmatrix}, \quad \begin{pmatrix} 1/2 & \sqrt{3}/2 \\ \sqrt{3}/2 & -1/2 \end{pmatrix},$$

$$\begin{pmatrix} -1 & 0 \\ 0 & 1 \end{pmatrix}, \quad \begin{pmatrix} -1/2 & -\sqrt{3}/2 \\ \sqrt{3}/2 & -1/2 \end{pmatrix}, \quad \text{and} \quad \begin{pmatrix} -1/2 & \sqrt{3}/2 \\ -\sqrt{3}/2 & -1/2 \end{pmatrix}. \tag{2.2}$$

Surprisingly, this group is isomorphic to the group of the six 3×3 permutation matrices of $\mathbf{S}_3$:

$$\begin{pmatrix} 1 & 0 & 0 \\ 0 & 1 & 0 \\ 0 & 0 & 1 \end{pmatrix}, \quad \begin{pmatrix} 0 & 1 & 0 \\ 1 & 0 & 0 \\ 0 & 0 & 1 \end{pmatrix}, \quad \begin{pmatrix} 0 & 0 & 1 \\ 0 & 1 & 0 \\ 1 & 0 & 0 \end{pmatrix},$$

$$\begin{pmatrix} 1 & 0 & 0 \\ 0 & 0 & 1 \\ 0 & 1 & 0 \end{pmatrix}, \quad \begin{pmatrix} 0 & 1 & 0 \\ 0 & 0 & 1 \\ 1 & 0 & 0 \end{pmatrix}, \quad \text{and} \quad \begin{pmatrix} 0 & 0 & 1 \\ 1 & 0 & 0 \\ 0 & 1 & 0 \end{pmatrix}.$$

Any matrix group consists of merely invertible matrices (also known as nonsingular matrices). A singular matrix (i.e., a matrix that has a determinant of zero) has no inverse.

2.4
Group Generators

Generators of a group consist of any subset $\{a, b, c, \ldots\}$ of the set S such that all the other elements of S can be written as one of the 'products' $aa, ab, ac, \ldots, ba, \ldots,$ $aaa, aab, \ldots$ Surprisingly, the whole permutation group $\mathbf{S}_n$ can be generated using only two (well-chosen) generators, such as the two permutations $(1,2)$ and $(1,2,3,\ldots,n)$. For example, for the case $n = 3$, we have the two generators $a = (1,2)$ and $b = (1,2,3)$. All six members of $\mathbf{S}_3$ can be written as a product:

$$() = 1$$
$$(1,2) = a$$
$$(1,3) = a*b$$
$$(2,3) = b*a$$
$$(1,2,3) = b$$
$$(1,3,2) = b*b .$$

Such decomposition is not unique. We may for example, write $() = a*a$ and also $(1,3,2) = a*b*a$.

As a second example, we consider all minterm functions f_1, f_2, f_4, and f_8 from Table 1.2, together with the operation XOR. These do not form a group, as the set is not closed. For example, $f_1 \oplus f_2$ equals f_3, which is not in the set $\{f_1, f_2, f_4, f_8\}$. The four minterms generate the full group $\{f_0, f_1, f_2, f_3, \ldots, f_{15}\}$. In general, the 2^n minterms of n variables, together with the operation XOR, generate the group of all 2^{2^n} functions of n variables.

Generators of a group are interesting since they act as building blocks for constructing arbitrary elements of the group. With a small set of building blocks (often called the 'library'), we can construct a huge number of combinations. It is sufficient to recall here that all $n!$ permutations can be built by successive applications of only two bricks: $a = (1,2)$ and $b = (1,2,3,\ldots,n)$. However, choosing such a small library is not a clever approach, since it can lead to very long cascades when realizing a particular permutation. For example, the permutation of Table 2.1b (where $n = 8$) requires at least 23 blocks:

$$(2,3)(4,8)(5,6) = b^2 ababab^2 ababab^3 ab^3 ab .$$

Therefore, it is often convenient to choose larger sets of generators, which guarantee shorter products. The challenge to the designer is to choose a clever generator set (i.e., not too small, but also not too large). A substantial part of the present book is devoted to this task. The task of the circuit designer is aided by the availability of dedicated computer algebra packages. Indeed, besides well-known computer algebra languages (such as Reduce, Maple, Mathematica, etc.), there are special-purpose languages that are dedicated to group theory. For finite groups, we should mention Magma [17, 18], Cayley [18, 19], and GAP [20]. For Lie groups, there is LiE [21, 22]. Many of the results given in this book were either discovered or verified by means of GAP.

2.5
Subgroups

One important aspect of a group is its *subgroups*. For example, the two matrices

$$\begin{pmatrix} 1 & 0 \\ 0 & 1 \end{pmatrix} \quad \text{and} \quad \begin{pmatrix} -1 & 0 \\ 0 & 1 \end{pmatrix} ,$$

which form a subset of the set (2.2), form a group of their own, isomorphic to S_2, the group of permutations of two objects. We say that this two-element group is a subgroup of the six-element group. We write:

$$S_2 \subset S_3 ,$$

which we may read as either 'S_2 is a subgroup of S_3' or 'S_3 is a supergroup of S_2'.
   If G is finite and a supergroup of H, then the ratio

$$\frac{\text{order}(G)}{\text{order}(H)}$$

is called the index of H in G. Lagrange's theorem (named after the Italian/French mathematician/astronomer Joseph-Louis Lagrange) says that such an index is always an integer. In other words, the order of a subgroup divides the order of its supergroup. This theorem strongly restricts the number of subgroups of a given group. Nevertheless, most groups have a wealth of subgroups. For example, the group S_4 (of order $4! = 24$) has 30 different subgroups, whereas S_8 (of order $8! = 40\,320$) has 151 221 subgroups [23].

2.6
Young Subgroups

Symmetric groups have a special class of subgroups, called *Young subgroups* (after the English priest/mathematician Alfred Young). These take advantage of the notion of the direct product of two groups. We introduce this product by giving an example of a Young subgroup of S_5. Assume that we have five objects a, b, c, d, and e. There are a total of $5! = 120$ permutations of these objects. However, let us also impose a restriction: we will only allow permutations that permute a, b, and c among each other and (simultaneously) permute d and e among each other. This allows 3! permutations of three objects, while (independently) allowing 2! permutations of two objects. The allowed permutations form a permutation group of order $3! \times 2! = 12$. We are allowed to 'combine' each element of S_3 with each element of S_2. Therefore, the group is called a *direct product* of S_3 and S_2, denoted $S_3 \times S_2$. We write

$$S_3 \times S_2 \subset S_5 .$$

The subgroup is based on a particular partition of the number 5:

$$3 + 2 = 5 .$$

In general, we may combine any group $\mathbf{G}_1$ with any group $\mathbf{G}_2, \ldots$, with any group $\mathbf{G}_m$. Of course, we have

$$\text{order}(\mathbf{G}_1 \times \mathbf{G}_2 \times \ldots \times \mathbf{G}_m) = \text{order}(\mathbf{G}_1) \times \text{order}(\mathbf{G}_2) \times \ldots \times \text{order}(\mathbf{G}_m) .$$

As an example, we consider the group formed by the set of all 2^{2^n} Boolean functions of n Boolean variables, together with the operation of XORing (see Sections 2.1 and 2.4). They form a group isomorphic to the direct product $\mathbf{S}_2 \times \mathbf{S}_2 \times \ldots \times \mathbf{S}_2$ with 2^n factors, with order

$$\text{order}(\mathbf{S}_2 \times \mathbf{S}_2 \times \ldots \times \mathbf{S}_2) = (\text{order}(\mathbf{S}_2))^{2^n} = 2^{2^n} .$$

Each factor $\mathbf{S}_2$ refers to what was called a minterm group in Section 2.1.

A Young subgroup [24–26] of the symmetric group $\mathbf{S}_n$ is defined as any subgroup that is isomorphic to $\mathbf{S}_{n_1} \times \mathbf{S}_{n_2} \times \ldots \times \mathbf{S}_{n_k}$, with $(n_1, n_2, \ldots, n_k)$ being a partition of the number n; that is, with

$$n_1 + n_2 + \cdots + n_k = n .$$

The order of this Young subgroup is $n_1! n_2! \ldots n_k!$.

The number of different Young subgroups of the group $\mathbf{S}_n$ is given by the Bell number B_n (named after the Scottish/American mathematician Eric Bell). For example, the group $\mathbf{S}_4$ has $B_4 = 15$ Young subgroups:

- One trivial subgroup isomorphic to $\mathbf{S}_4$,
- Three subgroups isomorphic to $\mathbf{S}_2 \times \mathbf{S}_2$,
- Four subgroups isomorphic to $\mathbf{S}_1 \times \mathbf{S}_3$,
- Six subgroups isomorphic to $\mathbf{S}_1 \times \mathbf{S}_1 \times \mathbf{S}_2$, and
- One trivial subgroup isomorphic to $\mathbf{S}_1 \times \mathbf{S}_1 \times \mathbf{S}_1 \times \mathbf{S}_1$.

The group $\mathbf{S}_8$ has $B_8 = 4140$ Young subgroups.

Because $\mathbf{S}_1$ is just the trivial group $\mathbf{I}$ with one element (i.e., the identity element i), Young subgroups of the form $\mathbf{S}_1 \times \mathbf{S}_k$ are often simply denoted by $\mathbf{S}_k$. Finally, Young subgroups of the form $\mathbf{S}_k \times \mathbf{S}_k \times \ldots \times \mathbf{S}_k$ (with m factors) will be written as $\mathbf{S}_k^m$.

2.7
Sylow *p*-Subgroups

Sylow p-subgroups, named after a third Norwegian group theorist, Ludwig Sylow, comprise another peculiar kind of subgroup. Let us assume an arbitrary (i.e., not necessarily symmetric) group $\mathbf{G}$. Its order, G (just like any integer number larger than 1), can be written as a prime factorization:

$$G = 2^{x_2} 3^{x_3} 5^{x_5} \ldots p^{x_p} \ldots ,$$

where all of the exponents x_p are integers (either 0 or positive). In this case, any subgroup **H** of **G**, with an order H that satisfies

$$H = p^{x_p} \, ,$$

is called a Sylow p-subgroup of **G**.

2.8
Cyclic Subgroups

We now consider an arbitrary element g of an arbitrary but finite group **G**, as well as the sequence $g, g^2, g^3, \ldots$ Because of the closeness property of the group (see Section 2.1), all of the powers g^j are members of the group **G**. In order to guarantee the finiteness of **G**, there must be an exponent n such that g^n equals the identity element i of **G**. Then, g^{n+1} is equal to g, whereas g^{n+2} is equal to g^2, etc., and there are only a finite number of different powers g^j. Thus, the infinite sequence $\{g, g^2, g^3, \ldots\}$ is periodic with a period of n. We call n the *order* of the element g. The finite sequence $\{g, g^2, g^3, \ldots, g^n\}$ forms a subgroup of **G** that is isomorphic to the group called the 'cyclic group of degree n' and denoted $\mathbf{Z}_n$. Because of Lagrange's theorem, any element g of **G** has an order that is a divisor of the group order.

The order of $\mathbf{Z}_n$ is equal to n. We have

$$\mathbf{Z}_n \subset \mathbf{S}_n \, ,$$

and, in particular,

$$\mathbf{Z}_2 = \mathbf{S}_2 \, .$$

All cyclic groups $\mathbf{Z}_n$ are Abelian.

2.9
Closing Remarks

This book is strongly grounded in a group-theoretical approach. This may surprise some readers. Group theory is sometimes considered to be overkill when discussing reversible computing. However, it is my feeling that groups in reversible computing are not introduced, let alone invented. They are merely discovered. Indeed, they are inherently present, whether one likes it or not. Unearthing them has two benefits:

- We see reversible computing as an example of more general mathematical schemes, and
- We can benefit from the many theorems discovered and tools developed by group theorists.

We discussed some of these theorems and tools above. More of them will be useful when investigating reversible computers, such as cosets, double cosets, conjugated subgroups, ... In order to ensure that the present chapter is relatively brief, and to allow us to focus on the subject of this book (i.e., reversible computers) as quickly as possible, we will introduce these concepts later on, when we actually need them.

One final (practical) remark. In the sections above, we adopted some conventions regarding group notation. For instance, a finite group is denoted by a bold-faced capital; the order of a group is denoted by a capital; and an element of a group is denoted by a lower-case letter. For example:

$$g \in \mathbf{G}$$
$$\text{order}(\mathbf{G}) = G \ .$$

For the rest of this book, we will (whenever possible) respect this convention.

2.10
Exercises for Chapter 2

Exercise 2.1
Prove that, in a group, we do not have to make any distinction between a 'right identity element' and a 'left identity element'. In other words, if i_1 and i_2 are two particular elements of a group, such that for all elements a of the group

$$\text{both} \quad a \, \Omega \, i_1 = a \quad \text{and} \quad i_2 \, \Omega \, a = a \ ,$$

then necessarily $i_1 = i_2$. This property also holds for non-Abelian groups!

Exercise 2.2
Prove that a group can only have one identity element. In other words, if i_1 and i_2 are two particular elements of a group, such that for all elements a of the group

$$\text{both} \quad a \, \Omega \, i_1 = a \quad \text{and} \quad a \, \Omega \, i_2 = a \ ,$$

then necessarily $i_1 = i_2$.

Exercise 2.3
Prove that there is no distinction between 'right inverse' and 'left inverse'.

Exercise 2.4
Prove that an element of a group can have only one inverse.

Exercise 2.5

In S_3 (see Sections 2.2 and 2.3), what is the inverse of each of the six elements? In other words, what are $()^{-1}$, $(1,2)^{-1}$, $(1,3)^{-1}$, $(2,3)^{-1}$, $(1,2,3)^{-1}$, and $(1,3,2)^{-1}$? Or: what are

$$\begin{pmatrix} 1 & 0 \\ 0 & 1 \end{pmatrix}^{-1}, \quad \begin{pmatrix} 1/2 & -\sqrt{3}/2 \\ -\sqrt{3}/2 & -1/2 \end{pmatrix}^{-1}, \quad \begin{pmatrix} 1/2 & \sqrt{3}/2 \\ \sqrt{3}/2 & -1/2 \end{pmatrix}^{-1},$$

$$\begin{pmatrix} -1 & 0 \\ 0 & 1 \end{pmatrix}^{-1}, \quad \begin{pmatrix} -1/2 & -\sqrt{3}/2 \\ \sqrt{3}/2 & -1/2 \end{pmatrix}^{-1}, \quad \text{and} \begin{pmatrix} -1/2 & \sqrt{3}/2 \\ -\sqrt{3}/2 & -1/2 \end{pmatrix}^{-1}?$$

Or: what are

$$\begin{pmatrix} 1 & 0 & 0 \\ 0 & 1 & 0 \\ 0 & 0 & 1 \end{pmatrix}^{-1}, \quad \begin{pmatrix} 0 & 1 & 0 \\ 1 & 0 & 0 \\ 0 & 0 & 1 \end{pmatrix}^{-1}, \quad \begin{pmatrix} 0 & 0 & 1 \\ 0 & 1 & 0 \\ 1 & 0 & 0 \end{pmatrix}^{-1},$$

$$\begin{pmatrix} 1 & 0 & 0 \\ 0 & 0 & 1 \\ 0 & 1 & 0 \end{pmatrix}^{-1}, \quad \begin{pmatrix} 0 & 1 & 0 \\ 0 & 0 & 1 \\ 1 & 0 & 0 \end{pmatrix}^{-1}, \quad \text{and} \begin{pmatrix} 0 & 0 & 1 \\ 1 & 0 & 0 \\ 0 & 1 & 0 \end{pmatrix}^{-1}?$$

Exercise 2.6

In S_3, what is the order of each of the six elements?

Exercise 2.7

A derangement is a permutation where no object is mapped to itself. In other words, all objects are 'moved'. Demonstrate that the derangements of n objects *do not* form a subgroup of the group S_n; that is, the group of all the permutations of those n objects.

Exercise 2.8

Demonstrate that S_3 is not Abelian, but that Z_3 is Abelian.

3
Reversible Computing

3.1
Introduction

What is a reversible computer? Figure 3.1 explains by means of a counterexample. We see a small calculator that has been designed for one particular task: computing the sum of two numbers. This computation is logically irreversible because, if we forget the input values (i.e., 3 and 1), knowledge of the output value (i.e., 4) is not sufficient to recover the inputs, since 4 could equally well have been generated from $2 + 2$ or $4 + 0$ or $0 + 4$ or ...

Figure 3.2 gives an actual example of a reversible computer. Again we have a pocket calculator, designed for a particular task: computing the sum of and the difference between two numbers. This computation is reversible because, if we forget the input values (3 and 1), knowledge of the output values (4 and 2) is sufficient to recover the inputs. If A and B designate the two input numbers and P and Q the two output numbers, then the knowledge that

$$P = A + B$$
$$Q = A - B \qquad\qquad (3.1)$$

is sufficient to be able to work out that

$$A = \frac{1}{2}(P + Q)$$
$$B = \frac{1}{2}(P - Q) \ .$$

Thus, the outputs contain enough information to reconstruct the inputs. In other words: the outputs contain the same information as the inputs.

It is important to realize that all of the computers that are currently on the market are irreversible. Thus, to perform an experiment with a reversible computer, we must build such a machine ourselves. The building blocks of a digital computer are called digital circuits. The building blocks of a digital circuit are called logic gates. To build a reversible computer, the safest approach is to use only reversible building-blocks, and thus exclusively reversible logic gates.

Reversible Computing. Alexis De Vos
Copyright © 2010 WILEY-VCH Verlag GmbH & Co. KGaA, Weinheim
ISBN: 978-3-527-40992-1

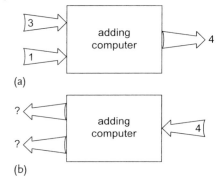

(a)

(b)

Figure 3.1 A logically irreversible computer.

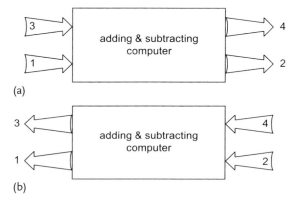

(a)

(b)

Figure 3.2 A logically reversible computer.

In the present chapter, we will demonstrate the application of group theory to the detailed design of reversible circuits from reversible gates. Such reversible logic gates are distinguished from conventional logic gates by two properties:

- The number of output bits always equals the number of input bits, and
- For each pair of different input words, the two corresponding output words are different.

For instance, it is clear that an AND gate (see the truth table in Table 1.3a) is not reversible, as

- It has two input bits but only one output bit, and
- For three different input words (i.e., for 00, 01, and 10), the three corresponding output words are equal.

Table 3.1 Truth tables of three reversible logic circuits of width 2: (a) an arbitrary reversible circuit r, (b) the identity gate i, and (c) the inverse r^{-1} of circuit r.

$A\ B$	$P\ Q$
0 0	0 0
0 1	1 0
1 0	1 1
1 1	0 1

(a)

$A\ B$	$P\ Q$
0 0	0 0
0 1	0 1
1 0	1 0
1 1	1 1

(b)

$A\ B$	$P\ Q$
0 0	0 0
0 1	1 1
1 0	0 1
1 1	1 0

(c)

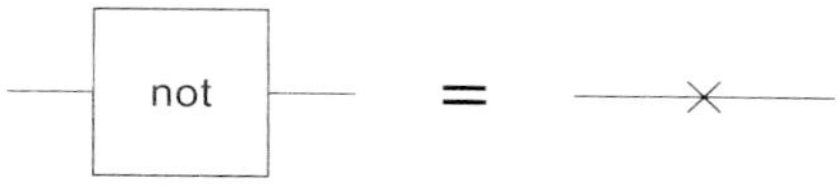

Figure 3.3 The NOT gate.

If, for example, we know that the output of the AND gate is 0, but we have forgotten the input values, knowledge of the output value is not sufficient to recover what the inputs have been. Indeed, 0 could equally well have been 0 AND 0 or 0 AND 1 or 1 AND 0. Analogously, neither the OR gate (Table 1.3b) nor the NAND gate nor the NOR gate are reversible.

In contrast, Table 1.1d is an example of a reversible gate: the NOT gate, also known as the *inverter*. This building-block is usually represented by a cross; see Figure 3.3. Table 3.1a gives another example of a reversible gate. Also here, the number of inputs equals the number of outputs (two). This number is called the *width* or logic width w of the reversible circuit r. The table gives all possible input words (A, B). We can see how all of the corresponding output words (P, Q) are different. Thus, the four (P, Q) words are merely a permutation of the four (A, B) words. This particular truth table may be replaced by a set of w Boolean equations:

$$P(A, B) = A \oplus B$$
$$Q(A, B) = A .$$

This is equally well represented by the cycle notation $(2,3,4)$ of the permutation of the four objects 1, 2, 3, and 4 (i.e., the four objects 00, 01, 10, and 11).

In contrast to arbitrary logic circuits, reversible logic circuits form a group. Remember that, for a group, we need a set (S) as well as an operation under which each pair (x, y) of elements of the set corresponds to a third element of the set (written xy). In our case, the operation applied to the two circuits is the cascading of the two circuits. Table 3.1b gives the truth table of the identity gate i (also known as the *follower*), and Table 3.1c gives r^{-1}; that is, the inverse of circuit r. The reader can easily verify that both the cascade rr^{-1} and the cascade $r^{-1}r$ equal i.

Note that, in each of the truth tables of Table 3.1, the functions $P(A, B)$ and $Q(A, B)$ are both balanced. It is not difficult to prove the general property that, in a reversible truth table, all w functions $P_j(A_1, A_2, \ldots, A_w)$ are balanced.[6] The restriction that all columns P_j are balanced is a necessary, though not sufficient, condition for reversibility.

3.2
Reversible Circuits

All reversible circuits of the same width w (Figure 3.4) form a group. The truth table of an arbitrary reversible circuit has 2^w rows. As all of the output words have to be different, they can merely be a repetition of the input words in a different order. In other words, the 2^w output words are a permutation of the 2^w input words. The $(2^w)!$ permutations of 2^w objects form the reversible group **R**, isomorphic to the symmetric group $\mathbf{S}_{2^w}$. Thus there are exactly $R(w) = (2^w)!$ different reversible logic circuits of width w. We recall here that the number 2^w is called the degree of the group and the number $(2^w)!$ is called the order of the group **R**. According to Section 2.3, each element of **R** can be represented by a $2^w \times 2^w$ permutation matrix. For example, Table 3.1a is represented by the 4×4 matrix

$$
\begin{pmatrix}
1 & 0 & 0 & 0 \\
0 & 0 & 1 & 0 \\
0 & 0 & 0 & 1 \\
0 & 1 & 0 & 0
\end{pmatrix} .
$$

For small values of w, the order R of the group is given in Table 3.2. It is well known that the exponential function grows rapidly; it is also well known that the factorial function grows rapidly. It thus is no surprise that $R(w)$, a factorial of an exponential, grows *very* rapidly. Stirling's asymptotic formula

$$
n! \approx \sqrt{2\pi}\, n^{n+1/2} e^{-n}
$$

(named after the Scottish mathematician James Stirling) is well known. The following inequalities [27]:

$$
\sqrt{2\pi}\, n^{n+1/2} e^{-n} < n! < \sqrt{2\pi}\, n^{n+1/2} e^{-n} \left(1 + \frac{1}{4n}\right)
$$

contain somewhat more information. We use them to deduce an interval for the order of the symmetric group $\mathbf{S}_{2^w}$:

$$
2^{\left[w - \frac{1}{\log(2)}\right]2^w + \frac{w}{2} + 1} < (2^w)! < 2^{\left[w - \frac{1}{\log(2)}\right]2^w + \frac{w}{2} + 2} , \tag{3.2}
$$

6) Besides using the notation $A, B, C, \ldots$ for the input bits and $P, Q, R, \ldots$ for the output bits, we will also use the letters $A_1, A_2, \ldots, A_n$ for the inputs and $P_1, P_2, \ldots, P_n$ for the outputs whenever this is more convenient. See also the footnote in Section 1.2.

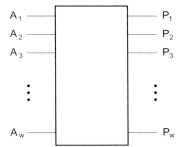

Figure 3.4 A circuit of logic width w.

Table 3.2 The number R of different reversible circuits, the number C of different conservative reversible circuits, the number L of different linear reversible circuits, the number AL of different affine linear reversible circuits, the number E of different exchanging circuits, and the number AE of different affine exchanging circuits, all as a function of the circuit width w.

w	R	C	L	AL	E	AE
1	2	1	1	2	1	2
2	24	2	6	24	2	8
3	40 320	36	168	1344	6	48
4	20 922 789 888 000	414 720	20 160	322 560	24	384

where 'log' stands for the natural logarithm. We note in passing that, in the prime factorization of the order; that is, in

$$(2^w)! = 2^{x_2} 3^{x_3} 5^{x_5} \dots \tag{3.3}$$

the exponent x_2 of the prime factor 2 is easily computed: it equals the number of even factors in the factorial $1 \times 2 \times 3 \times 4 \times \dots \times (2^w - 1) \times 2^w$, augmented by the number of quadruple factors in it, etc. Thus:

$$x_2 = \frac{2^w}{2} + \frac{2^w}{4} + \dots + 1 = 2^w - 1 . \tag{3.4}$$

As discussed in Chapter 2, the symmetric group has a wealth of properties. For example, it has a lot of subgroups, most of which have been studied in detail. Some of these subgroups naturally make their appearance in the study of reversible computing.

3.3
Conservative Circuits

One example of a subgroup of **R** is the subgroup **C** of *conservative* logic circuits. Conservative gates have been studied by Sasao and Kinoshita [28], and conservative reversible gates have been studied by Fredkin and Toffoli [29] and by Cattaneo *et al.* [30]. Table 3.3a gives the truth table of an example. In each of its rows, the output $(P, Q, R, \ldots)$ contains a number of 1s equal to the number of 1s in the corresponding input $(A, B, C, \ldots)$. We see how 000 remains 000, whereas the objects 001, 010, and 100 are permuted among each other, and so are the three objects 011, 101, and 110, while 111 is fixed. Such permutations are elements of the direct product $\mathbf{S}_1 \times \mathbf{S}_3 \times \mathbf{S}_3 \times \mathbf{S}_1$, with an order equal to $1!3!3!1! = 36$.

The conservative gates thus form a Young subgroup of $\mathbf{S}_{2^w}$, isomorphic to $\mathbf{S}_1 \times \mathbf{S}_w \times \mathbf{S}_{w(w-1)/2} \times \cdots \times \mathbf{S}_w \times \mathbf{S}_1$. This is based on the binomial partition of the number 2^w:

$$2^w = 1 + \binom{w}{1} + \binom{w}{2} + \cdots + \binom{w}{w-1} + 1 .$$

Table 3.2 gives $C(w)$, the number of conservative logic circuits of width w.

3.4
Monotonic Circuits

A logic circuit is monotonic iff each of its outputs $P, Q, \ldots$ is a monotonic function of the inputs $A, B, \ldots$ (see Section 1.6). The circuit of Table 3.3a is not monotonic. Indeed, $P(A, B, C)$ is not a monotonic function, as $P(1, 1, 0) < P(0, 1, 0)$. In contrast, Table 3.3b is monotonic, as all three functions $P(A, B, C)$, $Q(A, B, C)$, and $R(A, B, C)$ are monotonic.

The reversible monotonic circuits of width w form a group; that is, a subgroup of $\mathbf{R}$. We will not discuss it here in detail, for reasons that will become clear later (in Theorem C.5 of Appendix C).

3.5
Linear Circuits

One important subgroup of $\mathbf{R}$ is the subgroup of linear reversible circuits. Linear reversible circuits have been studied in detail by Patel *et al.* [31]. A logic circuit is linear iff each of its outputs $P, Q, \ldots$ is a linear function of the inputs $A, B, \ldots$ (see Section 1.4). The reversible circuit of Table 3.3a is not linear. It can be written as a set of three Boolean equations:

$$P = B \oplus AB \oplus AC$$
$$Q = A$$
$$R = C \oplus AB \oplus AC .$$

While the function $Q(A, B, C)$ is linear, the function $P(A, B, C)$ is clearly not (its Reed–Muller expansion contains two second-degree terms). Table 3.3c, on the other

Table 3.3 Truth tables of four reversible logic circuits of width 3: (a) a conservative circuit, (b) a monotonic circuit, (c) a linear circuit, and (d) an affine linear circuit.

ABC	PQR	ABC	PQR	ABC	PQR	ABC	PQR
0 0 0	0 0 0	0 0 0	0 0 0	0 0 0	0 0 0	0 0 0	1 0 0
0 0 1	0 0 1	0 0 1	1 0 0	0 0 1	0 1 0	0 0 1	1 1 0
0 1 0	1 0 0	0 1 0	0 0 1	0 1 0	1 0 1	0 1 0	0 0 1
0 1 1	1 0 1	0 1 1	1 0 1	0 1 1	1 1 1	0 1 1	0 1 1
1 0 0	0 1 0	1 0 0	0 1 0	1 0 0	1 0 0	1 0 0	0 0 0
1 0 1	1 1 0	1 0 1	1 1 0	1 0 1	1 1 0	1 0 1	0 1 0
1 1 0	0 1 1	1 1 0	0 1 1	1 1 0	0 0 1	1 1 0	1 0 1
1 1 1	1 1 1	1 1 1	1 1 1	1 1 1	0 1 1	1 1 1	1 1 1

| (a) | (b) | (c) | (d) |

hand, is an example of a linear circuit:

$$P = A \oplus B$$
$$Q = C$$
$$R = B \; .$$

This relationship may be written in matrix form:

$$\begin{pmatrix} P \\ Q \\ R \end{pmatrix} = \begin{pmatrix} 1 & 1 & 0 \\ 0 & 0 & 1 \\ 0 & 1 & 0 \end{pmatrix} \begin{pmatrix} A \\ B \\ C \end{pmatrix} . \tag{3.5}$$

The relation between the inputs $A, B, C, \ldots$ and the outputs $P, Q, R, \ldots$ is thus fully determined by means of a square $w \times w$ matrix (with all entries from $\mathbb{B} = \{0, 1\}$).

Linear reversible circuits form a group **L** that is isomorphic to what is called in mathematics the *general linear group* **GL**$(w, \mathbb{B})$. Its order equals $2^{(w-1)w/2} w!_2$, where $w!_2$ is the bifactorial of w; the q-factorial is a generalization of the ordinary factorial $w! = w!_1$:

$$w!_q = 1(1 + q)(1 + q + q^2) \ldots (1 + q + \cdots + q^{w-1}) \; .$$

Appendix A provides a calculation of the order. Table 3.2 provides the number $L(w)$ of different linear reversible circuits. For large values of the logic width w, the order of the group is of magnitude $a2^{w^2}$, where $a \approx 0.29$. This is demonstrated in Appendix B.

The group **L** of linear reversible circuits is thus isomorphic to the group of $w \times w$ nonsingular square matrices with all entries equal to either 0 or 1.

3.6
Affine Linear Circuits

Table 3.3d is an example of an affine linear circuit:

$$P = 1 \oplus A \oplus B$$
$$Q = C$$
$$R = B \, .$$

All functions $P(A, B, \ldots)$, $Q(A, B, \ldots), \ldots$ are affine linear (see Section 1.5). Such a circuit is described by two matrices: a $w \times w$ square matrix and a $w \times 1$ column matrix, both containing entries from $\mathbb{B} = \{0, 1\}$. Table 3.3d may be written as

$$\begin{pmatrix} P \\ Q \\ R \end{pmatrix} = \begin{pmatrix} 1 \\ 0 \\ 0 \end{pmatrix} \oplus \begin{pmatrix} 1 & 1 & 0 \\ 0 & 0 & 1 \\ 0 & 1 & 0 \end{pmatrix} \begin{pmatrix} A \\ B \\ C \end{pmatrix} \, ,$$

where the XORing of two column vectors is simply defined as the bitwise XOR:

$$\begin{pmatrix} X \\ Y \\ Z \end{pmatrix} \oplus \begin{pmatrix} U \\ V \\ W \end{pmatrix} = \begin{pmatrix} X \oplus U \\ Y \oplus V \\ Z \oplus W \end{pmatrix} \, .$$

Affine linear reversible circuits form a group **AL** that is isomorphic to what is called in mathematics the *affine general linear group* **AGL**$(w, \mathbb{B})$. Its order is $2^{(w+1)w/2} \, w!_2$. Table 3.2 gives order(**AGL**$(w, \mathbb{B})$); that is, the number $AL(w)$ of different affine linear reversible circuits.

Affine linear circuits are particularly interesting because of a property they do *not* have. An arbitrary Boolean function can be synthesized by (loop-free and fanout-free) wiring together a finite number of *identical* reversible gates, provided that this type of gate is *not* affine linear. Appendix C gives the proof of this remarkable theorem. The initial part of the proof (Appendix C.3) is due to Kerntopf [32], while the latter part (Section C.4) is due to De Vos and Storme [33, 34]. In other words: any reversible circuit that is not affine linear can be used as a universal building block. Thus, affine-linear reversible circuits are 'weak' circuits. Indeed, any wiring of affine linear circuits (reversible or not, identical or not) can only yield affine linear Boolean functions as its outputs. We see from Table 3.2 that (at least for $w > 2$) the vast majority of the reversible circuits are not affine linear and thus can act as universal gates.

The group **AL** is simultaneously a supergroup of **L** and a subgroup of **R**:

$$\mathbf{R} \supset \mathbf{AL} \supset \mathbf{L} \, .$$

3.7
Exchange Gates

We now descend through the hierarchy of subgroups by imposing the rule that *each of the outputs equals one of the inputs*. Table 3.4a is such a circuit:

$$P = B$$
$$Q = A$$
$$R = C, \tag{3.6}$$

as depicted in Figure 3.5a. Such circuits are called *exchangers* (or exchange gates). They form a subgroup **E** that is isomorphic to the symmetric group $\mathbf{S}_w$ of order $w!$ (this number is given in Table 3.2 too). The group is also isomorphic to the group of $w \times w$ permutation matrices. This symmetric group should not be confused with the symmetric group $\mathbf{S}_{2^w}$ of order $(2^w)!$.

Like any reversible truth table, Table 3.4a can be seen as a permutation of its 2^w rows. Because Table 3.4a represents an exchange gate, it can also be interpreted as a permutaion of the w columns. Thus, the gate defined by the set (3.6) can be described by a $w \times w$ permutation matrix, but also (just like any reversible circuit

Table 3.4 Truth tables of two reversible logic circuits of width 3: (a) an exchange gate and (b) an affine exchange gate.

ABC	PQR
0 0 0	0 0 0
0 0 1	0 0 1
0 1 0	1 0 0
0 1 1	1 0 1
1 0 0	0 1 0
1 0 1	0 1 1
1 1 0	1 1 0
1 1 1	1 1 1

(a)

ABC	PQR
0 0 0	0 1 0
0 0 1	0 1 1
0 1 0	1 1 0
0 1 1	1 1 1
1 0 0	0 0 0
1 0 1	0 0 1
1 1 0	1 0 0
1 1 1	1 0 1

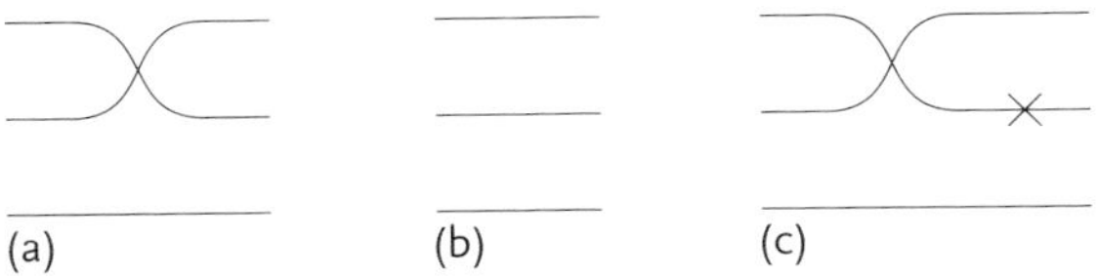

(b)

(a)   (b)   (c)

Figure 3.5 Three reversible circuits of width $w = 3$: (a) an exchange gate, (b) the identity gate, and (c) an affine exchange gate.

of width w) by a $2^w \times 2^w$ permutation matrix:

$$\begin{pmatrix} P \\ Q \\ R \end{pmatrix} = \begin{pmatrix} 0 & 1 & 0 \\ 1 & 0 & 0 \\ 0 & 0 & 1 \end{pmatrix} \begin{pmatrix} A \\ B \\ C \end{pmatrix} \quad \text{and}$$

$$\begin{pmatrix} p \\ q \\ r \\ s \\ t \\ u \\ v \\ w \end{pmatrix} = \begin{pmatrix} 1 & 0 & 0 & 0 & 0 & 0 & 0 & 0 \\ 0 & 1 & 0 & 0 & 0 & 0 & 0 & 0 \\ 0 & 0 & 0 & 0 & 1 & 0 & 0 & 0 \\ 0 & 0 & 0 & 0 & 0 & 1 & 0 & 0 \\ 0 & 0 & 1 & 0 & 0 & 0 & 0 & 0 \\ 0 & 0 & 0 & 1 & 0 & 0 & 0 & 0 \\ 0 & 0 & 0 & 0 & 0 & 0 & 1 & 0 \\ 0 & 0 & 0 & 0 & 0 & 0 & 0 & 1 \end{pmatrix} \begin{pmatrix} a \\ b \\ c \\ d \\ e \\ f \\ g \\ h \end{pmatrix},$$

where a stands for 000, b stands for 001, ..., and h stand for 111, and the same for $p, q, \ldots$ Group theorists say that we have two different *representations* of the same group here. In order to avoid confusion, in the present book, variables in the $w \times w$ representation are denoted by uppercase letters, whereas variables in the $2^w \times 2^w$ representation are denoted by lowercase letters. The distinction between the $w \times w$ world and the $2^w \times 2^w$ world is very important. It will reappear in the present book again and again.

Because we have a permutation of w objects, we may use the cycle notation (Section 2.2). However, in order to distinguish it from the permutation of 2^w objects, we will use semicolumns instead of commas. Thus, Table 3.4a is the permutation $(1;2)$, as the first and the second bits are interchanged. We may write:

$$(1;2) = (3,5)(4,6) ,$$

where $(1;2)$ represents a permutation of the three truth table columns and $(3,5)(4,6)$ represents a permutation of the eight truth table rows.

Finally, we can impose the rule that each of the outputs equals the corresponding input:

$$P = A$$
$$Q = B$$
$$R = C .$$

This results in the trivial subgroup **I** of order 1 (isomorphic to $\mathbf{S}_1$) consisting of just one circuit; that is, the identity gate i (Figure 3.5b).

We have thus constructed a chain of subgroups:

$$\mathbf{R} \supset \mathbf{AL} \supset \mathbf{L} \supset \mathbf{E} \supset \mathbf{I} \tag{3.7}$$

isomorphic to

$$\mathbf{S}_{2^w} \supset \mathbf{AGL}(w, \mathbb{B}) \supset \mathbf{GL}(w, \mathbb{B}) \supset \mathbf{S}_w \supset \mathbf{I} ,$$

with the subsequent orders

$$(2^w)! > 2^{(w+1)w/2}w!_2 > 2^{(w-1)w/2}w!_2 > w! > 1 \,,$$

where we have tacitly assumed $w > 1$. Here, the symbol $\supset$ corresponds to *is a proper supergroup of*. For the example of $w = 3$, this becomes:

$$\mathbf{S}_8 \supset \mathbf{AGL}(3, \mathbb{B}) \supset \mathbf{GL}(3, \mathbb{B}) \supset \mathbf{S}_3 \supset \mathbf{I} \,,$$

with the subsequent orders

$$40\,320 > 1\,344 > 168 > 6 > 1 \,.$$

3.8
SWAP Gates

Exchange gates where only two bit wires are interchanged are called SWAP gates. There are $\binom{w}{2} = w(w-1)/2$ such gates. In fact, Table 3.4a is a SWAP gate, as (3.6) reveals that A and B are swapped.

SWAP gates do *not* form a group. Suffice it to say that the cascade of two SWAP gates is always an exchanger, but not necessarily a SWAP gate. For example,

$$(1;3)*(2;3)=(1;2;3) \,.$$

The SWAP gates form a set of generators of the exchangers.

Actually, there are two different symbols for the SWAP gate. Figure 3.6a is an icon that is self-explanatory: two wires crossing each other. Figure 3.6b is an alternative icon, which may be advantageous in two cases: when a circuit contains a lot of SWAPs, and when two distant wires are swapped. In the present book, we will only apply the iconography of Figure 3.6a.

3.9
Affine Exchange Gates

Just as linear circuits (Section 3.5) are generalized to affine linear circuits (Section 3.6), we can generalize exchangers (Section 3.7) to *affine exchangers*. Table 3.4b and Figure 3.5c is just such a circuit. In matrix notation it looks like

$$\begin{pmatrix} P \\ Q \\ R \end{pmatrix} = \begin{pmatrix} 0 \\ 1 \\ 0 \end{pmatrix} \oplus \begin{pmatrix} 0 & 1 & 0 \\ 1 & 0 & 0 \\ 0 & 0 & 1 \end{pmatrix} \begin{pmatrix} A \\ B \\ C \end{pmatrix} \,. \tag{3.8}$$

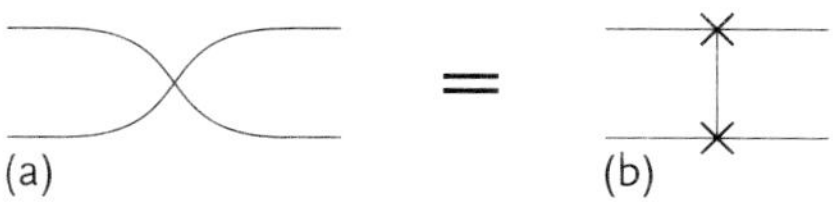

(a)   =   (b)

Figure 3.6 Two symbols for the same SWAP gate.

They form the subgroup **AE** of order $w!2^w$ (this number $AE(w)$ is also given in Table 3.2).

This group is a subgroup of the group of affine linear circuits and a supergroup of the group of exchangers. However, it cannot be inserted into chain (3.7), as it is neither a subgroup nor a supergroup of the group of linear circuits. Instead of a chain, we obtain what mathematicians call a *partial ordering*:

$$\mathbf{R} \supset \mathbf{AL} \begin{Bmatrix} \supset & \mathbf{L} & \supset \\ \supset & \mathbf{AE} & \supset \end{Bmatrix} \mathbf{E} \supset \mathbf{I} . \tag{3.9}$$

Figure 3.7 illustrates this by means of a Venn diagram (named after the British logician John Venn). Note that the group **E** is the intersection of **L** and **AE**:

$$\mathbf{E} = \mathbf{L} \cap \mathbf{AE} .$$

Affine exchangers allow us to illustrate the non-Abelian nature of reversible circuits. Figure 3.8 shows two circuits, each a cascade of an inverter and an exchanger. By straightforward construction of the truth tables, we find the $2^w \times 2^w$ permutation matrices of the two building-blocks; that is, the matrix I of the inverter and the matrix E of the exchanger:

$$I = \begin{pmatrix} 0 & 0 & 1 & 0 & 0 & 0 & 0 & 0 \\ 0 & 0 & 0 & 1 & 0 & 0 & 0 & 0 \\ 1 & 0 & 0 & 0 & 0 & 0 & 0 & 0 \\ 0 & 1 & 0 & 0 & 0 & 0 & 0 & 0 \\ 0 & 0 & 0 & 0 & 0 & 0 & 1 & 0 \\ 0 & 0 & 0 & 0 & 0 & 0 & 0 & 1 \\ 0 & 0 & 0 & 0 & 1 & 0 & 0 & 0 \\ 0 & 0 & 0 & 0 & 0 & 1 & 0 & 0 \end{pmatrix} \quad \text{and}$$

$$E = \begin{pmatrix} 1 & 0 & 0 & 0 & 0 & 0 & 0 & 0 \\ 0 & 1 & 0 & 0 & 0 & 0 & 0 & 0 \\ 0 & 0 & 0 & 0 & 1 & 0 & 0 & 0 \\ 0 & 0 & 0 & 0 & 0 & 1 & 0 & 0 \\ 0 & 0 & 1 & 0 & 0 & 0 & 0 & 0 \\ 0 & 0 & 0 & 1 & 0 & 0 & 0 & 0 \\ 0 & 0 & 0 & 0 & 0 & 0 & 1 & 0 \\ 0 & 0 & 0 & 0 & 0 & 0 & 0 & 1 \end{pmatrix} .$$

The reader can easily verify that the two matrix products give different results:

$$I E \neq E I . \tag{3.10}$$

Thus, neither matrix multiplication nor the cascading of reversible gates are commutative. We now introduce another inverter (that inverts the first bit, not the sec-

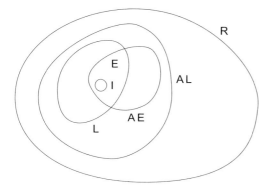

Figure 3.7 Venn diagram of reversible circuits, affine linear reversible circuits, linear reversible circuits, affine exchange gates, exchange gates, and the identity gate.

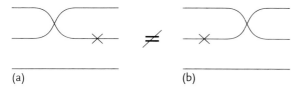

(a)   (b)

Figure 3.8 Two different cascades (with $w = 3$) of an inverter and an exchanger, representing two different affine exchangers.

ond bit):

$$J = \begin{pmatrix} 0 & 0 & 0 & 0 & 1 & 0 & 0 & 0 \\ 0 & 0 & 0 & 0 & 0 & 1 & 0 & 0 \\ 0 & 0 & 0 & 0 & 0 & 0 & 1 & 0 \\ 0 & 0 & 0 & 0 & 0 & 0 & 0 & 1 \\ 1 & 0 & 0 & 0 & 0 & 0 & 0 & 0 \\ 0 & 1 & 0 & 0 & 0 & 0 & 0 & 0 \\ 0 & 0 & 1 & 0 & 0 & 0 & 0 & 0 \\ 0 & 0 & 0 & 1 & 0 & 0 & 0 & 0 \end{pmatrix}.$$

The reader can now verify the equality

$$I E = E J .$$

See Figure 3.9.

Reading Figure 3.8a in the 'conventional' way (from left to right), the exchanger E comes first and the inverter I comes after. Forward computations are performed in that order. Thus, circuit schematics are read from left to right, according to engineering tradition. Unfortunately, mathematicians follow the other convention, writing and reading operations from right to left. This is why, on the left-hand side of (3.10), the inverter is the matrix furthest to the left in the product and the exchanger is the matrix furthest to the right. It is no surprise that the difference between the two order conventions often leads to unpleasant errors...

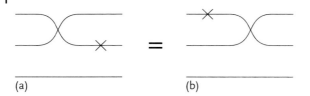

(a)   (b)

Figure 3.9 Two different cascades (with $w = 3$) of an inverter and an exchanger, representing the same affine exchanger.

Whereas Figure 3.8a can be written with $w \times w$ and $w \times 1$ matrices by (3.8), Figure 3.8b can be written with $w \times w$ and $w \times 1$ matrices by

$$\begin{pmatrix} P \\ Q \\ R \end{pmatrix} = \begin{pmatrix} 0 & 1 & 0 \\ 1 & 0 & 0 \\ 0 & 0 & 1 \end{pmatrix} \left[\begin{pmatrix} 0 \\ 1 \\ 0 \end{pmatrix} \oplus \begin{pmatrix} A \\ B \\ C \end{pmatrix} \right] ,$$

whereas Figure 3.9b can be written

$$\begin{pmatrix} P \\ Q \\ R \end{pmatrix} = \begin{pmatrix} 0 & 1 & 0 \\ 1 & 0 & 0 \\ 0 & 0 & 1 \end{pmatrix} \left[\begin{pmatrix} 1 \\ 0 \\ 0 \end{pmatrix} \oplus \begin{pmatrix} A \\ B \\ C \end{pmatrix} \right] . \tag{3.11}$$

3.10
Control Gates

We now introduce a special class of reversible logic circuits, called *control gates*. They will play a pivotal role in the present book. We define them by means of their relationship between the w outputs $P_1, P_2, \ldots, P_w$ and the w inputs $A_1, A_2, \ldots, A_w$.

In a control gate, we always have $P_1 = A_1$, $P_2 = A_2, \ldots, P_u = A_u$, where u is an integer that obeys $0 < u < w$. The other outputs, in other words $P_{u+1}, P_{u+2}, \ldots,$ and P_w, are controlled via some Boolean function f of the u inputs $A_1, A_2, \ldots, A_u$:

- If $f(A_1, A_2, \ldots, A_u) = 0$, then we additionally have $P_{u+1} = A_{u+1}$, $P_{u+2} = A_{u+2}, \ldots, P_w = A_w$.
- If, however, $f(A_1, A_2, \ldots, A_u) = 1$, then the values of $P_{u+1}, P_{u+2}, \ldots, P_w$ follow from the values of $A_{u+1}, A_{u+2}, \ldots, A_w$ by the application of a reversible circuit g of width $v = w - u$.

In other words, if $f = 0$, then we apply the w-bit follower to $A_1, A_2, \ldots, A_w$; otherwise, we apply the u-bit follower to $A_1, A_2, \ldots, A_u$, together with v-bit circuit g to $A_{u+1}, A_{u+2}, \ldots, A_w$. See Figure 3.10.

We call $A_1, A_2, \ldots, A_u$ the controlling bits and $A_{u+1}, A_{u+2}, \ldots, A_{u+v}$ the controlled bits. Whereas w is the width, u is the controlling width and v is the controlled width. We call f the control function and g the controlled circuit.

We stress that any Boolean function f is allowed. There are 2^{2^u} Boolean functions f of u binary variables. Together with the XOR operation, they form a group

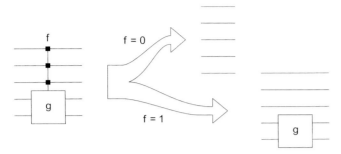

Figure 3.10 A control gate with $u = 3$ and $v = 2$ (and thus $w = 5$).

Table 3.5 Truth tables of three reversible logic circuits of width 3: (a) an arbitrary circuit, (b) a controlled NOT gate, and (c) a twin circuit.

$A_1 A_2 A_3$	$P_1 P_2 P_3$
0 0 0	1 0 0
0 0 1	1 0 1
0 1 0	1 1 0
0 1 1	0 0 0
1 0 0	1 1 1
1 0 1	0 1 1
1 1 0	0 1 0
1 1 1	0 0 1

(a)

$A_1 A_2 A_3$	$P_1 P_2 P_3$
0 0 0	0 0 1
0 0 1	0 0 0
0 1 0	0 1 1
0 1 1	0 1 0
1 0 0	1 0 1
1 0 1	1 0 0
1 1 0	1 1 0
1 1 1	1 1 1

(b)

$A_1 A_2 A_3$	$P_1 P_2 P_3$
0 0 0	0 0 1
0 0 1	0 1 1
0 1 0	0 1 0
0 1 1	0 0 0
1 0 0	1 0 0
1 0 1	1 0 1
1 1 0	1 1 1
1 1 1	1 1 0

(c)

isomorphic to the Young subgroup $\mathbf{S}_2 \times \mathbf{S}_2 \times \cdots \times \mathbf{S}_2 = \mathbf{S}_2^{2^u}$ (see Section 2.6). There-fore, the control gates with the same controlled gate g also form a group isomorphic to $\mathbf{S}_2^{2^u}$. Its order is 2^{2^u}. However, the reader is invited to check that the group con-ditions (Section 2.1) are only fulfilled provided $g^2 = i$, where i denotes the v-bit identity gate.[7] Figure 3.11a illustrates the first group condition: the cascade of two control gates (with the same controlled circuit g, one with a control function f_1, the other with a control function f_2) is also a control gate (with a control function $f_1 \oplus f_2$). Figure 3.11b illustrates the other group conditions: a control gate is its own inverse, and the identity gate may be interpreted as the control gate with a control function equal to the zero function.

We assign an icon to the control gate: Figure 3.12b (where $u = 4$ and $v = 2$, such that $w = 6$). Note that each of the controlling bits is labeled

7) Circuits satisfying $g^2 = i$ are sometimes called *involutary*. For the case where $g^2 \neq i$, in other words the case where order $(g) \neq 2$, the reader is referred to the 'control circuits' of Section 7.5.

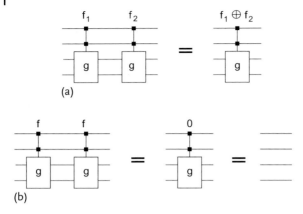

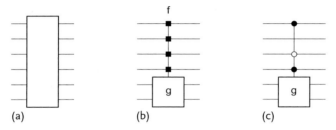

Figure 3.11 Group properties of the control gates with $u = v = 2$ (and thus $w = 4$).

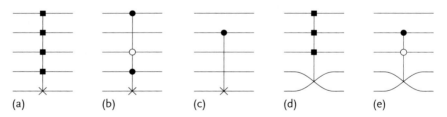

Figure 3.12 Symbols for reversible circuits of width $w = 6$: (a) an arbitrary circuit, (b) a control gate with an arbitrary control function f, and (c) a control gate with an AND control function.

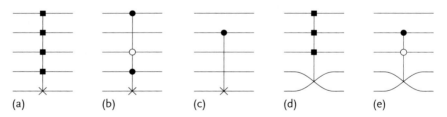

Figure 3.13 Symbols for control gates: (a) arbitrary controlled NOT gate, (b) specific TOFFOLI gate, (c) specific FEYNMAN gate, (d) arbitrary controlled SWAP gate, and (e) specific FREDKIN gate.

with a small black square. However, in the special case where the controlling function $f(A_1, A_2, \ldots, A_u)$ is an AND of some controlling bits, whether inverted or not, then circular tags are used: a filled circle if the variable is not inverted, an open circle if the variable is inverted. Figure 3.12c shows an example: $f(A_1, A_2, A_3, A_4) = A_1 \overline{A_3} A_4$.

We consider two special cases in detail:

- If $v = 1$, then there are only two possibilities for the controlled circuit g: either it is the trivial follower or it is the inverter. We only have to consider the latter choice. Then, in accordance with Figure 3.3, the controlled circuit g is represented by a cross: see Figure 3.13a. We call such gates controlled NOTs. An example is given in Table 3.5b. Its controlling function is $f(A_1, A_2) = \overline{A}_1 + \overline{A}_2$. This means: if $\overline{A}_1 + \overline{A}_2 = 0$ then $P_3 = A_3$, else $P_3 = \overline{A}_3$. Note that, in the truth table of a controlled NOT, the first two rows are either permuted or not, the second two rows are either permuted or not, etc. This reminds us of the fact that the controlled NOTs form a subgroup that is isomorphic to $\mathbf{S}_2 \times \mathbf{S}_2 \times \cdots \times \mathbf{S}_2$ of order $2^{2^{w-1}}$ [35].

  If the controlled NOT's control function f is an AND function, we call it a TOFFOLI gate (named after the Italian/American physicist/engineer Tommaso Toffoli, pioneer of reversible computing [29]). In Figure 3.13b, we show an example with the control function $f = A_1 \overline{A}_3 A_4$. Finally, if the control function is a single variable (i.e., if $f = A_j$), we call it a FEYNMAN gate [36, 37] (after the American physicist Richard Feynman, pioneer of quantum computing [38, 39]). See Figure 3.13c.

- If $v = 2$, then, at first sight, there are $4! = 24$ possibilities for the controlled circuit g. However, the restriction $g^2 = i$ lowers the number of candidates to 10. The most interesting case is where g is the SWAP gate. The controlled gate is then represented by a crossover: see Figure 3.13d. We call such gates controlled SWAPs. They form a subgroup of order $2^{2^{w-2}}$.

  If additionally the SWAP's control function is an AND function, we call it a FREDKIN gate (named after the American computer scientist Edward Fredkin, pioneer of reversible computing [29]). In Figure 3.13e, we show an example with the control function $f = A_2 \overline{A}_3$. In accordance with Figure 3.6, a controlled SWAP may also be written as in Figure 3.14b. This icon should not be confused with two controlled NOTs (Figure 3.14c)! Anyway, we will not be using symbols in the style of Figure 3.14b in this book.

Note that the functionality of the controlled NOT gate can be written as a set of w Boolean equations:

$$P_1 = A_1$$
$$P_2 = A_2$$
$$\ldots$$
$$P_{w-1} = A_{w-1}$$
$$P_w = f(A_1, A_2, \ldots, A_{w-1}) \oplus A_w \,, \tag{3.12}$$

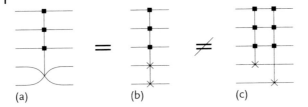

Figure 3.14 Two different icons for the controlled SWAP gate.

and so can the functionality of the controlled SWAP gate:

$$P_1 = A_1$$
$$P_2 = A_2$$

$$\cdots$$

$$P_{w-2} = A_{w-2}$$
$$P_{w-1} = f(A_1, A_2, \ldots, A_{w-2})(A_{w-1} \oplus A_w) \oplus A_{w-1}$$
$$P_w = f(A_1, A_2, \ldots, A_{w-2})(A_{w-1} \oplus A_w) \oplus A_w . \tag{3.13}$$

Also note that, in (3.12), even if the control function f is not a balanced function of $A_1, A_2, \ldots, A_{w-1}$, the function $f \oplus A_w$ is automatically a balanced function of $A_1, A_2, \ldots, A_w$. Analogously, in (3.13), even if the control function f is not a balanced function of $A_1, A_2, \ldots, A_{w-2}$, the functions $f(A_{w-1} \oplus A_w) \oplus A_{w-1}$ and $f(A_{w-1} \oplus A_w) \oplus A_w$ are automatically balanced functions of $A_1, A_2, \ldots, A_w$.

So far, we have discussed control gates where the uppermost u wires are the controlling wires and the lowest v wires are the controlled wires. In particular, we considered the controlled NOT, where bits #1, #2, ..., and #$w - 1$ are the controlling bits, whereas bit #w is the controlled bit. However, there is nothing to prevent us from also considering controlled NOTs where wire #k is controlled by wires $1, 2, \ldots, k - 1, k + 1, \ldots, w - 1$, and w. Figure 3.15a shows an example for $w = 5$: a controlled NOT where the NOT is on the fourth wire ($k = 4$) and the controlling wires are #1, #2, #3, and #5.

Just as controlled NOTs where the controlled bit is equal to bit #w form a group (of order $2^{2^{w-1}}$), controlled NOTs where the controlled bit is equal to bit #k also form a group (equally of order $2^{2^{w-1}}$). If $k \neq w$, then these two subgroups of **R** are different. Because k can take any value from $\{1, 2, \ldots, w\}$, we thus have w dif-

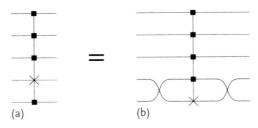

Figure 3.15 A controlled NOT gate.

ferent subgroups $\mathbf{H}_k$ of $\mathbf{R}$. Although all different, they greatly resemble each other. These w subgroups are said to be *conjugate* to each other. This means that one subgroup $\mathbf{H}_j$ can be obtained from another one $\mathbf{H}_k$ as follows:

$$\mathbf{H}_j = c\mathbf{H}_k c^{-1} \, ,$$

where c is some particular member of the supergroup $\mathbf{R}$. In our case we have that $c = c^{-1}$ is a SWAP gate exchanging the wires #j and #k. Figure 3.15b illustrates how $\mathbf{H}_4$ can be deduced from $\mathbf{H}_5$ as the cascade $c\mathbf{H}_5 c^{-1}$.

We note that the present set of w conjugate subgroups overlap very little, as two of the conjugate subgroups have only one element in common; that is, the identity element (or w-bit follower):

$$\mathbf{H}_j \cap \mathbf{H}_k = \mathbf{I} \quad \text{if} \quad j \neq k \, .$$

This small overlap must nevertheless be taken into account when counting the number of controlled NOTs with arbitrary controlled wires: there are *not* w times $2^{2^{w-1}}$ different control gates, only $w(2^{2^{w-1}} - 1) + 1$. These gates do *not* form a group. They, in fact, form a set of generators that generate the full group $\mathbf{R}$ of reversible circuits. In the next few sections, these building blocks will play a central role in the synthesis of an arbitrary reversible circuit.

3.11
Sylow Circuits

We can generalize the idea of the controlled NOT by cascading w controlled NOTs of ever-decreasing width: a controlled NOT of width w, one of width $w - 1, \dots$, and finally one of unit width; see Figure 3.16 (with $w = 4$). Such a circuit obeys the set of equations

$$P_j = f_j(A_1, A_2, \dots, A_{j-1}) \oplus A_j \quad \text{for} \quad 1 \leq j \leq w \, ,$$

where each of the w functions f_j is an arbitrary Boolean function of the $j - 1$ binary variables $A_1, A_2, \dots,$ and A_{j-1}. The w functions f_j are called the control functions of the circuit. Table 3.6a gives an example (where $w = 3$):

$$P_1 = 1 \oplus A_1$$
$$P_2 = A_1 \oplus A_2$$
$$P_3 = \overline{A_1} A_2 \oplus A_3 \, ,$$

with three control functions: $f_1 = 1$, $f_2(A_1) = A_1$, and $f_3(A_1, A_2) = \overline{A_1} A_2$.

For the function f_1, there are two possible choices (either $f_1 = 0$ or $f_1 = 1$); for the function f_2, there are four possible choices ($f_2 = 0$, $f_2 = A_1$, $f_2 = 1 \oplus A_1$, and $f_2 = 1$); for f_3, there are 16 possible choices; etc. The total number of possible combinations is thus

$$2 \times 2^2 \times 2^{2^2} \times \cdots \times 2^{2^{w-1}} = 2^{1+2+2^2+\cdots+2^{w-1}} = 2^{2^w - 1} \, .$$

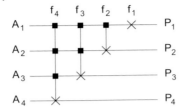

Figure 3.16 A Sylow cascade of $w = 4$ control gates.

Table 3.6 Truth table of two Sylow reversible logic circuits of width 3.

$A\,B\,C$	$P\,Q\,R$		$A\,B\,C$	$P\,Q\,R$
0 0 0	1 0 0		0 0 0	0 0 1
0 0 1	1 0 1		0 0 1	0 1 0
0 1 0	1 1 1		0 1 0	0 1 1
0 1 1	1 1 0		0 1 1	1 0 0
1 0 0	0 1 0		1 0 0	1 0 1
1 0 1	0 1 1		1 0 1	1 1 0
1 1 0	0 0 0		1 1 0	1 1 1
1 1 1	0 0 1		1 1 1	0 0 0

(a)   (b)

One can check that each combination gives a different (reversible) truth table. Taken together, all of these circuits form a group [35]. The order of the group is thus 2^{2^w-1}, which is exactly the factor 2^{x_2} in the prime factorization (3.3)–(3.4). This proves that the group is a Sylow 2-subgroup of the group $\mathbf{R}$ of reversible circuits of width w. Because of Lagrange's theorem (Section 2.5), no subgroup of $\mathbf{R}$ of order 2^y with $y > 2^w - 1$ can exist.

A controlled NOT, as described in the previous section (with a single control function f), is a special case where the first $w - 1$ functions f_j equal zero but the last function f_w equals f. Thus, the controlled NOTs form a subgroup of the Sylow group.

Reading from left to right, the crosses in Figure 3.16 are positioned from bottom to top. Other orders are possible, with each ordering generating another Sylow subgroup. These $w!$ Sylow groups are conjugate subgroups of the supergroup $\mathbf{R}$. In particular, ordering the crosses from top-left to bottom-right leads to an interesting example: the circuit of Figure 3.17. Here, all control gates are TOFFOLI gates, as all control functions are AND functions:

$$P_j = A_{j+1}A_{j+2}\ldots A_w \oplus A_j \quad \text{for} \quad 1 \le j \le w-1$$
$$P_w = 1 \oplus A_w \,.$$

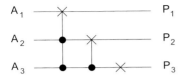

Figure 3.17 A $w = 3$ Sylow cascade of TOFFOLI gates.

This is called the *cyclic-shift circuit* [40, 41]. The case $w = 3$ illustrates why:

$$P_1 = A_2 A_3 \oplus A_1$$

$$P_2 = A_3 \oplus A_2$$

$$P_3 = 1 \oplus A_3 \,.$$

Table 3.6b gives the corresponding truth table. It shows how the value of the output word PQR equals the value of the input word one row below. The 2^w words are thus permuted according to the cyclic permutation $(1,\ 2,\ 3,\ \dots,\ 2^w)$.

3.12
Gate Cost and Logic Depth

In the next few sections, we will discuss the synthesis problem in detail. Given a truth table, synthesis involves constructing a cascade of simple circuits (i.e., gates) that performs the functionality of the table. There are usually many solutions; there is no unique synthesis. In order to evaluate the quality of a particular synthesis, we can use various *cost functions*. The lower the cost of the design, the more *efficient* the synthesis is considered to be.

Numerous cost functions have been defined for both conventional and reversible circuits, as well as for quantum circuits. We will present only two of them here:

- The gate cost, and
- The logic depth.

We will introduce a third at a later stage (Section 4.6):

- The switch cost.

There are different definitions of gate cost in the literature on reversible circuits. The price of an exchange gate in general and that of a SWAP gate in particular are matters of debate. Some authors consider any exchange gate to be free of cost. Other authors decompose an exchange circuit into a cascade of successive SWAP gates and attribute a gate cost equal to 3 to each SWAP gate. The gate cost of 3 units results from the fact that a SWAP gate can be constructed from three cascaded

Figure 3.18 The equivalence of a SWAP gate and three FEYNMAN gates.

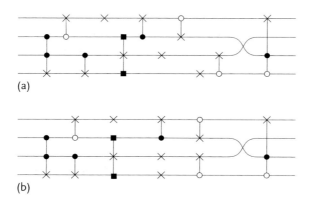

(a)

(b)

Figure 3.19 The same $w = 4$ logic circuit (a) before telescoping, (b) after telescoping.

FEYNMAN gates:

$$\begin{pmatrix} 0 & 1 \\ 1 & 0 \end{pmatrix} = \begin{pmatrix} 1 & 1 \\ 0 & 1 \end{pmatrix}\begin{pmatrix} 1 & 0 \\ 1 & 1 \end{pmatrix}\begin{pmatrix} 1 & 1 \\ 0 & 1 \end{pmatrix} \tag{3.14}$$

where the SWAP and the FEYNMANs, being linear gates, are represented by $2 \times 2 = w \times w$ matrices (Section 3.5); see Figure 3.18. For controlled SWAPs, a similar decomposition (into three controlled NOTs) exists.

In the present book, we will apply the following simple rules:

- Any exchanger has a gate cost and a logic depth equal to 0.
- Any control gate (NOT gate, FEYNMAN gate, TOFFOLI gate, or other controlled NOT, or FREDKIN gate, or other controlled SWAP) has a gate cost and logic depth equal to 1.

Therefore, the total gate cost of a circuit is equal to the number of control gates in it. Figure 3.19a shows an example: a sequence of twelve gates. We see a TOFFOLI gate, two FEYNMAN gates, a NOT gate, a controlled NOT gate, a FEYNMAN gate, a NOT gate, a FEYNMAN gate, a NOT gate, a FEYNMAN gate, a SWAP gate, and a TOFFOLI gate. Considering that the SWAP gate does not contribute to the gate cost, the circuit has a gate cost of 11.

Whereas the gate cost is a measure of the fabrication cost (and thus the purchase price) of a circuit, the logic depth is more related to the exploitation cost of the circuit. It provides a rough estimate of the effort and time necessary to perform a computation with the computer circuit. We assume that each control gate takes the same (short) time to perform its task. The logic depth gives a rough estimate of the total time needed by the circuit to perform the full computation. Nevertheless, the logic depth is not necessarily equal to the number of control gates. It is an integer that is smaller than or equal to the gate cost. Figure 3.19 explains the difference between gate cost and logic depth. As mentioned above, the circuit of Figure 3.19a has a gate cost equal to eleven. Nevertheless, the logic depth is only 6. Indeed, some computations may be performed 'simultaneously'. By sliding some of the small gates of Figure 3.19a, we obtain (the completely equivalent) Figure 3.19b. There, two or three simple computations are sometimes performed 'in parallel'. The whole calculation requires only six subsequent elementary steps.

3.13
Methods of Synthesis

The task of finding the circuit (i.e., the appropriate cascade of gates) that realizes a given truth table is known as the *synthesis problem*. However, we must distinguish between two different synthesis problems:

- Either we want to implement an arbitrary (but given) Boolean function $f(A_1, A_2, \ldots, A_n)$; that is, we want to translate a truth table with n input columns and one output column,
- Or we want to implement a given reversible Boolean truth table (with w input columns and w output columns), i.e., we want to realize w Boolean functions $P_1(A_1, A_2, \ldots, A_w), P_2(A_1, A_2, \ldots, A_w), \ldots, P_w(A_1, A_2, \ldots, A_w)$.

The former problem is discussed in Sections 3.20 to 3.22; we will discuss the latter first, in Sections 3.14 to 3.19.

A lot of tools are available for the synthesis of conventional logic circuits (i.e., not necessarily reversible circuits). These tools can be applied to design reversible circuits. However, such an approach has a few inconvenient aspects. The resulting circuit may provide the requested reversible logic function, but be built from irreversible building blocks. For example, the (sub)circuits in Figure 1.1 contain the irreversible AND gate, OR gate, and XOR gate. Such hardware can only be applied in the forward direction. Backward computation is then impossible. Therefore, we must take the necessary precautions to ensure that only reversible gates are applied. For example, the Davio circuit of Figure 1.1b can be replaced by a single TOFFOLI gate [42, 43]: see Figure 3.20.

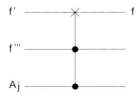

Figure 3.20 Davio decomposition by means of a TOFFOLI gate.

Even with the above precautions, conventional methods may not be the best choice. Indeed, assume that we would like to synthesize the circuit of Table 3.5a. We could apply Davio decompositions to each of the three logic functions $P_1(A_1, A_2, A_3)$, $P_2(A_1, A_2, A_3)$, and $P_3(A_1, A_2, A_3)$. Then, however, we apply general-purpose techniques that do not take advantage of several properties of these functions P_1, P_2, and P_3. Because Table 3.5a is reversible, the three columns P_1, P_2, and P_3 contain the same amount of information as the columns A_1, A_2, and A_3 do. Therefore, $P_1(A_1, A_2, A_3)$, $P_2(A_1, A_2, A_3)$, and $P_3(A_1, A_2, A_3)$ are not independent functions, and so synthesizing them separately may be a nonoptimal approach. Standard tools do not take into account that the eight output rows of Table 3.5a form a permutation of the eight input rows. They not even take into account that each of the functions $P_j(A_1, A_2, A_3)$ is balanced.

A lot of effort has been made to fix the above problems, often leading to successful results. In the present book, however, we will start from scratch and look for synthesis tools that are specially dedicated to reversible logic. Such tools may exploit the fact that reversible circuits form a group. Indeed, group theory provides us with a lot of theorems and tools. It would be a waste not to make use of them. One tool – subgroups – has already been encountered in the previous chapter. In the next few sections, we will introduce even more powerful tools: *cosets* and *double cosets*. Analogous to the Davio decomposition (which reduces one big original problem to two smaller problems; see Section 1.8), (double) cosets will enable us to decompose the original synthesis problem into one, two, or four smaller problems.

3.14
Cosets

Subgroups are at the heart of cosets. If **H** (with order H) is a subgroup of the group **G** (with order G), then **H** partitions **G** into $\frac{G}{H}$ classes, all of the same size H. These equipartition classes are called cosets. The number of cosets is $\frac{G}{H}$. Note that $\frac{G}{H}$ is always an integer because of Lagrange's theorem (Section 2.5). The number is called the index.

We can distinguish between left cosets and right cosets. The left coset of the element a of **G** is defined as all of the elements of **G** that can be written as a cascade ba, where b is an arbitrary element of **H**. This left coset forms an equipartition class because of the following property: if c is member of the left coset of a, then a is member of the left coset of c. Right cosets are defined in an analogous way. Note that **H** itself is one of the left cosets of **G**, as well as one of its right cosets. Moreover, **H** is the only coset that is a subgroup of **G**. Suffice it to say that **H** is the only coset containing the identity element.

Why should we want to define cosets? The answer is that they are very handy in synthesis. Assume that we want to make an arbitrary element of the group **G** in hardware. Instead of solving this problem for each of the G cases, we only synthe-size

- The H circuits b of **H**, and
- A single representative r_j of each of the $\frac{G}{H} - 1$ other left cosets $\left(1 \leq j \leq \frac{G}{H} - 1\right)$.

If we can make each of these $H + \frac{G}{H} - 1$ circuits, we can make all of the other circuits of **G** by merely creating a short cascade $b r_j$. If we choose the subgroup **H** cleverly, we can guarantee that $H + \frac{G}{H} - 1$ is much smaller than G. We call the set of $H + \frac{G}{H} - 1$ building blocks the *library* for synthesizing the G circuits of **G**.

Choosing the subgroup **H** of **G** cleverly presents a challenge to the designer. He/she can for example, aim to minimize the size of the library: $d(H + \frac{G}{H} - 1)/dH = 0$, which leads to $H = \sqrt{G}$. Of course, **G** will seldom have a subgroup of order $\sqrt{G}$. In most cases, $\sqrt{G}$ is not even an integer; it is an irrational number. In such cases, the designer has to look for a subgroup with an order that is 'in the neighborhood' of $\sqrt{G}$. Note in passing that the condition $H = \sqrt{G}$ can be rewritten as

$$\frac{\log(G)}{\log(H)} = 2 \; .$$

Ratios of logarithms of sizes will play more important parts in our story; see Appendix D.

Maslov and Dueck [44] present a method for synthesizing an arbitrary reversible circuit of width 3. They propose as a subgroup **H** of the group $\mathbf{G} = \mathbf{S}_8$ all circuits with output (P, Q, R) equal $(0, 0, 0)$ in the case of the input $(A, B, C) = (0, 0, 0)$ (thus having a truth table with the first row equal to 000 | 000). This subgroup is isomorphic to $\mathbf{S}_7$. Thus, the supergroup has order $G = 8! = 40\,320$, whereas the subgroup has order $H = 7! = 5040$. The subgroup partitions the supergroup into eight cosets. Interestingly, the procedure can be repeated: to design each of the 5040 members of $\mathbf{S}_7$, Maslov and Dueck choose a subgroup of $\mathbf{S}_7$. They chose all reversible circuits where (P, Q, R) equals $(0, 0, 0)$ in the case $(A, B, C) = (0, 0, 0)$ and equals $(0, 0, 1)$ in the case $(A, B, C) = (0, 0, 1)$. This is a subgroup that is isomorphic to $\mathbf{S}_6$ of order $6! = 720$, which partitions $\mathbf{S}_7$ into seven cosets, etc. Figure 3.21a illustrates one step in the procedure: the 24 elements of $\mathbf{S}_4$ are fabricated by means of the six elements of its subgroup $\mathbf{S}_3$ plus the representatives of the three other cosets in which $\mathbf{S}_4$ is partitioned by $\mathbf{S}_3$. Thus, Maslov and Dueck apply the following chain of subgroups:

$$\mathbf{S}_8 \supset \mathbf{S}_7 \supset \mathbf{S}_6 \supset \mathbf{S}_5 \supset \mathbf{S}_4 \supset \mathbf{S}_3 \supset \mathbf{S}_2 \supset \mathbf{S}_1 = \mathbf{I} \; , \qquad (3.15)$$

with subsequent orders

$$40\,320 > 5040 > 720 > 120 > 24 > 6 > 2 > 1 \; . \qquad (3.16)$$

To synthesize all 40 320 members of $\mathbf{S}_8$, they need a library of only $(7 + 6 + \ldots + 1) + 1 = 29$ elements (identity gate included). Their procedure also works for an arbitrary logic width w. For an arbitrary circuit width w, the synthesis of all $(2^w)!$ members of $\mathbf{S}_{2^w}$ requires a library of $2^{2w-1} - 2^{w-1} + 1$ elements, leading to cascades that are never longer than $2^w - 1$.

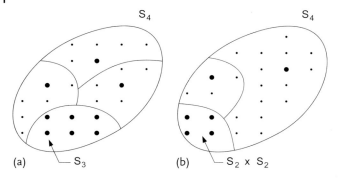

Figure 3.21 The symmetric group $\mathbf{S}_4$ partitioned (a) as the four left cosets of $\mathbf{S}_3$, and (b) as the three double cosets of $\mathbf{S}_2 \times \mathbf{S}_2$. Each *dot* depicts an element of the supergroup, while the *bold-faced dots* depict the elements of the subgroup and the representatives of the (double) cosets.

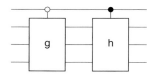

Figure 3.22 A twin circuit of width 4: if $A_1 = 0$ then apply g, else apply h.

Van Rentergem *et al.* [41, 45] also present a coset method for synthesis, although theirs is based on the following subgroup $\mathbf{H}$: all circuits from $\mathbf{R} = \mathbf{S}_{2^w}$ that possess the property $P_1 = A_1$. In other words, whereas Maslov and Dueck choose $\mathbf{H}$ with truth tables where the first output row equals the first input row, Van Rentergem *et al.* choose $\mathbf{H}$ with truth tables where the first output column equals the first input column. Note that, in the truth table of such a circuit, the upper 2^{w-1} rows are permuted among themselves, as are the bottom 2^{w-1} rows. Such circuits consist of the cascade of two control gates with $u = 1$ and $v = w - 1$; see Figure 3.22. If $A_1 = 0$, then g is applied to $A_2, A_3, \ldots,$ and A_w; otherwise (thus if $A_1 = 1$) h is applied. We will call such a circuit a twin circuit. An example is given in Table 3.5c.

The twin circuits form a subgroup that is isomorphic to $\mathbf{S}_{2^{w-1}} \times \mathbf{S}_{2^{w-1}}$. The twin circuits of width 3 form a group isomorphic to $\mathbf{S}_4 \times \mathbf{S}_4 = \mathbf{S}_4^2$ of order $(4!)^2 = 576$. The subgroup $\mathbf{S}_4^2$ partitions its supergroup $\mathbf{S}_8$ into 70 cosets. Like the Maslov–Dueck approach, the present decomposition can be applied recursively. Indeed, the members of $\mathbf{S}_4$ are subsequently partitioned into six cosets using its subgroup $\mathbf{S}_2^2$, etc. Thus, finally, Van Rentergem *et al.* apply the following chain of subgroups:

$$\mathbf{S}_8 \supset \mathbf{S}_4^2 \supset \mathbf{S}_2^4 \supset \mathbf{S}_1^8 = \mathbf{I} \,, \tag{3.17}$$

with subsequent orders

$$40\,320 > 576 > 16 > 1 \,. \tag{3.18}$$

The reader can easily generalize to an arbitrary value of w.

If we denote 2^w by n, then Dueck *et al.* apply the subgroup $\mathbf{S}_{n-1}$ of the group $\mathbf{S}_n$, whereas Van Rentergem *et al.* apply the subgroup $\mathbf{S}_{\frac{n}{2}} \times \mathbf{S}_{\frac{n}{2}}$. We note that both the group $\mathbf{S}_{n-1}$ (which can also be written $\mathbf{S}_{n-1} \times \mathbf{S}_1$) and the group $\mathbf{S}_{\frac{n}{2}} \times \mathbf{S}_{\frac{n}{2}}$ are Young subgroups of $\mathbf{S}_n$. See Section 2.6.

3.15
Double Cosets

Double cosets are even more powerful than cosets. The double coset of a, element of $\mathbf{G}$, is defined as the set of all elements of $\mathbf{G}$ that can be written as a cascade $b_1 a b_2$, where both b_1 and b_2 are members of the subgroup $\mathbf{H}$. One surprising fact is that, in general, the double cosets into which $\mathbf{G}$ is partitioned by $\mathbf{H}$ are of different sizes (ranging from H to H^2). Therefore, the number of double cosets into which $\mathbf{G}$ is partitioned by $\mathbf{H}$ is not easy to predict. It is some number between $\frac{G}{H^2}$ and $\frac{G}{H}$. This number is much smaller than $\frac{G}{H}$, leading to the (appreciated!) fact that there are far fewer double cosets than there are cosets. This results in smaller libraries for synthesis. However, there is a price to pay for this small library. Indeed, if the chain of subgroups considered is of length m, then the length of the synthesized cascade (i.e., the logic depth) is $2^m - 1$ (instead of m, as in single coset synthesis).

The subgroup $\mathbf{S}_{n-1}$ partitions its supergroup $\mathbf{S}_n$ into only two double cosets, a small one of size $(n - 1)!$ and a large one of size $(n - 1)!(n - 1)$. Therefore, a double coset approach using the Maslov–Dueck subgroup chain (3.15) needs only 2^w library elements. However, a synthesized cascade can be $2^{2^w} - 1$ gates long.

To address the problem of synthesizing all members of $\mathbf{S}_8$, Van Rentergem, De Vos and Storme [46] choose the double cosets of the subgroup obeying $P_1 = A_1$ (and discussed in the previous section). They conclude that, to synthesize all 40 320 members of $\mathbf{S}_8$, they need a library of only $(4 + 2 + 1) + 1 = 8$ elements. For an arbitrary circuit width w, the synthesis of all $(2^w)!$ members of $\mathbf{S}_{2^w}$ requires a library of 2^w elements.

Figure 3.21b illustrates one step in the procedure: the 24 elements of $\mathbf{S}_4$ are fabricated by means of the four elements of its subgroup $\mathbf{S}_2 \times \mathbf{S}_2$ plus the representatives of the two other double cosets in which $\mathbf{S}_4$ is partitioned by $\mathbf{S}_2 \times \mathbf{S}_2$. Figure 3.23a shows how an arbitrary member g of $\mathbf{S}_{16}$ is decomposed with the help of two members (b_1 and b_2) of $\mathbf{S}_8 \times \mathbf{S}_8$ and one representative of the double coset of g. Van Rentergem *et al.* have demonstrated that it is *always* possible to construct a representative that is a controlled NOT gate:

$$P_1 = f(A_2, A_3, \ldots, A_w) \oplus A_1$$
$$P_2 = A_2$$
$$P_3 = A_3$$
$$\ldots\ldots$$
$$P_w = A_w \, ,$$

where A_1 is the controlled bit ($k = 1$ in Section 3.10). A proof is given in Appendix E. The proof is based on the following remarkable theorem from combinatorics:

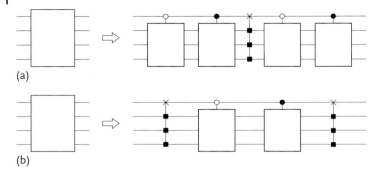

(a)

(b)

Figure 3.23 An arbitrary circuit g (member of the group $\mathbf{S}_{16}$), decomposed as $b_1 a b_2$ with the help of double cosets generated by (a) its subgroup $\mathbf{S}_8^2$ and (b) its subgroup $\mathbf{S}_2^8$.

If an integer n can be factorized as $p \times q$, then any permutation of n objects can be performed by subsequently applying

- q permutations, each of p objects,
- p permutations, each of q objects, and
- q permutations, each of p objects.

This theorem is (one of the many variants of) Birkhoff's theorem, named after the American mathematician Garrett Birkhoff. In particular, the above circuit decomposition is based on the theorem for the special case $n = 2^w$, $p = 2^{w-1}$, and thus $q = 2$.

We conclude that the present synthesis of an arbitrary circuit of width w consists of the cascade of

- A first twin circuit,
- A controlled NOT gate, and
- A second twin circuit.

We illustrate the procedure with an example where $\mathbf{G} = \mathbf{S}_8$ and $\mathbf{H}$ is isomorphic to $\mathbf{S}_4^2$, and thus $G = 40\,320$ and $H = 24^2 = 576$. We choose the truth table of Table 3.5a. Figure 3.24a shows the result of repeatedly applying the procedure until all controlled circuits are members of $\mathbf{S}_2$; that is, they are equal to either the one-bit identity gate or the one-bit inverter. The nested schematic can easily be translated into a chain of controlled NOTs; in other words, the conventional way of writing down a reversible circuit;[8] see Figure 3.24b. This particular circuit consists of eight controlled NOT gates, of which seven are simply TOFFOLI gates. Both the gate cost and the logic depth of circuit 3.24b is therefore 8. When we apply the same procedure to each of the 8! = 40 320 circuits of the group $\mathbf{S}_8$, we obtain a statistical

---

8) The reader should note that there is a handy special-purpose LaTeX package, called Q-Circuit, for writing such reversible (or quantum) networks [47]. However, that package was not used in this book.

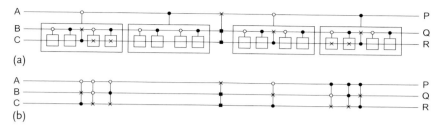

(a)

(b)

Figure 3.24 Decomposition of the example circuit of width 3 (Table 3.5a): (a) as nested control gates; (b) as a chain of controlled NOTs.

Figure 3.25 Photomicrograph (700 μm × 100 μm) of a 0.35-μm constructal reversible adder.

distribution of gate costs, ranging from 0 to 19, with an average gate cost of about 10.1.

The recursive procedure is illustrated by Figure 3.25, which shows a hardware implementation of a $w = 4$ circuit in silicon technology [48]. Although the details of such electronic implementations will be discussed in the next chapter, this photograph is shown here because it reveals the basic structure of the synthesis procedure. We see the controlled NOT gate, representative of the double coset, in the middle. Around it are four satellites that form the two twin circuits (compare with Figure 3.23a). In the middle of each satellite circuit, we again see a controlled NOT surrounded by four blocks, etc. The photograph reveals the fractal structure of the circuit. According to the proposal by Bejan [49], this is termed *constructal geometry* (instead of *fractal geometry*).

Finally, for an arbitrary w, we note that the present double coset approach may end up with a chain of cost of the order 4^w. Detailed calculations [50] reveal that both the gate cost and the logic depth are $\frac{1}{3}(4^w - 1)$ or less.

3.16
The Synthesis Algorithm

Instead of applying a subgroup $\mathbf{H}$ isomorphic to the Young subgroup $\mathbf{S}_{2^{w-1}} \times \mathbf{S}_{2^{w-1}} = \mathbf{S}_{2^{w-1}}^2$ and taking in each double coset a representative which is a member of $\mathbf{S}_2 \times \mathbf{S}_2 \times \cdots \times \mathbf{S}_2 = \mathbf{S}_2^{2^{w-1}}$, we can also work the other way around: choose a subgroup $\mathbf{H}$ isomorphic to the Young subgroup $\mathbf{S}_2^{2^{w-1}}$ and check whether there is a representative that is a member of $\mathbf{S}_{2^{w-1}}^2$ in each double coset; see Figure 3.23b. Indeed, this is always possible [51–53]. Again, a proof is provided by Birkhoff's theorem (Appendix E), but this time with $n = 2^w$, $p = 2$, and thus $q = 2^{w-1}$.

Therefore, we can conclude that a synthesis of an arbitrary circuit of width w can consist of the cascade of

- A first controlled NOT gate,
- A twin circuit, and
- A second controlled NOT gate.

Note that Figure 3.23b is like Figure 3.23a inside out. We say that the two circuits are each other's dual. They are indeed based on two different Young subgroups. These subgroups are based on two dual partitions of the number 2^w (i.e., the degree of the supergroup $\mathbf{S}_{2^w}$):

$$
\begin{aligned}
2^w &= 2^{w-1} + 2^{w-1} \\
&= 2 + 2 + \cdots + 2 \quad (2^{w-1} \text{ terms}) .
\end{aligned}
$$

The synthesis based on the former partition is discussed in the previous section, and its detailed synthesis algorithm is given in [46]. Because the latter partition leads to a far more efficient synthesis, it is much more important. Therefore, we now discuss the synthesis algorithm [51, 52] obtained using the latter partition in detail.

3.16.1
Basic Idea of the Algorithm

In the algorithm, we use notations like $A_i(j)$, where the subscript i refers to the column in the truth table, whereas the number j refers to the row. Thus, these counters obey $1 \leq i \leq w$ and $1 \leq j \leq 2^w$. To find the three parts of the decomposition as in Figure 3.23b, we proceed as follows. We add two extra sets of columns F and J to the given truth table (consisting of w input columns A and w output columns P). These are filled in three steps:

- First, we fill in the $w - 1$ columns $F_2, F_3, \ldots, F_w$ by merely copying columns $A_2, A_3, \ldots, A_w$; analogously, we fill in the $w-1$ columns $J_2, J_3, \ldots, J_w$ by merely copying columns $P_2, P_3, \ldots, P_w$.
- We then fill in the remaining two columns F_1 and J_1:
  - We construct a *coil* of 0s and 1s, starting from $F_1(1) = 0$;
  - Then we construct a second coil, starting from the unfilled $F_1(j)$ with the lowest j, etc., until all F_1 (and thus also all J_1) are filled in.

The coil referred to above consists of a finite number of 'windings'. Here, a winding is a four-bit sequence $F_1(k) = X$, $F_1(l) = \overline{X}$, $J_1(l) = \overline{X}$, and $J_1(m) = X$, where the row number l results from the condition that the string $F_2(l), F_3(l), \ldots, F_w(l)$ must be equal to the string $F_2(k), F_3(k), \ldots, F_w(k)$, and where the row number m results from the condition that the string $J_2(m), J_3(m), \ldots, J_w(m)$ must be equal to the string $J_2(l), J_3(l), \ldots, J_w(l)$.

A_1 A_2	F_1 F_2	J_1 J_2	P_1 P_2
0 0	0 0	0 1	0 1
0 1	1 1	1 1	1 1
1 0	1 0	1 0	0 0
1 1	0 1	0 0	1 0

Figure 3.26 A synthesis according to the basic algorithm ($w = 2$): expanded truth table.

Although the above text might suggest that the algorithm is complicated, it is in fact very straightforward. Figure 3.26 provides an illustration of this fact, by showing in detail the synthesis of a reversible circuit of width $w = 2$; that is, the circuit with two inputs (A_1 and A_2) and two outputs ($P_1 = A_2$ and $P_2 = \overline{A}_1$ in this particular case). First, we insert the four empty columns (F_1, F_2) and (J_1, J_2) between the columns (A_1, A_2) and (P_1, P_2) of the truth table. Subsequently, columns F_2 and J_2 are filled by simply copying columns A_2 and P_2, respectively. This step is displayed in boldface. Next comes the tricky part: filling the columns F_1 and J_1. To do this, we start at $F_1(1)$. We can set this bit arbitrarily, but we will choose to set it to 0. This starting choice is marked by a small square in Figure 3.26. As a consequence, we can automatically fill a lot of other bits into columns F_1 and J_1. Indeed, as all computations need to be reversible, $F_1(1) = 0$ automatically leads to $F_1(3) = 1$. Then we impose $J_1(3) = F_1(3)$; that is, $J_1(3) = 1$. Again, reversibility requires that $J_1(3) = 1$ infers $J_1(4) = 0\dots$, and so on, until we come back to the starting point $F_1(1)$. The arrows in Figure 3.26 show the order of filling. Everything is filled in when the route followed closes up, so this synthesis is finished after a single coil (with two windings). This example illustrates that, during the application of the algorithm, we 'walk in circles' while assigning the bit sequence

$$0, 1, 1, 0, 0, 1, 1, \dots, 1, 1, 0, 0, 1, 1, 0 .$$

If the first coil is closed before the two columns J_1 and F_1 are completely filled, the designer just starts a second coil, and so on.

The fact that the above algorithm always comes to an end with the extended truth table being completely filled provides additional proof that the theorem of Appendix E is true for the special case $p = 2$ (and thus $q = 2^{w-1}$).

As a result, the algorithm yields a decomposition of an arbitrary reversible circuit a (Figure 3.27a) into the desired cascade (Figure 3.27b) of

- A first controlled NOT gate with the controlled bit on the first wire,
- A twin circuit a_1 with the first bit left unaffected (its $P_1 = $ its A_1), and
- A second controlled NOT gate with the controlled bit on the first wire.

Note that circuit a_1 in Figure 3.27b is simpler than circuit a in Figure 3.27a, as a_1 obeys $P_1 = A_1$.

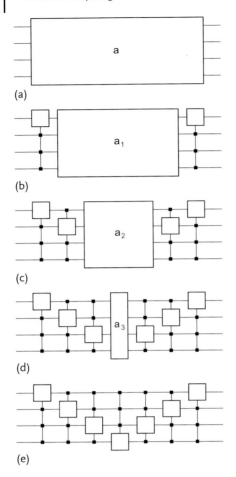

Figure 3.27 Step-by-step decomposition of a reversible logic circuit of width $w = 4$: (a) original logic circuit; (b), (c), and (d) intermediate steps; (e) final decomposition.

3.16.2
Working Out the Algorithm

The algorithm can now be 'deepened' as follows. By applying the decomposition of a_1 into three circuits, we obtain Figure 3.27c, where the circuit a_2 is again simpler than the circuit a_1, because it fulfils both $P_1 = A_1$ and $P_2 = A_2$. We continue like this, until we obtain Figure 3.27d, where the circuit a_{w-1} obeys $P_1 = A_1$, $P_2 = A_2$, ..., and $P_{w-1} = A_{w-1}$. These properties reveal that a_{w-1} is simply a control gate with a controlled bit A_w. Therefore, Figure 3.27d is equivalent to Figure 3.27e, such that we have decomposed a into $2w - 1$ controlled NOT gates. This procedure automatically leads us to the detailed algorithm.

We add to the given truth table (consisting of w input columns A and w output columns P) not two extra sets of columns, but $2(w-1)$ sets of columns. We call them $A^1, A^2, \ldots, A^{w-2}, A^{w-1}, P^{w-1}, P^{w-2}, \ldots, P^2$, and P^1. Together they make $2(w-1)w$ new columns. These are filled in according to the following steps:

- First, we fill all A^1 columns except column A^1_1 by copying the $w-1$ corresponding A columns; analogously, we fill all P^1 columns except column P^1_1 by copying the $w-1$ corresponding P columns.
- Then we fill the two columns A^1_1 and P^1_1 by constructing a coil starting from bit $A^1_1(1)$, and then constructing a new coil starting at the unfilled $A^1_1(j)$ with the lowest j, etc., until all A^1_1 (and thus also all P^1_1) are filled in.
- Then, we fill all A^2 columns except column A^2_2 by copying the $w-1$ corresponding A^1 columns; analogously, we fill all P^2 columns except column P^2_2 by copying the $w-1$ corresponding P^1 columns.
- Then we fill the two columns A^2_2 and P^2_2 by constructing the appropriate number of coils, starting from bit $A^2_2(1)$ until all A^2_2 (and thus also all P^2_2) are filled in.
- And so on, until all A^{w-1}_{w-1} (and thus also all P^{w-1}_{w-1}) are filled in. We then have all $2w^2 2^w$ entries of the extended table.

We end the present section with a historical perspective. The Birkhoff theorem, the basis of the above synthesis procedure, is also the basis for 'Clos networks' [54] (named after the American engineer Charles Clos); or, more precisely, rearrangeable (nonblocking) Clos networks [55–57]. In the past, this approach has been successfully applied to telephone switching systems. Nowadays, it finds use in internet routing [58]. These conventional applications of the Birkhoff theorem are concerned with permutations of wires (or communication channels); that is, with the decomposition of the members of the subgroup of exchangers (isomorphic to $\mathbf{S}_w$). Here we apply the theorem not to the w wires, but to the 2^w possible messages; in other words, to the full group $\mathbf{S}_{2^w}$. Figure 3.27b is reminiscent of Clos networks, but the final figure, 3.27e, is reminiscent of so-called 'banyan networks' (named after an Asian tree species), but with $n = 2^w$ instead of $n = w$. Finally, the coil/winding procedure of Section 3.16.1 is reminiscent of the 'looping algorithm', as presented by Hui [56].

3.16.3
Results

We will illustrate our deepened procedure using the example circuit in Table 3.5a. By applying the above procedure, we obtain Table 3.7. The first step of the procedure is displayed in bold face, while the second step is emphasized in italic. (The reader can verify that this step requires two coils; the former with three windings, the latter with only one winding.) The third step of the algorithm is underlined.

The above procedure thus yields a decomposition of the logic circuit into five logic circuits (one computing A^1 from A, one computing A^2 from $A^1, \ldots,$ and one computing P from P^1). All five subcircuits are automatically controlled NOT

Table 3.7 Expanded truth table according to the algorithm.

$A_1 A_2 A_3$	$A_1^1 A_2^1 A_3^1$	$A_1^2 A_2^2 A_3^2$	$P_1^2 P_2^2 P_3^2$	$P_1^1 P_2^1 P_3^1$	$P_1 P_2 P_3$
0 0 0	*0* 0 0	0 0 0	0 0 0	*0* 0 0	1 0 0
0 0 1	*1* 0 1	1 0 1	1 0 1	*1* 0 1	1 0 1
0 1 0	*0* 1 0	0 1 0	0 1 0	0 1 0	1 1 0
0 1 1	*1* 1 1	1 1 1	1 1 0	1 0 0	0 0 0
1 0 0	*1* 0 0	1 1 0	1 1 1	1 1 1	1 1 1
1 0 1	*0* 0 1	0 0 1	0 0 1	0 1 1	0 1 1
1 1 0	*1* 1 0	1 0 0	1 0 0	1 1 0	0 1 0
1 1 1	*0* 1 1	0 1 1	0 1 1	0 0 1	0 0 1

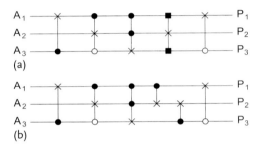

Figure 3.28 Decomposition of the example circuit of width 3 (Table 3.5a) according to the algorithm: (a) into controlled NOT gates; (b) into TOFFOLI gates.

gates. By merely inspecting Table 3.7, we find their successive control functions:
$f(A_2, A_3) = A_3$, $f\left(A_1^1, A_3^1\right) = A_1^1 \overline{A_3}^1$, $f\left(A_1^2, A_2^2\right) = A_1^2 A_2^2$, $f\left(P_1^2, P_3^2\right) = P_1^2 \oplus P_3^2$,
and $f\left(P_2^1, P_3^1\right) = \overline{P_3}^1$.

Figure 3.28a shows the final synthesis of Table 3.5a with its five controlled NOT gates. Note that this gate cost of 5 is lower than the gate cost of 8 in Figure 3.24b. It is worth noting the automatic V-shape of the positions of the five crosses (i.e., controlled NOTs) in the figure. When we apply the same procedure to each of the $8! = 40\,320$ circuits of the group $\mathbf{S_8}$, sometimes one or more of the five control functions equals 0. This means that one or more of the five controlled NOTs is the identity gate and so is in fact absent, leading to a total of less than five gates. We thus obtain a statistical distribution of gate costs ranging from 0 to $L = 2w - 1 = 5$. The average gate cost is found to be about 4.4. This number is substantially smaller than 10.1 (the average number found with the method of Section 3.15).

We note that Figure 3.18b is discovered automatically by applying our algorithm to the truth table of Figure 3.18a. This constitutes an example of a decomposition of a $w = 2$ circuit into three controlled NOTs; that is, into three FEYNMAN gates. If

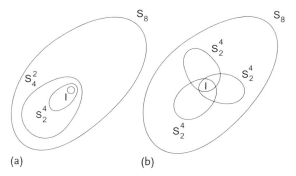

Figure 3.29 Two different sets of efficient subgroups: (a) a subgroup chain, and (b) a subgroup flower.

we apply the same procedure to each of the $4! = 24$ circuits of the group $\mathbf{S}_4$, this yields a statistical distribution of gate costs ranging from 0 to $L = 2w - 1 = 3$. The average gate cost is about 1.92.

We stress that a maximum gate cost of $2w - 1$ is very close to optimal. No synthesis method can guarantee better than $2w - 3$. This is proved in Appendix D. As subgroups isomorphic to $\mathbf{S}_2^{2^{w-1}}$ thus lead to (almost) optimal decompositions, we conclude that the controlled NOTs form a natural library for synthesis. We stress that such library is larger than libraries that only have TOFFOLI gates. The latter are of the type shown in Figure 3.13b, controlled by AND functions. In the synthesis approach presented here, we make full use of building blocks of the type shown in Figure 3.13a, controlled by arbitrary control functions.

While the synthesis method of Section 3.15 is based on a subgroup chain like (3.17), in other words on a set of w subgroups of ever-decreasing order, the algorithm of the present section is based on a set of w subgroups that are all of the same order $2^{2^{w-1}}$. These w subgroups are conjugate to each other; see the end of Section 3.10. Figure 3.29 illustrates the two approaches: the former with ever-smaller subgroups, and the latter with equally sized subgroups. In order to be efficient, the conjugate subgroups should overlap as little as possible. In our synthesis method, the overlap is indeed very small, as two subgroups have only one element in common: the identity element (or w-bit follower).

Sometimes, for practical purposes, the library of controlled NOT gates is considered too large. A library consisting only of TOFFOLI gates is then a possibility. In that case, we may proceed as follows: each controlled NOT is decomposed into TOFFOLI gates by merely replacing the control function by its Reed–Muller expansion. Such an expansion may contain up to 2^{w-1} terms. From Appendix D, we see that this expansion is not optimal. Better results can be obtained by applying one of the ESOP expansion algorithms [5, 6]. Figure 3.30 gives an example: the controlled NOT gate with the control function $f = A_1 + A_2$; that is, an OR function. The Reed–Muller expansion (Figure 3.30b) reads

$$f = A_1 \oplus A_2 \oplus A_1 A_2 .$$

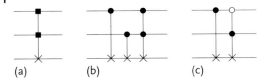

Figure 3.30 Decomposition of (a) a controlled NOT gate into (b) its Reed–Muller expansion and into (c) one of its minimal ESOP expansions.

whereas one of the minimal ESOP expansions (Figure 3.30c) is

$$f = A_1 \oplus \overline{A}_1 A_2 .$$

The minimal ESOP expansion thus often leads to cheaper circuits than the Reed–Muller expansion. However, it also has a disadvantage: there is no efficient algorithm to find the minimal ESOP for $w > 6$.

Applying either the Reed–Muller decomposition or a minimal ESOP expansion to the circuit of Figure 3.28a yields Figure 3.28b, with six TOFFOLI gates.

3.17
Variable Ordering

In Figure 3.27b, we have started the decomposition of Figure 3.27a by applying two controlled NOTs that control the first bit. Then, in Figure 3.27c, we have applied two control gates that control the second bit, etc. There really is no reason to follow this top-to-bottom order. We may equally well apply any other order. This means that in Figure 3.29b, we can apply the w subgroups in any of the $w!$ possible orders. This will lead to $w!$ (usually different) syntheses of the same truth table. For example, Figure 3.31 shows the result of applying the bottom-to-top order to Table 3.5a. In contrast to Figure 3.28a, the crosses in Figure 3.31 are not located in a V-shape but in a Λ-shape. The gate costs of the two hardware implementations (Figures 3.28a and 3.31) are the same: five units.

For a particular synthesis problem, the $w!$ synthesis solutions can have quite different hardware costs. On average, however, solving all $(2^w)!$ synthesis problems of width w, applying the optimum of the $w!$ wire orders instead of a single constant wire order, gives a moderate cost gain. For example, synthesizing all 24 circuits of width 2, trying both wire orderings, yields cascades with an average gate cost of about 1.83, only 4% better than the 1.92 achieved in the previous section. Synthe-

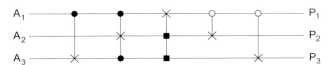

Figure 3.31 Decomposition of the example circuit of width 3 (Table 3.5a) into controlled NOT gates.

sizing all 40 320 circuits of width 3, trying all six wire orderings, yields cascades with an average gate cost of about 3.9; that is, 11% better than the 4.4 achieved in the previous section. We finally note that variable ordering may also be used in conjunction with other, for example, quite different synthesis algorithms.

3.18
Templates

Templates are small logic circuits that are used to simplify a given logic circuit. For an excellent introduction, the reader is referred to the papers by Maslov *et al.* [59–61]. Templates play an important role in automatic circuit synthesis. Synthesis algorithms, either straightforward or heuristic, usually do not yield an optimum design. Even the synthesis method of Sections 3.16 and 3.17 yields only 'almost optimum' circuits, which are therefore prone to post-synthesis improvement. Thus, after the actual circuit design step, a circuit simplification step is appropriate. It is here that templates are the appropriate tool to use.

Figure 3.32a is an example of a template of width 5 and depth 4. It consists of four reversible gates (four TOFFOLI gates) in cascade. We call it a template because it is equal to the five-bit follower or identity gate i:

$$a_1 a_2 a_3 a_4 = i .\tag{3.19}$$

The dashed lines on the left-hand and right-hand sides of the figure draw our attention to the fact that the figure has neither an actual beginning nor an actual end. Indeed, by multiplying (3.19) to the left by a_1^{-1} and to the right by a_1, we obtain an equivalent relation:

$$a_2 a_3 a_4 a_1 = i .$$

Proceeding further like this, the reader will produce two more such equations. Thus, Figure 3.32a has neither a head nor a tail, and is thus merely a linear representation of the 'circular' template of Figure 3.32b. Any partition of Figure 3.32b into two parts leads to circuit simplification. For example, the three gates on the right can be replaced by the single gate on the left. Figure 3.32d illustrates the equality obtained by multiplying (3.19) to the right by a_4^{-1}:

$$a_1 a_2 a_3 = a_4^{-1} .$$

However, the template tells us that the three gates at the top of Figure 3.32b can be equally well replaced by the single gate at the bottom: Figure 3.32e and

$$a_2 a_3 a_4 = a_1^{-1} .$$

Because, in this example, all a_i are TOFFOLI gates, these gates are their own inverses, such that a_4^{-1} equals a_4 and a_1^{-1} equals a_1, etc.

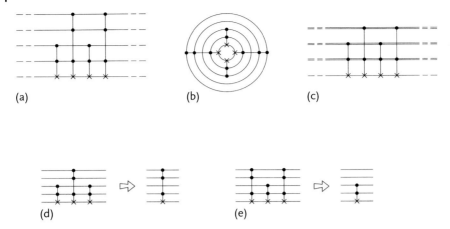

Figure 3.32 A template: (a) basic symbol, (b) circular symbol, (c) symbol using busbars, (d) derived circuit simplification, and (e) another derived circuit simplification.

Following Maslov *et al.*, we compact Figure 3.32a by bringing the lines A_1 and A_2 together into a set of lines: Figure 3.32c. As in electronics, a thick line thus represents a 'bus', in other words a set of wires (i.e., zero, one, two, or more wires), whereas a narrow line represents a single wire. Note that Figure 3.32c not only represents Figure 3.32a but a whole family of (infinitely many) templates, of which Figure 3.32a is but one representative.

The most obvious template consists of an arbitrary reversible circuit cascaded by its own mirror image. Figure 3.33a gives a $w = 3$ example: a cascade of eight gates. Inspection shows that the latter half of the figure is the mirror image of the former half. Such a circuit is equivalent to the three-bit identity gate i. The latter half does indeed perform the backward computation, reconstructing the inputs of the former half from its outputs. Therefore, the overall circuit has outputs that are equal to its inputs. We call such a construction a *do-undo scheme*: Figure 3.33b. If the synthesis of a circuit contains such a scheme, the do-undo part should be removed, thus replacing the overall circuit with an equivalent but cheaper one. Such post-synthesis optimization is usually performed by an expert artificial-intelligence system that searches for patterns to be simplified. In our example, the expert system will, for example, first recognize the presence of the small template of Figure 3.33c and then replace it by a two-bit identity. Subsequently, the system will detect the presence of the small template of Figure 3.33d and replace it by a three-bit follower, etc., until the whole circuit in Figure 3.33a is removed from the design.

Not all templates are of the mirror style. Figure 3.34 shows six templates of depth 6 or less, composed of TOFFOLIs and suggested by Maslov *et al.* We label them T1 through T6. Only T1 is of the mirror type. Note that our example in Figure 3.32c is simply template T2.

In order to further compact notation, we generalize TOFFOLI gates to controlled NOT gates (Section 3.10). It is clear that two control gates (one with a control func-

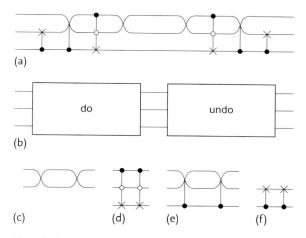

(a)

(b)

(c)   (d)   (e)   (f)

Figure 3.33 Do-undo circuits.

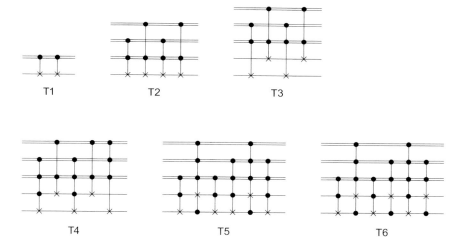

T1   T2   T3

T4   T5   T6

Figure 3.34 The six Maslov templates.

tion f, the other with a control function g) can be merged into a single gate with a control function $f \oplus g$. This leads us to the template U1 of Figure 3.35. Note that both templates, T1 and T2 (of Figure 3.34), can be deduced from this U1. Template T1 is the special case of template U1 with $f = g$; template T2 is obtained by applying U1 three times.

Combining buses and controlled NOTs leads us to template V1 of Figure 3.36. Here, f''' is the partial derivative of $f(A_1, A_2, \ldots, A_{w-1})$ with respect to A_{w-1}:

$$f'''(A_1, A_2, \ldots, A_{w-2}) = f(A_1, A_2, \ldots, A_{w-2}, 0) \oplus f(A_1, A_2, \ldots, A_{w-2}, 1) .$$

See Section 1.7. We note that template T3 is a special case of template V1, with $f''' = 0$. Template T4 is a consequence of U1 and V1 combined.

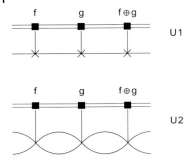

Figure 3.35 The U templates.

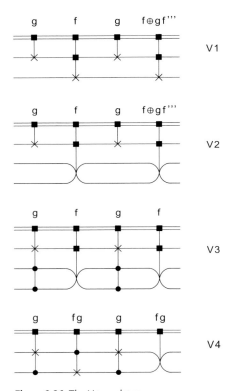

Figure 3.36 The V templates.

We now give an example of the beneficial use of templates: in Section 3.16.3, the synthesis method of Section 3.16.2 is applied to all reversible circuits of width 3. Applying post-synthesis optimization (for example, by means of template U1 only) lowers the gate cost by one unit in 255 of the 40 320 cases, thus reducing the average gate cost from 4.438 to 4.432.

Finally, there are also templates with controlled SWAP gates [62–65]. Figure 3.35 shows an example: template U2. Figure 3.36 shows three more examples: templates V2, V3, and V4. We note that Figure 3.18 is an application of template V4 (with $f = g = 1$).

3.19
The Linear Synthesis Algorithm

In Section 3.16, we presented an efficient synthesis method for an arbitrary reversible circuit of width w. It was a cascade of $2w - 1$ (or less) controlled NOTs, with controlled bits located successively on logic lines $1, 2, \ldots, w - 1, w, w - 1, w - 2, \ldots, 2, 1$; see Figure 3.27e. This method is 'almost optimal', as we can prove (see Appendix D) that any synthesis with less than $2w - 3$ controlled NOT gates is impossible.

As a linear reversible circuit is just a special kind of reversible circuit, the synthesis method is perfectly applicable to an arbitrary linear reversible circuit. However, this may yield cascades that contain nonlinear control gates. As a linear circuit can be built from exclusively linear building blocks, we must conclude that the approach of Section 3.16 is overkill in this case. Thus, there is need for a dedicated synthesis method for linear reversible circuits.

We will check whether a decomposition of linear reversible circuits into $2w - 1$ linear controlled NOTs is possible. To do this, we again follow the reasoning method of Appendix D; in particular (D1). Section 4 of this Appendix, with $N \approx 2^{w^2}$ and $B \approx w2^{w-1}$, yields the lower bound

$$L \approx \frac{\log(2)w^2}{\log(2)w} = w \ .$$

We conclude that a synthesis method that needs $2w - 1$ blocks from the linear library could work, but would not be efficient: the hardware overhead is of the order of a factor of 2. Thus, there is room for improvement.

Let Q be the $w \times w$ matrix representing the arbitrary linear circuit. We apply a matrix decomposition according to the scheme of Figures 3.27a and 3.27b. Thus:

$$Q = LMR$$

with a left and a right matrix that only affect the first bit:

$$L = \begin{pmatrix} 1 & L_{12} & L_{13} & L_{14} \\ 0 & 1 & 0 & 0 \\ 0 & 0 & 1 & 0 \\ 0 & 0 & 0 & 1 \end{pmatrix} \quad \text{and} \quad R = \begin{pmatrix} 1 & R_{12} & R_{13} & R_{14} \\ 0 & 1 & 0 & 0 \\ 0 & 0 & 1 & 0 \\ 0 & 0 & 0 & 1 \end{pmatrix}$$

and a middle matrix M that does not affect the first bit:

$$M = \begin{pmatrix} 1 & 0 & 0 & 0 \\ M_{21} & M_{22} & M_{23} & M_{24} \\ M_{31} & M_{32} & M_{33} & M_{34} \\ M_{41} & M_{42} & M_{43} & M_{44} \end{pmatrix}.$$

The $2w - 2$ numbers $L_{12}, L_{13}, \ldots, L_{1w}$ and $R_{12}, R_{13}, \ldots, R_{1w}$ (all $\in \mathbb{B}$) are called *lifting coefficients*. Because this decomposition is overkill, we can do better: it can be proven [66–68] that the following form of the matrix R, with a single lifting factor, is sufficient:

$$R = \begin{pmatrix} 1 & R_{12} & 0 & 0 \\ 0 & 1 & 0 & 0 \\ 0 & 0 & 1 & 0 \\ 0 & 0 & 0 & 1 \end{pmatrix},$$

although only on the condition that an extra (very simple) matrix is allowed; that is, a swap matrix S:

$$Q = LMRS, \tag{3.20}$$

where S is either the $w \times w$ identity matrix or a $w \times w$ permutation matrix that swaps two bits (i.e., a permutation matrix with only two off-diagonal 1s).

We apply matrix decomposition (3.20) $w - 1$ times and arrive at the decomposition into $3w - 2$ matrices, each of size $w \times w$:

$$Q = L_1 L_2 \ldots L_{w-1} L_w R_{w-1} S_{w-1} R_{w-2} S_{w-2} \ldots R_1 S_1. \tag{3.21}$$

We have thus demonstrated how an arbitrary linear reversible circuit can be decomposed into $2w - 1$ linear controlled NOT gates, among which $w - 1$ are particularly cheap ones. The circuit decomposition contains

- w or less linear controlled NOTs, each with up to $w - 1$ controlling bits,
- $w - 1$ or less FEYNMAN gates, and
- $w - 1$ or less SWAP gates.

Figure 3.37 visualizes the hardware gain, with respect to Figure 3.27e, in a case without SWAPs. Figure 3.38a shows the case of Table 3.3c, where the matrix decomposition according to (3.21) is

$$Q = L_1 L_2 L_3 R_2 S_2 R_1 S_1;$$

in this particular case, both L_1 and S_2 are equal to the identity matrix such that

$$\begin{pmatrix} 1 & 1 & 0 \\ 0 & 0 & 1 \\ 0 & 1 & 0 \end{pmatrix}$$

$$= \begin{pmatrix} 1 & 0 & 0 \\ 1 & 1 & 1 \\ 0 & 0 & 1 \end{pmatrix} \begin{pmatrix} 1 & 0 & 0 \\ 0 & 1 & 0 \\ 1 & 1 & 1 \end{pmatrix} \begin{pmatrix} 1 & 0 & 0 \\ 0 & 1 & 1 \\ 0 & 0 & 1 \end{pmatrix} \begin{pmatrix} 1 & 1 & 0 \\ 0 & 1 & 0 \\ 0 & 0 & 1 \end{pmatrix} \begin{pmatrix} 0 & 1 & 0 \\ 1 & 0 & 0 \\ 0 & 0 & 1 \end{pmatrix}.$$

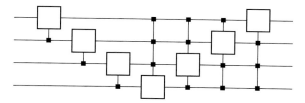

Figure 3.37 Decomposition of a linear reversible circuit of width $w = 4$ into $2w - 1 = 7$ linear control gates.

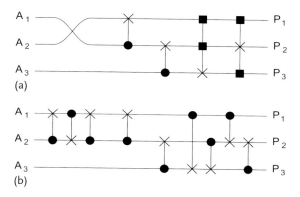

Figure 3.38 Decomposition of a linear reversible circuit into: (a) controlled NOTs and SWAPs; (b) FEYNMAN gates.

We indeed see

- Two (i.e., less than w) controlled NOTs with two controlling bits,
- Two (i.e., $w - 1$) FEYNMAN gates, and
- One (i.e., less than $w - 1$) SWAP gate.

The w control gates (each with a linear control function!) can be further decomposed into a total of $w(w - 1)$ or less FEYNMAN gates. There are two points of view regarding SWAP gates (see Section 3.12): either they are considered free of hardware costs, or they can be decomposed into three FEYNMANs (Figure 3.18). In the former case, we conclude that any linear reversible circuit can be decomposed into $w(w-1)+(w-1) = w^2-1$ or less FEYNMANs. In the latter case, we see that any linear reversible circuit can be decomposed into a total of $w(w - 1) + (w - 1) + 3(w - 1) = w^2 + 3w - 4$ or less FEYNMANs. Figure 3.38b shows the case of Table 3.3c. We see nine (i.e., less than $w^2 + 3w - 4 = 14$) FEYNMAN gates. Post-synthesis optimization, such as template matching (Section 3.18), can simplify this circuit. Note that the two subsequent and identical FEYNMANs may cancel each other (Template T1), leaving only seven FEYNMANs.

We check whether the above decomposition methodology is efficient. Again applying (D1), this time with the library of FEYNMANs, in other words with $B =$

$w(w-1)+1$, yields (according to Sect. 5 of Appendix D)

$$L \approx \frac{\log(2)}{2} \frac{w^2}{\log(w)} .$$

We must conclude that the above synthesis method (which needs a cascade length of the order w^2) is efficient, but not close to optimal. It has the same complexity as the factorization proposed by Beth and Rötteler [40]. In contrast, Patel *et al.* [31] have presented a somewhat different, more efficient algorithm, guaranteeing a decomposition with an asymptotic size that is proportional to $w^2/\log(w)$. However, the synthesis method presented here is shown in order to serve as comparison with the related synthesis methods for arbitrary reversible circuits (Section 3.16) and as a step towards analog reversible linear circuits (Chapter 5) and quantum circuits (Chapter 7).

3.20
Preset Bits and Garbage Bits

In the above sections, synthesis means 'finding a hardware implementation for a given reversible truth table'. However, a synthesis task is often defined by an irreversible truth table. Three such examples are discussed below:

- A duplicating circuit,
- A circuit calculating a single Boolean function of more than one Boolean variable, and
- A full-adder circuit.

3.20.1
Duplicating Circuit

The first example is the duplicator: see Table 3.8a. It has one binary input: the bit A, and two outputs: the bits P and Q. Basically, it replaces A with two copies of A; see Figure 3.39a. The truth table is definitely not reversible:

- The number of output bits is not equal to the number of input bits.

In order to implement this copying in a reversible computer, we have to expand the table such that the original table is embedded in a larger, reversible one; see, for example, the two possible embeddings in Tables 3.8b and 3.8c. All bit values from Table 3.8a are repeated (in boldface) in both Table 3.8b and Table 3.8c.

In order to get an equal number of input and output bits, Table 3.8b has an extra input column: bit F. By setting it equal to the constant 0, we make sure that both outputs P and Q are equal to input A: see Figure 3.39b. Table 3.8c has an extra output column: bit G. This bit is called a garbage bit. It is not required in

Table 3.8 Duplicators: (a) irreversible, (b) reversible, and (c) reversible.

A	PQ
0	0 0
1	1 1

(a)

AF	PQ
0 0	0 0
0 1	0 1
1 0	1 1
1 1	1 0

(b)

AF_1F_2	GPQ
0 0 0	0 0 0
0 0 1	0 0 1
0 1 0	0 1 0
0 1 1	1 0 0
1 0 0	0 1 1
1 0 1	1 0 1
1 1 0	1 1 0
1 1 1	1 1 1

(c)

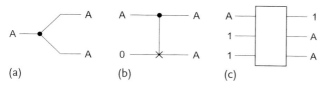

(a) (b) (c)

Figure 3.39 Duplicating a Boolean variable A: (a) by conventional fan-out, (b) by a reversible FEYNMAN gate, and (c) by a reversible gate of width 3.

the first place. Because there are now three output bits, there must be three input bits too. Therefore, we have added two additional input columns: the preset bits F_1 and F_2. For the desired application, F_1 and F_2 will always be placed equal to 1 (see Figure 3.39c). The fact that we have two different embeddings here indicates that there is no unique way to embed an irreversible table in a larger reversible table. The embedding should thus be done carefully, in order to minimize the resulting reversible hardware cost and hardware width.

In reversible logic circuits, a fan-out (Figure 3.39a) is not allowed. There is an analog to this 'no-fan-out theorem' of classical reversible circuits in quantum circuits: the 'no-cloning theorem' [69].

3.20.2
Controlled NOT

We note that a controlled NOT can be interpreted as a reversible embedding of the calculation of an irreversible Boolean function. Assume that we would like to calculate the Boolean function $f(A, B, C)$ of three Boolean variables, as defined by its truth table in Table 3.9a. The table is, of course, irreversible, because:

Table 3.9 Truth tables of a Boolean function $f(A, B, C)$: (a) irreversible; (b) reversible.

$A B C$	f
0 0 0	0
0 0 1	0
0 1 0	0
0 1 1	1
1 0 0	1
1 0 1	0
1 1 0	0
1 1 1	1

(a)

$A B C D$	$P Q R S$
0 0 0 0	0 0 0 0
0 0 0 1	0 0 0 1
0 0 1 0	0 0 1 0
0 0 1 1	0 0 1 1
0 1 0 0	0 1 0 0
0 1 0 1	0 1 0 1
0 1 1 0	0 1 1 1
0 1 1 1	0 1 1 0
1 0 0 0	1 0 0 1
1 0 0 1	1 0 0 0
1 0 1 0	1 0 1 0
1 0 1 1	1 0 1 1
1 1 0 0	1 1 0 0
1 1 0 1	1 1 0 1
1 1 1 0	1 1 1 1
1 1 1 1	1 1 1 0

(b)

- It has fewer output columns than input colums,
- An output row 0 appears no less than five times and an output row 1 appears three times.

Table 3.9b shows the truth table of the controlled NOT gate with control function $f(A, B, C)$, controlling bits A, B, and C, and a controlled bit as an extra input D. We have the following relations between outputs and inputs: $P = A$, $Q = B$, $R = C$, and $S = f(A, B, C) \oplus D$, in accordance with (3.12). The output S equals the desired function f if the input D is preset to zero. The extra outputs P, Q, and R are garbage outputs. We note that, unfortunately, the reversible embedding (Table 3.9b) has double the total number of columns of the original problem (Table 3.9a).

3.20.3
An Application: the Majority Circuit

In the previous Section, we needed a circuit with $n + 1$ inputs and $n + 1$ outputs in order to reversibly implement a single Boolean function $f(A_1, A_2, \ldots, A_n)$ of n variables. If the function f is balanced, we can do the job in a slightly cheap-

Table 3.10 Majority blocks: (a) irreversible; (b) reversible.

$A_1 A_2 A_3$	f
0 0 0	0
0 0 1	0
0 1 0	0
0 1 1	1
1 0 0	0
1 0 1	1
1 1 0	1
1 1 1	1

(a)

$A_1 A_2 A_3$	$G_1 G_2 f$
0 0 0	0 0 0
0 0 1	1 1 0
0 1 0	0 1 0
0 1 1	0 0 1
1 0 0	1 0 0
1 0 1	1 1 1
1 1 0	0 1 1
1 1 1	1 0 1

(b)

er way: with n inputs and n outputs. Table 3.10 shows an example. The function $f(A_1, A_2, A_3)$ is the majority function (Table 3.10a). For an arbitrary (but odd) n, the value of the majority function $f(A_1, A_2, \ldots, A_n)$ equals 0 iff the majority of the input bits $A_1, A_2, \ldots, A_n$ equal 0. In the case $n = 3$, we obtain the Reed–Muller expansion

$$f(A_1, A_2, A_3) = A_1 A_2 \oplus A_2 A_3 \oplus A_3 A_1 . \tag{3.22}$$

As usual, there are many ways to embed the function in a reversible table of width n. According to Yang *et al.* [70], there are 576 ways for $n = 3$. Table 3.10b shows one example.

To implement a reversible circuit with a single balanced output function $f(A_1, A_2, \ldots, A_n)$, we can proceed as follows. We embed the irreversible truth table in a larger reversible truth table, with outputs $G_1, G_2, \ldots, G_{n-1}, f$. We then apply the synthesis method of Section 3.16, resulting in a cascade of $2n - 1$ controlled NOTs. Figure 3.40a shows an example for $n = 3$, resulting in five control functions: $g(A_2, A_3)$, $h(A_1, A_3)$, $i(A_1, A_2)$, $j(A_1, A_3)$, and $k(A_2, A_3)$. We see how the lowermost bit (yielding the desired output f) is not affected by the last $n - 1$ NOT gates. We can therefore throw them away. This results in a cascade with a gate cost of only n (Figure 3.40b). Note that Figure 3.40b results in other garbage outputs than Figure 3.40a, but that is of no concern here.

In Figure 3.40, both of the garbage outputs $G_1, G_2, \ldots, G_{n-1}$ and $G_1', G_2', \ldots,$ G_{n-1}' will usually be completely useless functions. Therefore, it may be profitable to replace them with more useful garbage functions. Sometimes this is performed by replacing them with the simplest possible functions of $A_1, A_2, \ldots$; in other words, $A_1, A_2, \ldots$ themselves. This is achieved by undoing the computation; see Figure 3.40c. To do this, we add to Figure 3.40b its own mirror image (recall the do-

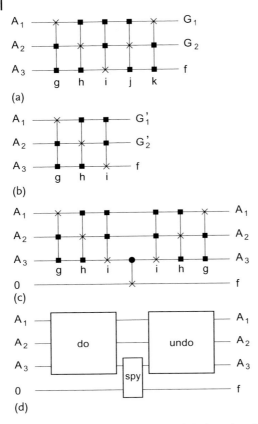

(a)

(b)

(c)

(d)

Figure 3.40 Reversible computation of a balanced Boolean function $f(A_1, A_2, A_3)$.

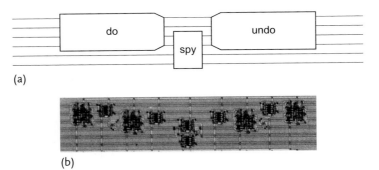

(a)

(b)

Figure 3.41 Prototype do-spy-undo circuit: (a) block diagram; (b) photomicrograph (180 μm × 40 μm).

undo scheme of Figure 3.33). However, so that the desired output f is not lost, we first copy it using a FEYNMAN gate; see Section 3.20.1. Figure 3.40d shows the resulting general scheme, called a do-spy-undo scheme, which was proposed by Fredkin and Toffoli [29]. The price we pay for this 'intelligent garbage' is a longer (depth $= 2n + 1$ instead of n) and wider (width $= n + 1$ instead of n) circuit. Figure 3.41 shows a hardware example, but with two useful functions of the same four variables: $f_1(A_1, A_2, A_3, A_4)$ and $f_2(A_1, A_2, A_3, A_4)$. It applies two 'spying' FEYNMAN gates.

3.21
Another Application: the Full Adder

One famous example of an irreversible truth table is the full adder; see Table 3.11a. It has three input bits: the augend bit A, the addend bit B, and the carry-in bit C_i; and two output bits: the sum bit S and the carry-out bit C_o. Basically, the table gives eight different additions of three numbers:

$$0 + 0 + 0 = 0$$
$$0 + 0 + 1 = 1$$
$$0 + 1 + 0 = 1$$
$$\cdots$$
$$1 + 1 + 0 = 2$$
$$1 + 1 + 1 = 3 \,.$$

Analyzing the truth table leads to the Reed–Muller expansions

$$C_o = A B \oplus B C_i \oplus C_i A$$
$$S = A \oplus B \oplus C_i \,.$$

We immediately recognize that $C_o(A, B, C_i)$ is a majority function (3.22). The truth table is definitely not reversible:

- The number of output bits is not equal to the number of input bits, and
- Various output words appear more than once in the table; for example, the output $C_o S = 10$ appears three times in Table 3.11a.

In order to implement this calculation in a reversible computer, we must expand the table such that the original table is embedded in a large reversible one; see for example Table 3.11b. All of the bits from Table 3.11a are repeated (in boldface) in Table 3.11b. The new table has two extra output columns:[9] the garbage bits G_1 and G_2. These are not requested in the first place, but are added in order to guarantee that all of the output words are different. Because there are now four

---

9) By now, the reader will realize that the number of extra columns we need is $\lceil \log_2(x) \rceil$, i.e., the smallest integer larger than or equal to $\log_2(x)$, where x is the maximum number of times the same output word appears in the original (irreversible) truth table. Here x equals 3, so we need two extra columns.

Table 3.11 Full adders: (a) irreversible and (b) reversible.

$A\,B\,C_i$	$C_o\,S$
0 0 0	0 0
0 0 1	0 1
0 1 0	0 1
0 1 1	1 0
1 0 0	0 1
1 0 1	1 0
1 1 0	1 0
1 1 1	1 1

(a)

$F\,A\,B\,C_i$	$C_o\,S\,G_1\,G_2$
0 0 0 0	0 0 0 0
0 0 0 1	0 1 0 1
0 0 1 0	0 1 1 0
0 0 1 1	1 0 1 1
0 1 0 0	0 1 0 0
0 1 0 1	1 0 0 1
0 1 1 0	1 0 1 0
0 1 1 1	1 1 1 1
1 0 0 0	1 0 0 0
1 0 0 1	1 1 0 1
1 0 1 0	1 1 1 0
1 0 1 1	0 0 1 1
1 1 0 0	1 1 0 0
1 1 0 1	0 0 0 1
1 1 1 0	0 0 1 0
1 1 1 1	0 1 1 1

(b)

output bits, there must be four input bits as well. Therefore, we have added one additional input column: the preset bit F. For the desired application, F will always be placed equal to 0. Again, note that there are many ways to embed the three-input two-output table (Table 3.11a) in a reversible four-input four-output table. Here we have chosen Table 3.11b such that the garbage outputs have a simple meaning: $G_1 = B$ and $G_2 = C_i$.

Applying the general synthesis algorithm of Section 3.16 to Table 3.11b leads to $2w - 1 = 7$ control gates, with the following seven control functions: 0, 0, 0, $C_i B \oplus B A \oplus A C_i$, $C_i \oplus B$, 0, and 0. Because five control functions equal 0, the circuit actually contains only two control gates; see Figure 3.42a. Inspection of the circuit reveals that it is a Sylow circuit consisting of two controlled NOTs. The four Sylow control functions (see Figure 3.16) are

$$f_4(C_i, B, A) = C_i B \oplus B A \oplus A C_i$$
$$f_3(C_i, B) = C_i \oplus B$$
$$f_2(C_i) = 0$$
$$f_1(.) = 0 \,.$$

Both the gate cost and the circuit depth are equal to 2.

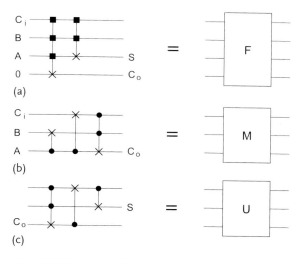

Figure 3.42 Three reversible circuits: (a) the full adder, (b) the majority circuit, and (c) the un-majority circuit.

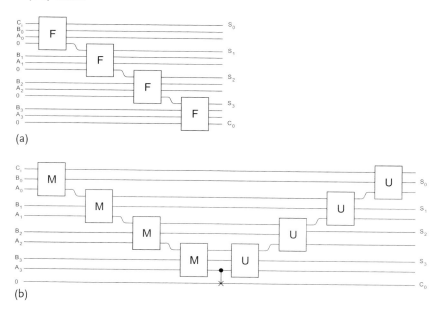

Figure 3.43 Four-bit reversible ripple adders: (a) with full adders; (b) with majority and unmajority circuits.

An n-bit adder is constructed with the help of n full adders; see Figure 3.43a. We see how the carry-out of a full adder is the carry-in of the next full adder. Carries thus 'ripple' from one full adder to the next, so this circuit is called a *ripple adder*.

3.22
Avoiding Garbage

Thus, reversible digital circuits have the disadvantage of generating a lot of garbage output, which is not desirable for the application. We are not allowed to throw them away. Therefore, we must take them all the way through the following computational steps. Just two garbage bits in a full adder is already a matter of great concern. Indeed, such a full adder is just a building block in, say, a 32-bit adder. The latter circuit will itself be a building block for a 32-bit multiplier. Such a multiplier is used many times in, for example, a digital filter. Many filters make up a filter bank; many filter banks make up, for example, a speech processor. Each time we step from one architectural level to the next, the number of garbage bits explodes. This proliferation of garbage will result in huge costs due to extra gates and extra interconnections. Therefore, the challenge is to design, at each level of abstraction, circuits that generate as little garbage as possible.

The clever adder design by Cuccaro *et al.* [71] avoids the need for one of the two garbage bits G_1 and G_2 in Table 3.11b, and is thus highly recommendable [72]. The trick here is to avoid to calculate the bits C_o and S simultaneously, in a single circuit. Cuccaro *et al.* first calculate C_o, and subsequently compute S from C_o when the information on C_o is not required anymore. Thus, the n-bit adder of Cuccaro *et al.* does not consist of n full adders. It is built from $2n$ blocks, of which n blocks (called *majority blocks*) are used to generate the carry-out bits, while the other n blocks (called *unmajority blocks*) are used to generate the sum bits. The two building blocks are shown in Figures 3.42b and c. Both circuits have gate costs and logic depths equal to 3. In fact, the unmajority block is the application of Template T1 (Section 3.18) to the cascade of the mirror image of the majority block (undoing the computation of C_o) and a small additional block that computes the sum bit S; see Figure 3.44.

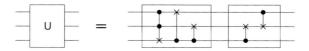

Figure 3.44 The unmajority circuit as a cascade.

Table 3.12 Two reversible *n*-bit adders: (a) with *n* full adders; (b) with *n* majority and *n* unmajority circuits.

Design	Gate Cost	Logic Depth	Logic Width
(a)	$2n$	$n + 1$	$3n + 1$
(b)	$6n + 1$	$5n + 1$	$2n + 2$

Table 3.13 Four-bit adder: (a) in binary notation; (b) in decimal notation.

F	$A_3 A_2 A_1 A_0$	$B_3 B_2 B_1 B_0$	C_i	$X_3 X_2 X_1 X_0$	$S_4 S_3 S_2 S_1 S_0$	G
0	0 0 0 0	0 0 0 0	0	0 0 0 0	0 0 0 0 0	0
0	0 0 0 0	0 0 0 0	1	0 0 0 0	0 0 0 0 1	1
0	0 0 0 0	0 0 0 1	0	0 0 0 0	0 0 0 0 1	0
...				...		
0	0 0 1 0	0 1 0 0	0	0 0 1 0	0 0 1 1 0	0
0	0 0 1 0	0 1 0 0	1	0 0 1 0	0 0 1 1 1	1
0	0 0 1 0	0 1 0 1	0	0 0 1 0	0 0 1 1 1	0
...				...		
0	0 1 0 1	1 1 0 1	0	0 1 0 1	1 0 0 1 0	0
0	0 1 0 1	1 1 0 1	1	0 1 0 1	1 0 0 1 0	1
0	0 1 0 1	1 1 1 0	0	0 1 0 1	1 0 0 1 1	0
...				...		
1	1 1 1 1	1 1 1 0	1	0 1 1 1	0 1 1 1 0	1
1	1 1 1 1	1 1 1 1	0	0 1 1 1	0 1 1 1 0	0
1	1 1 1 1	1 1 1 1	1	0 1 1 1	0 1 1 1 1	1

(a)

F	A	B	C_i	X	S	G
0	0	0	0	0	0	0
0	0	0	1	0	1	1
0	0	1	0	0	1	0
...				...		
0	2	4	0	2	6	0
0	2	4	1	2	7	1
0	2	5	0	2	7	0
...				...		
0	5	13	0	5	18	0
0	5	13	1	5	19	1
0	5	14	0	5	19	0
...				...		
1	15	14	1	15	14	1
1	15	15	0	15	14	0
1	15	15	1	15	15	1

(b)

The complete n-bit adder is shown in Figure 3.43b for the case $n = 4$. Note that the carry-out of the last M-block is copied using a FEYNMAN gate in order to get a carry-over bit; that is, the additional (fifth) sumbit S_4. From Table 3.12, it is clear that the Cuccaro adder is more costly in terms of number of gates than the full-adder adder. The logic depth is also much larger. However, the Cuccaro adder is superior in terms of logic width. This implies fewer metal interconnections on the chip, fewer pins on the chip encapsulation, and fewer interconnections on the printed circuit board. The advantage of the Cuccaro adder eclipses its disadvantages.

If we calculate the corresponding output vector for any input vector of Figure 3.43b, this analysis results in the full truth table. As the width w of the circuit is $2n + 2 = 10$, the table has $2w = 20$ columns and $2^w = 1024$ rows. Table 3.13a shows part of the table (i.e., only 12 rows). Table 3.13b shows the same table in decimal notation:

$$A = A_0 + 2A_1 + 4A_2 + 8A_3$$
$$B = B_0 + 2B_1 + 4B_2 + 8B_3$$
$$X = X_0 + 2X_1 + 4X_2 + 8X_3$$
$$S = S_0 + 2S_1 + 4S_2 + 8S_3 + 16S_4 \ .$$

We see that, if input F is preset to 0,

$$S = A + B + C_i$$
$$X = A \ .$$

3.23
Exercises for Chapter 3

Exercise 3.1
Check that (3.8) and (3.11) are the same.

Exercise 3.2
Is a TOFFOLI gate conservative? Is it linear? Is a FREDKIN gate conservative? Is it linear?

Exercise 3.3
Consider all circuits of width w that can be constructed with (an arbitrary number of) just one type of building block: the (uncontrolled) NOT gate. Demonstrate that they form a group (say **A**). What is the order of this group of inverters? Demonstrate that the group **A** is a subgroup of the group **AE** of affine exchangers (Section 3.9).[10] Fit **A** within the partial ordering (3.9).

10) Because an inverter and an exchanger do not commute, we are not allowed to say that **AE** is the direct product **A** × **E** of the group **A** and the group **E**. We say instead that **AE** is the semidirect product of **A** and **E**, with notation **A** : **E**.

Exercise 3.4

Elements of the group **R**, which satisfy $g^2 = i$ (where i is the identity element of **R**), are sometimes called 'involutions'. Do these involutions form a subgroup of **R**?

Exercise 3.5

Do the TOFFOLI gates form a subgroup of the group of controlled NOT gates?

Exercise 3.6

The controlled NOTs (with order $2^{2^{w-1}}$, according to Section 3.10) form a subgroup of the Sylow circuits (with order 2^{2^w-1}, according to Section 3.11). Check that these orders fulfil Langrange's theorem. What is the index of the subgroup?

Exercise 3.7

Prove the equivalence in Figure 3.18, not by applying the multiplication of $w \times w = 2 \times 2$ matrices, but by applying the multiplication of $2^w \times 2^w = 4 \times 4$ permutation matrices.

Exercise 3.8

Demonstrate that, if **G** is an Abelian group and **H** is an arbitrary subgroup, then the left cosets, the right cosets and the double cosets are one and the same set of sets.

Exercise 3.9

Choose a truth table for $w = 2$ and apply the algorithm of Section 3.16.1 in order to decompose it into three or less FEYNMAN gates.

Exercise 3.10

Choose a truth table for $w = 3$ and apply the algorithm of Section 3.16.2 in order to decompose it into five or less controlled NOTs.

Exercise 3.11

Find the decomposition with three crosses in a Λ-configuration, equivalent to Figure 3.18, where the crosses are in a V-configuration.

Exercise 3.12

Explain the number 576 in Section 3.20.3.

4
Low-power Computing

Let us now consider a reversible circuit with inputs $A_1, A_2, \ldots, A_w$ and outputs $P_1, P_2, \ldots, P_w$. Let a_1 be the probability that the input word $A_1 A_2 \ldots A_{w-1} A_w$ equals $00 \ldots 00$; let a_2 be the probability that the input word equals $00 \ldots 01$; $\ldots$; let a_{2^w} be the probability that the input word equals $11 \ldots 11$. In general, let a_k be the probability that the input word is the binary representation of the number $k - 1$.

In the previous chapter, a circuit had one particular input (leading to one particular output). Thus, all numbers a_j were equal to 0, except for one a_k which equalled 1. However, in this chapter, we will consider arbitrary sets of numbers $a_1, a_2, \ldots, a_{2^w-1}, a_{2^w}$ (of course, with the restrictions $0 \leq a_j \leq 1$ for all j and $\sum a_j = 1$). Automatically, the output word will also be stochastic, with probabilities $p_1, p_2, \ldots, p_{2^w}$ of being equal to $00 \ldots 00$, $00 \ldots 01$, $\ldots$, $11 \ldots 11$. Such an approach will lead to far-reaching results. No less than an encounter between informatics and physics materializes. The link between these two worlds will be the quantity known as entropy.

4.1
Entropy

We will first consider a single Boolean variable A. Its value is not known. We donote the probability[11] that $A = 0$ by a. The probability that $A = 1$ is denoted by b. We define the entropy associated with A as

$$S_A = k[-a \log(a) - b \log(b)] ,$$

where k is a universal physical constant called Boltzmann's constant (after the Austrian physicist Ludwig Boltzmann). The value of k is 1.380662×10^{-23} J/K; that is, about 14 yoctojoules per kelvin.

11) In analogy to the footnotes of Sections 1.2 and 3.1, we switch here from the notations $a_1, a_2, a_3, \ldots, a_{2^w}$ and $p_1, p_2, p_3, \ldots, p_{2^w}$, to the notations $a, b, c, \ldots$ and $p, q, r, \ldots$ whenever appropriate.

If $a = b = 1/2$, in other words if $A = 0$ and $A = 1$ are equally probable, then

$$S_A = k \left[-\frac{1}{2} \log \left(\frac{1}{2} \right) - \frac{1}{2} \log \left(\frac{1}{2} \right) \right]$$

$$= k \log(2) .$$

This quantum of entropy (with a value of about 10 yoctojoules per kelvin) is called 'one bit of entropy' or 'one bit of information'.

Next, we consider two stochastic variables A and B. The probabilities that (A, B) equals $(0,0)$, $(0,1)$, $(1,0)$, and $(1,1)$ are denoted by a, b, c, and d, respectively. If A and B are statistically independent and both are either 0 or 1 with equal probability, then $a = b = c = d = 1/4$, and we have exactly two bits of information:[12]

$$S_{A,B} = k \left[-\frac{1}{4} \log \left(\frac{1}{4} \right) - \frac{1}{4} \log \left(\frac{1}{4} \right) - \frac{1}{4} \log \left(\frac{1}{4} \right) - \frac{1}{4} \log \left(\frac{1}{4} \right) \right]$$

$$= 2k \log(2) .$$

We recall that there are $2^4 = 16$ different functions $P = f(A, B)$ of the two logic variables; see Table 1.2. Table 1.3c shows a well-known example: the XOR gate. Its entropy properties are discussed in detail by Gershenfeld [74]. None of the 16 logic gates yield two bits of information at the output. The reader can easily verify that six truth tables (e.g., Table 1.3c) yield exactly 1 bit at the output: if the four possible inputs (A, B) all have probability 1/4, then the probability that P equals 0 is 1/2, and so is the probability that $P = 1$. Thus,

$$S_P = k \left[-\frac{1}{2} \log \left(\frac{1}{2} \right) - \frac{1}{2} \log \left(\frac{1}{2} \right) \right]$$

$$= k \log(2) .$$

Another eight tables (e.g., Tables 1.3a and 1.3b) yield output probabilities of $\frac{1}{4}$ and $\frac{3}{4}$, and thus

$$S_P = k \left[-\frac{1}{4} \log \left(\frac{1}{4} \right) - \frac{3}{4} \log \left(\frac{3}{4} \right) \right]$$

$$= k \left[2 \log(2) - \frac{3}{4} \log(3) \right]$$

$$= \left[2 - \frac{3}{4} \frac{\log(3)}{\log(2)} \right] k \log(2) ;$$

that is, only 0.811 bits. The remaining two tables yield zero bits. Anyway, all of the 16 gates cause information loss: 'two bits in' yield at most 'one bit out'. Thus, at least one bit of information is destroyed. None of these gates are logically reversible.

---

12) For the case where the numbers a, b, c, and d form an arbitrary distribution (with, of course, the restrictions $0 \le a \le 1$, $0 \le b \le 1$, $0 \le c \le 1$, $0 \le d \le 1$, and $a + b + c + d = 1$), the reader is referred to [73].

This is a general feature of logic calculations with w_i logic inputs and w_o outputs: if $w_o < w_i$, then at least $w_i - w_o$ bits are destroyed.

Even if $w_o = w_i$, information may be destroyed. Indeed, let us consider two cases with $w_o = w_i = 2$: Table 4.1 with a reversible truth table and an irreversible truth table. Again, let a, b, c, and d be the probabilities that (A, B) equals $(0,0)$, $(0,1)$, $(1,0)$, and $(1,1)$, respectively. Let p, q, r, and s be the probabilities that (P, Q) equals $(0,0)$, $(0,1)$, $(1,0)$, and $(1,1)$, respectively. Then we have:

$$\begin{pmatrix} p \\ q \\ r \\ s \end{pmatrix} = \begin{pmatrix} 1 & 0 & 0 & 0 \\ 0 & 1 & 0 & 0 \\ 0 & 0 & 0 & 1 \\ 0 & 0 & 1 & 0 \end{pmatrix} \begin{pmatrix} a \\ b \\ c \\ d \end{pmatrix} \tag{4.1}$$

for Table 4.1a and

$$\begin{pmatrix} p \\ q \\ r \\ s \end{pmatrix} = \begin{pmatrix} 1 & 0 & 0 & 0 \\ 0 & 1 & 0 & 0 \\ 0 & 0 & 1 & 1 \\ 0 & 0 & 0 & 0 \end{pmatrix} \begin{pmatrix} a \\ b \\ c \\ d \end{pmatrix} \tag{4.2}$$

for Table 4.1b. The matrix elements in (4.1) and (4.2) can be interpreted as conditional probabilities. For example, the element in the third row and fourth column is the probability that $(P, Q) = (1, 0)$, under the condition that $(A, B) = (1, 1)$. The reader can verify that, under the condition $a = b = c = d = 1/4$ (and thus $S_{A,B} = 2$ bits), we obtain $S_{P,Q} = 2$ bits for Table 4.1a, but only $S_{P,Q} = \frac{3}{2}$ bits for Table 4.1b.

Both of the matrices in (4.1) and (4.2) have the property that all column sums are equal to 1. We call such matrices *stochastic matrices*, because each column resembles a probability distribution. Stochastic matrices may or may not conserve entropy. Only stochastic matrices that are permutation matrices conserve entropy.[13]

We note that the square matrix in (4.1) is not only a permutation matrix, but that its inverse matrix is also a permutation matrix. In contrast, the square matrix in (4.2) does not even have an inverse, as its determinant is zero. A similar remark can be made concerning the reversible toy computer described in the 'Introduction'. Its stochastic matrix, in

$$\begin{pmatrix} p \\ q \end{pmatrix} = \begin{pmatrix} 0 & 1 \\ 1 & 0 \end{pmatrix} \begin{pmatrix} a \\ b \end{pmatrix} ,$$

is an invertible permutation matrix. The backward calculation obeys

$$\begin{pmatrix} a \\ b \end{pmatrix} = \begin{pmatrix} 0 & 1 \\ 1 & 0 \end{pmatrix} \begin{pmatrix} p \\ q \end{pmatrix} .$$

13) Permutation matrices are doubly stochastic, as all column *and* row sums are equal to 1.

Table 4.1 Truth tables of two Boolean circuits: (a) reversible; (b) irreversible.

A B	P Q
0 0	0 0
0 1	0 1
1 0	1 1
1 1	1 0

A B	P Q
0 0	0 0
0 1	0 1
1 0	1 0
1 1	1 0

(a)   (b)

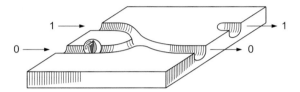

Figure 4.1 An irreversible toy computer.

In stark contrast, the toy computer of Figure 4.1 is irreversible. Its stochastic matrix, in

$$\begin{pmatrix} p \\ q \end{pmatrix} = \begin{pmatrix} 1 & 1 \\ 0 & 0 \end{pmatrix} \begin{pmatrix} a \\ b \end{pmatrix} ,$$

has zero determinant and is thus not invertible. One could describe the backward calculations by the matrix equation

$$\begin{pmatrix} a \\ b \end{pmatrix} = \begin{pmatrix} \pi & 0 \\ 1 - \pi & 0 \end{pmatrix} \begin{pmatrix} p \\ q \end{pmatrix} ,$$

with (according to the details of the figure) $\pi \approx 1/2$. This matrix is not invertible either; it is not even a stochastic matrix. We can convert it into a stochastic (but no longer square) matrix by disregarding the variable q:

$$\begin{pmatrix} a \\ b \end{pmatrix} = \begin{pmatrix} \pi \\ 1 - \pi \end{pmatrix} (p) .$$

4.2
Permutation Matrices

The previous section shows us that no entropy is destroyed in a reversible computer. Indeed, any reversible classical circuit of w bits can be represented by a $2^w \times 2^w$

permutation matrix:

$$
\begin{pmatrix} p_1 \\ p_2 \\ \vdots \\ p_{2^w} \end{pmatrix} = \begin{pmatrix} m_{11} & m_{12} & \cdots & m_{12^w} \\ m_{21} & m_{22} & \cdots & m_{22^w} \\ & \vdots & & \\ m_{2^w 1} & m_{2^w 2} & \cdots & m_{2^w 2^w} \end{pmatrix} \begin{pmatrix} a_1 \\ a_2 \\ \vdots \\ a_{2^w} \end{pmatrix} .
\tag{4.3}
$$

Subscripts run from 1 to 2^w. Remember that both a_j and p_k can be interpreted as probabilities:

$$
a_j = \text{prob}[(A_1, A_2, \ldots, A_w) = j - 1]
$$
$$
p_k = \text{prob}[(P_1, P_2, \ldots, P_w) = k - 1] ,
$$

where $(A_1, A_2, \ldots, A_w)$ and $(P_1, P_2, \ldots, P_w)$ are interpreted as binary representations of a number between 0 and $2^w - 1$. The -1 occurs at the end of each equation due to convention: rows, columns, and objects in general are labeled with the ordinal numbers $1, 2, 3, \ldots$ instead of $0, 1, 2, \ldots$

We recall that all $m_{jk} \in \{0, 1\}$, and that all line sums (i.e., row sums $\sum_{k=1}^{2^w} m_{jk}$ and column sums $\sum_{j=1}^{2^w} m_{jk}$) equal 1. Because the permutation matrix in (4.3) automatically implies that each p_k is equal to some a_j, we have

$$
\sum p_k = \sum a_j ,
$$

and because the input probabilities satisfy

$$
\sum_{j=1}^{2^w} a_j = 1 ,
$$

a similar property for the output words follows: $\sum_{j=1}^{2^w} p_j = 1$. Thus, the property that the total probability is one is conserved by the permutation matrix. Actually, there is more: let $\Phi(x)$ be an arbitrary function; we then have

$$
\sum_{j=1}^{2^w} \Phi(p_j) = \sum_{j=1}^{2^w} \Phi(a_j) .
$$

In particular, this property holds for the function $\Phi(x) = -x \log(x)$, such that

$$
\sum_{j=1}^{2^w} -p_j \log(p_j) = \sum_{j=1}^{2^w} -a_j \log(a_j) .
$$

Thus, entropy is also conserved.

4.3
Landauer's Theorem

Reversible computing [75, 76] is useful in low-power classical computing [77, 78]. According to Landauer's theorem (named after the German/American physicist

Rolf Landauer, pioneer of reversible computing), the only way to make classical digital computing lossless is to ensure that no information is lost at each stage of the computation. Each bit of information that is thrown away results in the consumption of a quantum of work and the generation of the same quantum of heat (of magnitude $kT \log(2)$, where T is the temperature of the computer hardware). The fact that consumption of work inevitably causes production of heat is a consequence of the first law of thermodynamics: that energy is conserved. The total energy U is the sum of the low-quality energy Q and the high-quality energy W:

$$U = Q + W \,.$$

The conversion of work W into heat Q can easily be described using thermodynamics. For instance, in the previous section, we saw that the single output $P(A, B)$ of a logic gate (with $w_i = 2$ and $w_o = 1$) contains less entropy than the two bits of information of the two independent random inputs A and B. Thus, the computation lowered the (macroscopic) entropy S. For example, the AND gate lowers the entropy from 2 bits to 0.811 bit. However, because of the second law of thermodynamics, the total amount of entropy σ in the universe must remain constant or increase. Therefore, at least $0.189 k \log(2)$ of entropy must be created simultaneously. This results in the generation of microscopic entropy s in the environment; that is, in the hardware of the computer. Thus, because of

$$\sigma = s + S \,,$$

whenever S decreases (e.g., because of an irreversible computation), s must increase. Microscopic entropy s manifests itself as a heat Q that is equal to Ts, where T is the temperature of the system. Therefore, $0.189 kT \log(2)$ of heat is released by the AND computation into the computer hardware [79–82]. For a rigorous analysis, see Appendix F.

As a result, if we want to avoid any heat generation in the computer circuits (and thus avoid any consumption of work by the computer), we must avoid any loss of information during the computational process. This means that we need to construct a logically reversible computer.

4.4
Thermodynamics

As stressed in the title of Landauer's notorious paper *Information is Physical* [83], computation is inevitably done by real physical objects, obeying the laws of physics in general, and the laws of thermodynamics in particular. Analogously, Nyíri [84] also remarks that microentropy is not a primitive quantity and thus cannot be transported alone; that is, without the transport of some extensive quantity. As already stressed in the 'Introduction', bare information particles (informatons) or bare entropy particles (entropons) do not exist. Both macroentropy and microentropy piggyback on other objects (electrons, ions, photons, phonons, ...).

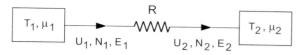

Figure 4.2 Thermodynamics.

We consider two thermodynamic reservoirs [85, 86]; see Figure 4.2. These are characterized by the (constant) values of their intensive parameters T (temperature) and μ (potential). They exchange fluxes of extensive quantities: energy flow U, particle flow N, and entropy flow E. We observe that N is the particle flux; that is, the flow rate of the 'physical objects' or 'material entities' mentioned at the beginning of the section. The intensive variable μ is the potential of the particles: either the chemical potential, the electrical potential, ...

Because of the laws of conservation (of energy and particles), we have $U_1 = U_2$ and $N_1 = N_2$. As there is no entropy conservation law, the entropy flux E_2 entering the latter reservoir need not necessarily equal the entropy flow E_1 leaving the former reservoir. The difference is the entropy creation rate:

$$s = E_2 - E_1 . \tag{4.4}$$

Any energy flux U consists of two parts: the high-quality part or work flow and the low-quality part or heat flow:

$$U = \mu N + TE ,$$

where both parts are now written as a product of an intensive variable (either μ or T) and the flow of an extensive variable (either N or E). From (4.4), we obtain

$$s = \frac{U_2 - \mu_2 N_2}{T_2} - \frac{U_1 - \mu_1 N_1}{T_1} , \tag{4.5}$$

where μ_1 and T_1 are the potential and the temperature of reservoir #1, and μ_2 and T_2 are the potential and the temperature of reservoir #2.

In Figure 4.2, the particle flow is restricted by the presence of a resistor R. We assume a linear transport law: the particle flow is proportional to the potential difference:

$$N_1 = N_2 = \frac{1}{R} (\mu_1 - \mu_2) .$$

Assuming additionally that $T_1 = T_2 = T$, we obtain from (4.5) that

$$s = \frac{1}{T} \frac{1}{R} (\mu_1 - \mu_2)^2 , \tag{4.6}$$

which is a positive quantity whatever the direction of motion: rightwards ($\mu_1 > \mu_2$) or leftwards ($\mu_2 > \mu_1$). This is in agreement with our experience (i.e., the second law of thermodynamics) that entropy always increases.

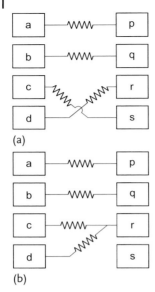

(a)

(b)

Figure 4.3 Thermodynamics of (a) a reversible computer and (b) an irreversible computer.

In our computer model, we consider 2^w left reservoirs (one for each possible input message $(A, B, C, \ldots)$) and 2^w right reservoirs (one for each possible output message $(P, Q, R, \ldots)$); see Figure 4.3, where $w = 2$. Each resistor is responsible for creating

$$s_j = a_j \, \frac{1}{T} \, \frac{1}{R} \, (\mu_1 - \mu_2)^2$$

of entropy, where $1 \leq j \leq 2^w$. Summing yields

$$s = \sum s_j = \frac{1}{T} \, \frac{1}{R} \, (\mu_1 - \mu_2)^2 \, .$$

The total entropy creation rate, however, is not just this quantity s. This sum plays the role of the microentropy s in the previous section and in Appendix F. The total entropy σ contains both the microentropy and the macroentropy S. We have

$$\sigma = \sum s_j + S \, .$$

While s has the same value in Figure 4.3a and b, the contribution

$$S = k[-p \log(p) - q \log(q) - r \log(r) - s \log(s)] \\ - k[-a \log(a) - b \log(b) - c \log(c) - d \log(d)]$$

is different in the two cases; in Figure 4.3a (representing (4.1)) we have $S = 0$, whereas in Figure 4.3b (representing (4.2)) we have $S = -k(c + d) \log(c + d) + k[\, c \log(c) + d \log(d)]$. The additional entropy created S is always negative or zero. It is related to the entropy of mixing in physical chemistry [85].

Whereas $s = \sum s_j$ is entropy creation associated with the friction (of the particles) within the individual resistors (and thus with the *transport* of information), S is associated with the topology of the interconnection of the resistors (and thus with the *loss* of information).

In our toy model, the particles are marbles and their potentials μ are gravitational potentials gh (product of the constant gravitational acceleration g and the variable height h).

4.5
An Application: Prototype Chips

From Chapter 3, we know the following: we can apply either left cosets, right cosets, or double cosets in the synthesis procedure; we can choose one subgroup or another. Whatever choices we make, we obtain a procedure for synthesizing an arbitrary circuit by cascading a small number of standard cells from a limited library. By choosing the representatives of the (double) cosets appropriately, we can see to it that all building blocks in the library are members of either of the two following special sets:

- The subgroup of controlled NOT gates, with a controlled bit on the wth wire, and
- The set of SWAP gates, which swap an arbitrary wire with the wth wire.

Recall Figure 3.15b. Among the controlled NOT gates, we note three special elements:

- If the control function f is identically zero, then P_w is always equal to A_w. The gate is then the identity gate i.
- If f is identically one, then P_w always equals $1 \oplus A_w$. The gate is then an inverter or NOT gate: $P_w = \overline{A_w}$.
- If $f(A_1, A_2, \ldots, A_{w-1})$ equals the $(w-1)$-bit AND function $A_1 A_2 \ldots A_{w-1}$, the gate is a TOFFOLI gate: whenever $A_1 A_2 \ldots A_{w-1}$ equals 0, P_w simply equals A_w, but whenever $A_1 A_2 \ldots A_{w-1}$ equals 1, P_w equals NOT A_w.

Dual logic is very convenient for physically implementing such rules. This means that, within the hardware, any logic variable X is represented by two physical quantities; the first representing X itself, and the other representing NOT X. Thus, for example, the physical gate that realizes the logic gate of Table 4.1a has four physical inputs: A, NOT A, B, and NOT B; or, in shorthand notation: A, $\overline{A}$, B, and $\overline{B}$. It also has four physical outputs: P, $\overline{P}$, Q, and $\overline{Q}$. Such an approach is common in electronics, where it is called dual-line or dual-rail electronics. Some quantum computers also make use of dual-rail qubits [87]. However, dual engineering is also applied in everyday mechanics: weight and counterweight, biceps and triceps, . . .

As a result, half of the input pins of the electronic circuit are at logic 0, and the other half are at logic 1, and the same is true for the output pins. In this way, dual electronics is physically conservative: the number of 1s at the output equals the number of 1s at the input (both being equal to w), even if the truth table of the reversible logic gate is not conservative. As a result, we get the advantages of conservative logic without having to restrict ourselves to conservative circuits (see Section 3.3).

Dual-line hardware allows very simple implementation of the inverter. It is sufficient to interchange its two physical lines in order to invert a variable. In other words, in order to hardwire the NOT gate,

- Output P is simply connected to input $\overline{A}$, and
- Output $\overline{P}$ is simply connected to input A.

Controlled NOTs are implemented as NOT gates, which are controlled by switches. A first example is the controlled NOT gate with a single controlling bit (here the bit A); that is, the FEYNMAN gate:

$$P = A$$
$$Q = A \oplus B .$$

These two logic relationships are implemented in the physical world as follows:

- Output P is simply connected to input A,
- Output $\overline{P}$ is simply connected to input $\overline{A}$,
- Output Q is connected to input B if $A = 0$, but connected to $\overline{B}$ if $A = 1$, and
- Output $\overline{Q}$ is connected to input $\overline{B}$ if $A = 0$, but connected to B if $A = 1$.

The last two implementations are shown in Figure 4.4a. In the figure, the arrowheads show the positions of the switches if the accompanying label is equal to 1. A second example is a TOFFOLI gate with two controlling bits (i.e., the bit A and the bit B):

$$P = A$$
$$Q = B$$
$$R = AB \oplus C .$$

Its logic relationships are implemented in the physical world as follows:

- Output P is simply connected to input A,
- Output $\overline{P}$ is simply connected to input $\overline{A}$,
- Output Q is simply connected to input B,
- Output $\overline{Q}$ is simply connected to input $\overline{B}$,
- Output R is connected to input C if either $A = 0$ or $B = 0$, but connected to $\overline{C}$ if both $A = 1$ and $B = 1$, and
- Output $\overline{R}$ is connected to input $\overline{C}$ if either $A = 0$ or $B = 0$, but connected to C if both $A = 1$ and $B = 1$.

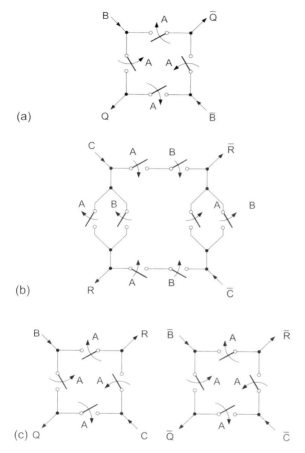

(a)

(b)

(c)

Figure 4.4 Implementations of (a) a controlled NOT gate ($u = 1$, $v = 1$), (b) a controlled NOT gate ($u = 2$, $v = 1$), and (c) a controlled SWAP gate ($u = 1$, $v = 2$).

The last two implementations are shown in Figure 4.4b. Note that in both Figures 4.4a and 4.4b, switches always appear in pairs in which one is closed whenever the other is open and vice versa. It is clear that the above design philosophy can be extrapolated to a controlled NOT gate with an arbitrary control function f. It is sufficient to write f as a combination of ANDs and ORs and to wire a square circuit as in Figures 4.4a and 4.4b, with the appropriate series and parallel connections of switches.

If, for example, we apply such hardware wiring to the controlled NOT with the control function $f = A + B$, we realize that the direct implementation of Figure 3.30a requires eight switches. In contrast, Figure 3.30b requires sixteen switches and Figure 3.30c twelve switches. This fact illustrates that decomposing a controlled NOT into TOFFOLIs is not necessarily advantageous.

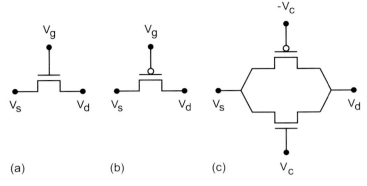

Figure 4.5 Schematic icons: (a) n-MOS transistor, (b) p-MOS transistor, (c) c-MOS transmission gate.

Now that we have an implementation approach, we can realize any reversible circuit in hardware. This can happen in different technologies. In mechanics, a controlled switch is called a door or a clutch; in hydraulics, a controlled switch is called a tap; in pneumatics, a controlled switch is called a valve. Here, however, we will demonstrate some examples of implementation on an electronic chip. In electronic circuits, a switch is realized using a so-called *transmission gate*; that is, two MOS transistors in parallel (one n-MOS transistor and one p-MOS transistor) – see Figure 4.5, where V_s stands for source voltage, V_g stands for gate voltage, V_d stands for drain voltage, and V_c stands for control voltage. Here, MOS stands for metal oxide semiconductor, whereas n refers to 'negative' type and p to 'positive' type. Circuits containing both n-type transistors and p-type transistors are called c-MOS circuits, where c stands for complementary. In electronic circuits, the role of the potential μ of the previous section is played by the electrical potential qV, the product of the elementary charge q (1.602189 × 10^{-19} C) and the voltage V. The role of the particle current N is played by i/q, where i is the electric current.

Readers familiar with electronics will notice that circuits like those in Figure 4.4 are not of the conventional style, called 'restoring logic' or 'static c-MOS', but a less well-known style called 'pass-transistor logic' [88–92]. The pass-transistor logic families allow good control of leakage currents and therefore cause less energy consumption [93]. Figure 4.6 shows a detailed electronic schematic of the building blocks. We stress that these circuits have no power supply inputs, so there are neither power nor ground busbars. Note also the complete absence of clock lines. Thus, all signals (voltages and currents) and all energy provided at the outputs originate from the inputs. Figure 4.7 illustrates the differences between restoring logic (Figures 4.7a and c) and pass-transistor logic (Figures 4.7b and d). In conventional c-MOS circuits, electrical currents flow vertically (from top to bottom), whereas information currents flow horizontally (from left to right); in pass-transistor c-MOS circuits, both electrical currents and information currents flow horizontally (either from left to right or from right to left).

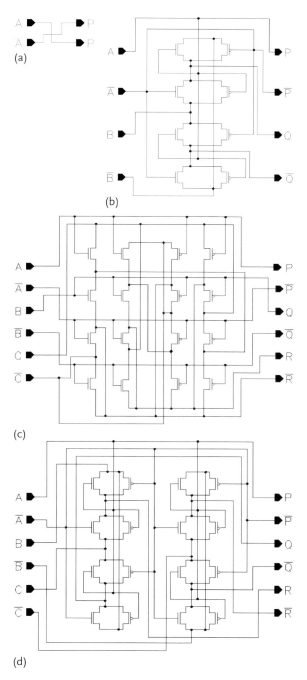

Figure 4.6 c-MOS schematics of basic circuits: (a) the NOT gate, (b) the FEYNMAN gate, (c) the TOFFOLI gate, and (d) the FREDKIN gate.

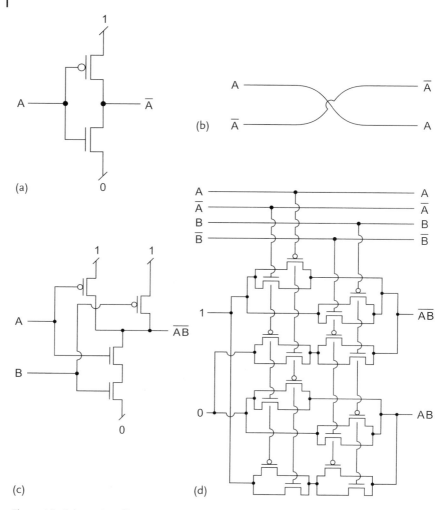

Figure 4.7 Schematics of logic gates: (a) conventional NOT gate, (b) reversible NOT gate, (c) conventional NAND gate, and (d) reversible NAND gate.

As an example, Figure 4.8 shows the actual FEYNMAN and TOFFOLI gates, implemented in silicon technology. An application is shown in Figure 4.9: a four-bit reversible ripple adder [94], implemented in full-custom 2.4 μm standard c-MOS technology and consisting of eight FEYNMANs and eight TOFFOLIs, with a total of $8 \times 8 + 8 \times 16 = 192$ transistors. This prototype chip was fabricated in 1998. The circuit functions equally well from left to right and from right to left. Conventional digital chips do not have this property. The reader is invited to compare Figure 4.9 to Figure 3.43a.

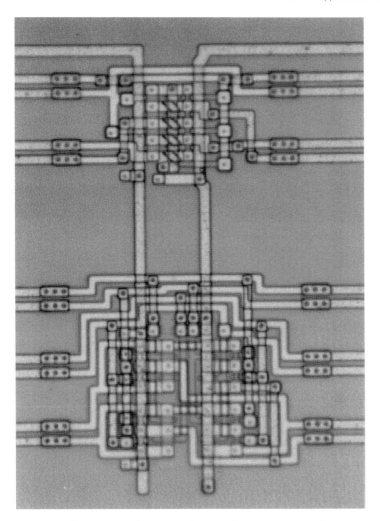

Figure 4.8 Photomicrograph (24 μm × 36 μm) of a FEYNMAN gate and a TOFFOLI gate.

A second application [95] (Figure 4.10) was fabricated in 2000, in submicron technology: a four-bit carry-look-ahead adder, implemented in 0.8 μm standard c-MOS technology, containing four FEYNMANs, four controlled NOTs of width $w = 3$, and one complex controlled NOT of width $w = 13$. It contains a total of 320 transistors.

We can use switches to decide not only whether or not an input variable is inverted, but also whether or not two input variables should be swapped. This concept leads to the implementation of the controlled SWAP gate, such as the FREDKIN

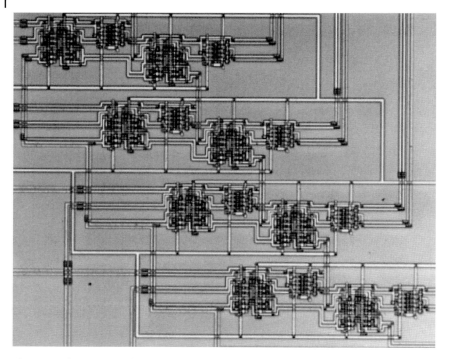

Figure 4.9 Photomicrograph (140 μm × 120 μm) of a 2.4-μm four-bit reversible ripple adder.

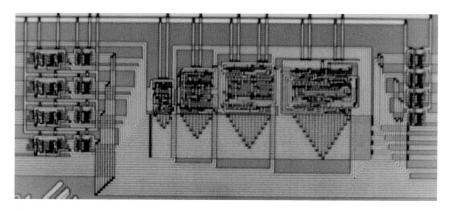

Figure 4.10 Photomicrograph (610 μm × 290 μm) of a 0.8-μm four-bit reversible carry-look-ahead adder.

gate:

$$P = A$$
$$Q = A(B \oplus C) \oplus B$$
$$R = A(B \oplus C) \oplus C \, ,$$

where A is the controlling bit and B and C are the two controlled bits. This set of equations corresponds to (3.13), with a control function $f(A) = A$. Figures 4.4c and 4.6d show the physical implementation. The reader can easily extrapolate the design philosophy to reversible logic gates of width $w = u + v$, where u controlling bits decide, by means of a control function f, whether or not the v controlled bits are subjected to some swapping and/or inverting.

4.6
Switch Cost

In Section 3.12 we introduced the gate cost of a circuit. We will now introduce another cost function: the *switch cost*. The switch cost of a circuit is simply the number of switches in the hardware realization. For example, the gate cost of a FEYNMAN gate is one unit, but its switch cost is four units; the gate cost of a TOFFOLI gate is 1, but its switch cost is $4u$, where u is the number of controlling bits. As another example, the gate cost of the full-adder circuit in Figure 3.42a is 2, but its switch cost [96] is 36. Whether the gate cost or the switch cost is the better cost function depends on (the economics of) the implementation technology.

In the case of silicon technology, twice the switch cost gives the number of transistors, and is therefore a good measure of the silicon area and thus the price of the chip. It is therefore interesting to investigate whether we can find syntheses of the building blocks F, M, and U other than those in Figure 3.42 that will yield lower switch costs. This leads to the optimal designs [97] shown in Figure 4.11. Table 4.2 makes a quantitative comparison between the two approaches. Inserting the optimized designs of Figure 4.11 into Figure 3.43 results in Table 4.3, which replaces Table 3.12.

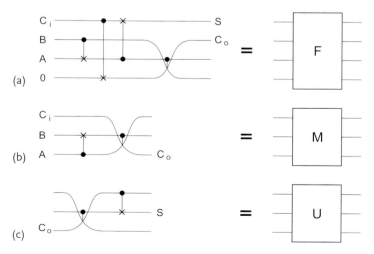

Figure 4.11 Three optimized reversible circuits: (a) the full adder, (b) the majority circuit, and (c) the unmajority circuit.

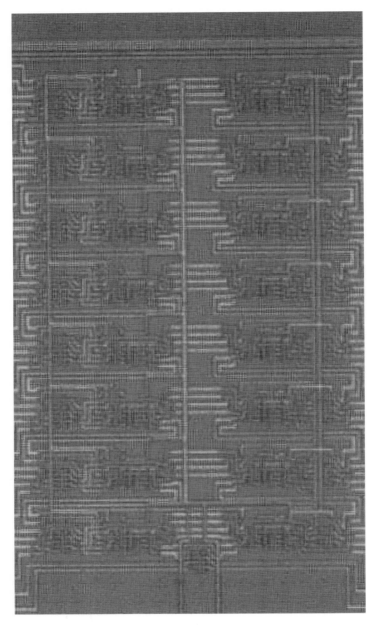

Figure 4.12 Photomicrograph (140 μm × 230 μm) of a 0.35-μm eight-bit reversible Cuccaro adder.

Table 4.2 Cost comparison of two different designs of three building blocks.

Building block	Cost function	Figure 3.42	Figure 4.11
F	Gate cost	2	4
	Switch cost	36	20
M	Gate cost	3	2
	Switch cost	16	12
U	Gate cost	3	2
	Switch cost	16	12

Table 4.3 Two reversible n-bit adders: (a) with n full adders; (b) with n majority and n unmajority circuits.

Design	Gate cost	Logic depth	Logic width	Switch cost
(a)	$4n$	$2n$	$3n + 1$	$20n$
(b)	$4n + 1$	$3n + 2$	$2n + 2$	$24n + 4$

One application [72] (Figure 4.12) is an eight-bit Cuccaro adder, implemented in 0.35 μm standard c-MOS technology, containing 16 FREDKIN and 17 FEYNMAN gates. It thus contains a total of $16 \times 16 + 17 \times 8 = 392$ transistors. The prototype chip was fabricated in 2004. We recognize eight majority circuits M at the left and eight unmajority circuits U at the right. At the bottom, we have one small spy circuit (see Section 3.20.3).

4.7
Moore's Law

According to Moore's law (named after the American engineer Gordon Moore) [98], electronic chips produced by the semiconductor industry contain an increasing number of transistors over time, because the transistors become smaller all the time. From the examples shown in the previous section, the reader will have observed that full-custom prototyping at a university lab also follows Moore's law, although with a delay of a couple of years with respect to the semiconductor industry. Indeed, many commercial chips now use transistors as small as 0.18 or 0.13 μm. Some companies have already entered the nanoscale era by introducing 90 nm, 65 nm, and 45 nm products [99] to the market.

Moore's law – the continuous decrease in transistor size – also leads to a continuous decrease in the energy dissipation per computational step. This electricity consumption and associated heat generation Q is of the order of magnitude of $C V_t^2$,

Table 4.4 Dimensions L, W, and t, and threshold voltage V_t, as well as resulting capacitance C and heat dissipation Q, of three different standard c-MOS technologies.

Technology L (μm)	L (μm)	W (μm)	t (nm)	V_t (V)	C (fF)	Q (fJ)
2.4	2.4	2.4	42.5	0.9	46.8	38
0.8	0.8	2.0	15.5	0.75	3.6	2.0
0.35	0.35	0.5	7.4	0.6	0.82	0.30

where V_t is the threshold voltage of the transistors and C is the total capacitance of the capacitors in the logic gate [100]. The quantity C is of the order of magnitude of $\epsilon_0 \epsilon \frac{LW}{t}$, where L, W, and t are the length, the width, and the oxide thickness of the transistors, whereas ϵ_0 is the permittivity of vacuum (8.854188×10^{-12} F/m) and ϵ is the dielectric constant of the oxide (either 3.9 for silicon oxide SiO_2, or 22 for hafnium oxide HfO_2). Table 4.4 gives some typical numbers. Note that a technology is named after its value for the transistor length L. We see how Q becomes smaller and smaller as L shrinks. However, this dissipation in electronic circuits is still about four orders of magnitude greater than the Landauer quantum $k T \log(2)$, which is (for $T = 300$ K) about 3×10^{-21} J, or 3 zeptojoules.

Shrinking L and W and reducing V_t still further will ultimately lead to a Q value in the neighborhood of $k T \log(2)$. According to the *International Technolo-*

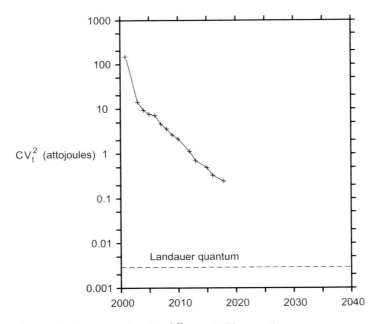

Figure 4.13 Heat generation Q in different c-MOS generations.

gy Roadmap of Semiconductors [101], Moore's law will continue to hold in the near future. Figure 4.13 shows how CV_t^2 will continue to decrease, ultimately approaching Landauer's quantum around the year 2034.

By that point, there will be a strong drive for digital electronics to be reversible, as logic reversibility is required in order to cross the Landauer barrier. This, however, does not mean that reversible MOS circuits are useless today. Indeed, as they are a reversible form of pass-transistor topology, they are particularly well suited for adiabatic addressing [102], leading to substantial power savings. In practice, such a procedure leads to a reduction in power of about a factor of 10 [100]; see the next section. The reduction in power dissipation is even more impressive if standard c-MOS technology is replaced by SOI (silicon-on-insulator) technology. In the latter process, the threshold voltage V_t can be controlled more precisely, making low-V_t technologies possible [103, 104].

4.8
Quasi-adiabatic Addressing

Power dissipation in electronic circuits is attributed to charge transfer [105, 106]. Figure 4.14a shows the basic circuit: a source voltage $v(t)$ charges a capacitor (with capacitance C) to a voltage $u(t)$. Between the voltage source and the capacitor, we have a switch. Its off-resistance is assumed to be infinite; its on-resistance is R. This R is of the order of magnitude of $\sigma \frac{Wd}{L}$, where d is the channel thickness of the transistors, whereas σ is the conductivity of the semiconductor (in most cases silicon Si). In practice, the switch is a transmission gate; that is, the parallel

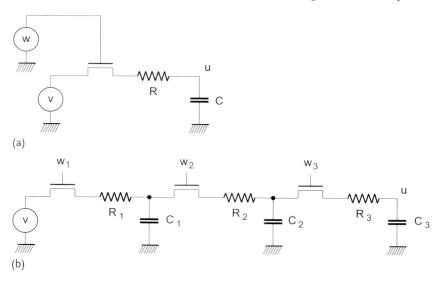

(a)

(b)

Figure 4.14 Basic RC model.

connection of an n-MOS transistor and a p-MOS transistor. We call $w(t)$ the *control voltage* of the switch.

The analog input signals $v(t)$ and $w(t)$ as well as the analog output signal $u(t)$ represent binary digital signals: V, W, and U, respectively. Thus, as usual, we denote logic values with capital letters. For example, an arbitrary binary variable X is either 0 or 1. The analog signal (say, the voltage) that represents the logic variable X is denoted by the lowercase letter x. In the ideal case, $X = 0$ is materialized by $x = -V_{dd}/2$ and $X = 1$ by $x = V_{dd}/2$. Here, V_{dd} is the power voltage (e.g., the battery voltage). Nonideal analog signals are interpreted as follows: if $x < 0$, it is interpreted as $X = 0$; if $x > 0$, it is interpreted as $X = 1$.

An ideal switch is open whenever $w < 0$ and closed whenever $w > 0$. Unfortunately, a transmission gate is not ideal. It works as follows:

- Whenever the gate voltage w exceeds $v + V_t$, the switch is closed, because the n-MOS transistor is on.
- Whenever the gate voltage $-w$ sinks below $v - V_t$, the switch is closed, because the p-MOS transistor is on.

Thus the switch is always closed, except if both transistors are off; that is, if

$$w < \min(v + V_t, -v + V_t) .$$

We compare this rule with the law of the ideal switch: an ideal switch is always closed except if $w < 0$.

Let V be an input signal that changes from $V = 0$ to $V = 1$ at time $t = 0$. For this purpose, let $v(t)$ be a ramp voltage:

$$
\begin{aligned}
v(t) &= -\frac{V_{dd}}{2} \quad \text{for} \quad t \leq -\frac{\tau}{2} \\
&= at \quad \text{for} \quad -\frac{\tau}{2} \leq t \leq \frac{\tau}{2} \\
&= \frac{V_{dd}}{2} \quad \text{for} \quad t \geq \frac{\tau}{2} .
\end{aligned}
\tag{4.7}
$$

Thus V_{dd} is the height of the ramp, τ is the rise time, and $a = V_{dd}/\tau$ is the slope of the ramp. We stress that such an addressing strategy is not optimal from an energy consumption perspective [107, 108]. However, among all possible functions $v(t)$ that rise from the value $-V_{dd}/2$ to the value $V_{dd}/2$ in a finite time τ, its performance is very close to being optimal. Because the above v profile is a simple time function and is independent of the circuit parameters C, R, and V_t, it is very often applied as the pseudo-optimal addressing of logic [109, 110]. The mathematical tool necessary to prove this statement is well known in optimal control theory, and is called the calculus of variations [102, 111–113]. This strategy is often called *adiabatic* charge transfer [114], although 'quasi-adiabatic' is perhaps a more correct name [115].

Note that it is not only input signals that change their binary values either from 0 to 1 (like in (4.7)) or from 1 to 0 that have to follow a controlled time-dependence, but also input signals that do not change their Boolean values. Figure 4.15 shows

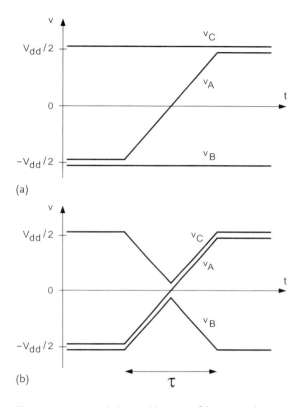

Figure 4.15 Quasi-adiabatic addressing of three input bits A, B, and C: (a) wrong; (b) right.

an example where the input vector (A, B, C) changes from $(0, 0, 1)$ to $(1, 0, 1)$: addressing only the input bit A by a smooth voltage function $v_A(t)$ (Figure 4.15a) is not sufficient; the inputs B and C (which remain at 0 and 1, respectively) have to be addressed by the smooth functions $v_B(t)$ and $v_C(t)$ (Figure 4.15b).

Power consumption is equal to voltage multiplied by current:

$$[v(t) - u(t)]i(t) , \tag{4.8}$$

where the electric current i is assumed to be zero, unless the switch is closed, in which case it obeys a linear transport law called Ohm's law (after the German physicist Georg Ohm) instead:

$$i = \frac{1}{R}(v - u) .$$

The total energy consumption is found by integrating the power dissipation:

$$Q = \int \frac{1}{R} [v(t) - u(t)]^2 \, dt , \tag{4.9}$$

with the integrand $\frac{1}{R}[v(t) - u(t)]^2$ reminding us of expression (4.6). By solving the appropriate differential equation, substituting the result $u(t)$ into formula (4.9), and evaluating the integral, we obtain Q as a polynomial in τ divided by a polynomial in τ [100]:

$$Q(\tau) \approx \frac{1}{2} \, C \, V_{dd}^2 \, \frac{8 + 2(1 + 2\alpha)z + \alpha^2 z^2}{(4 + z)(2 + z)}$$

$$\text{with} \quad z = (1 - \alpha) \, \frac{\tau}{RC} \,,$$

(4.10)

where α is the ratio

$$\alpha = V_t / V_{dd}$$

between the threshold voltage and the step voltage. Usually this voltage ratio is about 1/4. We recognize three modes of operation:

$$Q \approx \frac{1}{2} C V_{dd}^2 \quad \text{if} \quad \tau \ll RC$$

$$\approx \frac{1}{2} C V_{dd}^2 \frac{2}{z} \quad \text{if} \quad RC \ll \tau \ll RC/\alpha^2$$

$$\approx \frac{1}{2} C V_{dd}^2 \alpha^2 = \frac{1}{2} \, C \, V_t^2 \quad \text{if} \quad \tau \gg RC/\alpha^2 \,.$$

It is important to note [91] that this result can also be applied to an RC ladder circuit; that is, a cascade of m sections, each with a resistance R_i and a capacitance C_i (see Figure 4.14b for $m = 3$). It is sufficient to use the following values for the effective capacitance C and the effective resistance R:

$$C = \sum_{i=1}^{m} C_i \quad \text{and} \quad R = \frac{\sum_{i=1}^{m} R_i \left(\sum_{j=i}^{m} C_j \right)^2}{\left(\sum_{i=1}^{m} C_i \right)^2} \,.$$

This theory has been checked using a reversible full adder consisting of a total of $m = 20$ switches (Figure 4.11a) in 0.35 μm standard c-MOS technology. The power voltage V_{dd} is 3.6 V. Whenever the input signals change from one input vector to another (according to the procedure of Figure 4.15b), switches open and close in subsequent gates, like dominoes, transferring the new information from the inputs to the outputs of the circuit [91]. Figure 4.16 shows an example of a quasi-adiabatic experiment [116]. We see two transient signals: one from the input variables and one from the resulting output bits. Figure 4.17 shows, for τ values ranging from 100 ps to 10 μs, a curve-fit according to (4.10). We clearly recognize the three modes. Figure 4.16 displays the third regime: an input signal $v(t)$ and an output signal $u(t)$ for $\tau = 500$ μs.

Only for zero-V_t technologies does the parameter α equal 0. In that case, (4.10) simplifies to

$$Q \approx \frac{1}{2} C V_{dd}^2 \frac{2}{2 + z} \,,$$

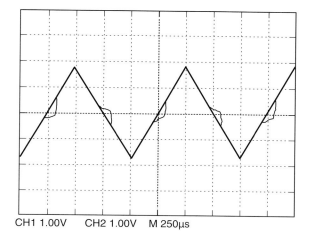

Figure 4.16 Oscilloscope view of a 0.35-μm c-MOS full adder.

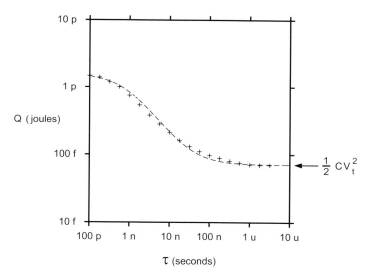

Figure 4.17 Heat generation Q as a function of rise time τ.

leaving only two modes [117]:

$$Q \approx \frac{1}{2} C V_{dd}^2 \quad \text{if} \quad \tau \ll RC$$

$$\approx C V_{dd}^2 \frac{RC}{\tau} \quad \text{if} \quad \tau \gg RC . \tag{4.11}$$

Note that $\lim_{\tau \to \infty} Q = 0$ and $\lim_{R \to 0} Q = 0$. Thus, Q can be made smaller than any value provided that we choose τ to be long enough or R to be small enough. This is no surprise, as any physical process can only happen infinitely smoothly provided that it either happens infinitely slowly or with infinitely low friction.

In the slow regime (4.11), both the factor $v(t) - u(t)$ and the factor $i(t)$ in the product (4.8) are approximately constant during the time interval $-\frac{\tau}{2} \leq t \leq \frac{\tau}{2}$:

$$i(t) \approx C V_{dd}/\tau$$
$$v(t) - u(t) \approx R C V_{dd}/\tau .$$

In finite-time thermodynamics, such a regime is sometimes called *equipartition* [108]. In Figure 4.16, we are clearly *not* in this mode: the voltage difference $v - u$ is not constant. It remains approximately 3 μV, except when $-V_t/2 < v(t) < V_t/2$ (i.e., when $-0.3\,\mathrm{V} < v < 0.3\,\mathrm{V}$). During that time interval, $v - u$ is unfortunately much larger.

4.9
Exercises for Chapter 4

Exercise 4.1
Explain the gate cost of 36 in Section 4.6 for the full adder of Figure 3.42a.

Exercise 4.2
For Figure 3.42a, Section 3.21 mentions that the two garbage outputs have values B and C_i, respectively. What are the garbage outputs of Figure 4.11a of Section 4.6?

Exercise 4.3
Assume that the transistor parameters L, W, t, and V_t change because of Moore's law, but not the parameter ϵ. Also assume that, from one c-MOS generation to the next, L shrinks by a factor κ: if the transistor length is L_0 in a certain generation, then it is L_0/κ in the next generation (with $\kappa > 1$). Each time that L is divided by κ, the other parameters are divided by some factor κ^n. Consider three different scaling laws [118, 119]:

Table 4.5 Three different scaling laws: (a) constant-voltage scaling, (b) constant-electric-field scaling, and (c) historic scaling.

Parameter		(a)	(b)	(c)
Length	L	κ^1	κ^1	κ^1
Width	W	κ^1	κ^1	κ^1
Oxide thickness	t	κ^1	κ^1	$\kappa^{0.77}$
Threshold voltage	V_t	κ^0	κ^1	$\kappa^{0.23}$
Energy consumption	Q	κ^2	κ^2	κ^2

(a) The ideal constant-voltage scaling,
(b) The ideal constant-electric-field scaling, and
(c) The historic scaling,

with κ^n according to Table 4.5.

If the energy dissipation is Q_0 in a certain generation, then it is Q_0/κ^m in the next generation. What is the exponent m for each of the three models?

Exercise 4.4

Consider Table 4.4 as three subsequent generations of MOS transistors. What is the value of κ between the first and the second generations? What is its value when stepping from the second to the third generations? Does the evolution of the energy consumption Q follow model (a), (b), or (c) of the previous exercise?

Exercise 4.5

Derive from (4.11), for long τ values, the expression for the product $Q\tau$. What happens with this result if you replace the charge $C\,V_{dd}$ by the elementary charge q and the resistance R by the von Klitzing constant $h/q^2 = 25.81281\,\mathrm{k}\Omega$ (named after the German physicist Klaus von Klitzing)? Here, h is Planck's constant $6.626176 \times 10^{-34}\,\mathrm{J\,s}$ (named after the German physicist Max Planck).

5
Analog Computing

5.1
Computing with Real Numbers

The vast majority of computers are digital computers. In them, input pins and output pins can have only two distinguishable values: both $A_j \in \mathbb{B}$ and $P_j \in \mathbb{B}$, where $\mathbb{B} = \{0, 1\}$. Nevertheless, analog computers do exist [120]. In such a machine, signals can take any real value from $-\infty$ to $+\infty$; thus, $A_j \in \mathbb{R}$ and $P_j \in \mathbb{R}$. One important kind of analog computer is the neural computer [121, 122], which mimics the performance of the brain.

Below, we will mostly restrict ourselves to linear relationships between analog outputs and analog inputs:

$$\begin{pmatrix} P_1 \\ P_2 \\ \ldots \\ P_w \end{pmatrix} = \begin{pmatrix} M_{11} & M_{12} & \ldots & M_{1w} \\ M_{21} & M_{22} & \ldots & M_{2w} \\ \ldots & & & \\ M_{w1} & M_{w2} & \ldots & M_{ww} \end{pmatrix} \begin{pmatrix} A_1 \\ A_2 \\ \ldots \\ A_w \end{pmatrix} . \tag{5.1}$$

In contrast to (3.5), where all matrix elements $M_{jk} \in \mathbb{B}$, here we have $M_{jk} \in \mathbb{R}$. In contrast to (4.3), where the variables p_j, m_{jk}, and a_k had subscripts running from 1 to 2^w, here we use the uppercase letters P_j, M_{jk}, and A_k, with subscripts running from 1 to w. The coefficients M_{jk} are called weight factors. In the case of neural computing, we may even call them synaptic weights. The matrix elements can be fixed-point positive numbers, but they can equally well be negative numbers, irrational numbers, etc.

Instead of a finite number of possible matrices, we now have an infinite number of possibilities; a continuous spectrum of matrices M. Indeed, all w^2 matrix elements M_{jk} can take all possible real values between $-\infty$ and $+\infty$, with the only reversibility restriction being

$$\det(M) \neq 0 .$$

Thus, there are ∞^{w^2} reversible weight matrices (where ∞ stands for a nondenumerable infinity, often called 'the cardinality of the reals', and where w^2 is the dimension of the matrix space). Table 5.1 compares the number ∞^{w^2} with the finite

Reversible Computing. Alexis De Vos
Copyright © 2010 WILEY-VCH Verlag GmbH & Co. KGaA, Weinheim
ISBN: 978-3-527-40992-1

Table 5.1 The number of different classical linear reversible circuits as a function of the circuit width w.

w	Digital	Analog
1	1	∞
2	6	∞^4
3	168	∞^9
4	20 160	∞^{16}

order L of the digital linear reversible group **L** (Table 3.2). The nonsingular (i.e., invertible) real matrices form a group $\boldsymbol{A}$, spanning a w^2-dimensional space. The infinite group is isomorphic to the Lie group [13, 123] known as the general linear group $\mathbf{GL}(w, \mathbb{R})$. This group is the set of nonsingular real $w \times w$ matrices, together with the standard matrix multiplication.

Analogously to Section 3.10, we introduce control gates:

$$
\begin{pmatrix} P_1 \\ P_2 \\ \cdots \\ P_{w-1} \\ P_w \end{pmatrix} = \begin{pmatrix} 1 & 0 & \cdots & 0 & 0 \\ 0 & 1 & \cdots & 0 & 0 \\ \cdots & & & & \\ 0 & 0 & & 1 & 0 \\ L_1 & L_2 & \cdots & L_{w-1} & 1 \end{pmatrix} \begin{pmatrix} A_1 \\ A_2 \\ \cdots \\ A_{w-1} \\ A_w \end{pmatrix},
\tag{5.2}
$$

where the weights L_k are called lifting coefficients. This, of course, is the linear version of the more general control gate

$$P_1 = A_1$$
$$P_2 = A_2$$
$$\cdots$$
$$P_{w-1} = A_{w-1}$$
$$P_w = f(A_1, A_2, \ldots, A_{w-1}) + A_w,
\tag{5.3}$$

where f stands for an arbitrary real function. Note that the addition sign (+) replaces the XOR in (3.12). However, as stressed by Yokoyama $et\ al.$ [1], XOR is its own inverse, whereas the inverse of + is −. In (5.2), we have a linear control function:

$$f(A_1, A_2, \ldots, A_{w-1}) = L_1 A_1 + L_2 A_2 + \cdots + L_{w-1} A_{w-1}.$$

The linear control gates (with the same controlled wire) form a $(w-1)$-dimensional Abelian subgroup $\boldsymbol{\Xi}$ of $\mathbf{GL}(w, \mathbb{R})$. The group $\boldsymbol{\Xi}$ is isomorphic to the group of real $w \times w$ matrices with all diagonal elements equal to 1 and all off-diagonal elements equal to 0, except in one particular row. Whereas in Section 3.19 the linear control gates (with an arbitrary controlled bit) generate the whole group **L**, here (in the case of real numbers) the linear control gates (with an arbitrary controlled wire) do *not* generate the whole group $\boldsymbol{A}$, only a subgroup of $\boldsymbol{A}$. Since all control gates have a unit determinant, and $\det(AB) = \det(A)\det(B)$, they can only generate circuits with unit determinants. These circuits form a subgroup of Λ; that is, Σ, isomorphic to the so-called special linear group [123] **SL** $(w, \mathbb{R})$, of dimension $w^2 - 1$:

$$\mathbf{SL}(w, \mathbb{R}) \subset \mathbf{GL}(w, \mathbb{R}) . \tag{5.4}$$

The group **SL** is the set of nonsingular real $w \times w$ matrices with determinant equal to 1, together with the operation of matrix multiplication.

Therefore, in order to generate the whole group Λ, we need extra generators, which is why we introduce SCALE gates:

$$\begin{pmatrix} P_1 \\ P_2 \\ \dots \\ P_{w-1} \\ P_w \end{pmatrix} = \begin{pmatrix} 1 & 0 & \dots & 0 & 0 \\ 0 & 1 & \dots & 0 & 0 \\ \dots & & & & \\ 0 & 0 & & 1 & 0 \\ 0 & 0 & \dots & 0 & S \end{pmatrix} \begin{pmatrix} A_1 \\ A_2 \\ \dots \\ A_{w-1} \\ A_w \end{pmatrix} ,$$

where the weight S is called the scaling coefficient. These form a one-dimensional group isomorphic to **GL**$(1, \mathbb{R})$. Thus, the w^2-dimensional space of **GL**$(w, \mathbb{R})$ consists of the $(w^2 - 1)$-dimensional space of **SL**$(w, \mathbb{R})$ and the one-dimensional space of **GL**$(1, \mathbb{R})$.

Besides SCALE gates that scale the number A_w, we can also consider SCALE gates that scale another real input A_k.

5.2
Synthesis

We note that the synthesis of an arbitrary circuit from **GL**$(w, \mathbb{R})$ requires only one SCALE gate plus the synthesis of an appropriate member from **SL**$(w, \mathbb{R})$. We can illustrate this by a $w = 4$ example:

$$\begin{pmatrix} a & b & c & d \\ e & f & g & h \\ j & k & l & m \\ n & o & p & q \end{pmatrix} = \begin{pmatrix} 1 & 0 & 0 & 0 \\ 0 & 1 & 0 & 0 \\ 0 & 0 & \Delta & 0 \\ 0 & 0 & 0 & 1 \end{pmatrix} \begin{pmatrix} a & b & c & d \\ e & f & g & h \\ \frac{j}{\Delta} & \frac{k}{\Delta} & \frac{l}{\Delta} & \frac{m}{\Delta} \\ n & o & p & q \end{pmatrix} ,$$

where Δ is the determinant of the matrix on the left-hand side. The right matrix of the right-hand side automatically has a unit determinant. Here we have chosen the input A_3 as the number to be scaled. Of course, any other choice is equally good.

We can now focus on the synthesis of an arbitrary member of **SL**$(w, \mathbb{R})$. Can it, like the binary matrices in Section 3.19, be synthesized solely from control gates? The answer is 'yes', provided we are careful with the swap matrix S in the decomposition (3.20). Can a SWAP gate be decomposed into control gates? This is not obvious, as, for example, (3.14) does not hold in the real-number field. Indeed, in that case, we have

$$\begin{pmatrix} 1 & 1 \\ 0 & 1 \end{pmatrix} \begin{pmatrix} 1 & 0 \\ 1 & 1 \end{pmatrix} \begin{pmatrix} 1 & 1 \\ 0 & 1 \end{pmatrix} = \begin{pmatrix} 2 & 3 \\ 1 & 2 \end{pmatrix} . \tag{5.5}$$

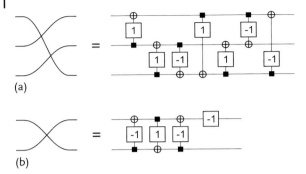

(a)

(b)

Figure 5.1 Decomposition of (a) an exchange gate and (b) a SWAP gate.

Only even wire permutations can be decomposed into control gates. An example is shown in Figure 5.1a:

$$\begin{pmatrix} 0 & 1 & 0 \\ 0 & 0 & 1 \\ 1 & 0 & 0 \end{pmatrix}$$

$$= \begin{pmatrix} 1 & 0 & -1 \\ 0 & 1 & 0 \\ 0 & 0 & 1 \end{pmatrix} \begin{pmatrix} 1 & 0 & 0 \\ -1 & 1 & 1 \\ 0 & 0 & 1 \end{pmatrix} \begin{pmatrix} 1 & 0 & 0 \\ 0 & 1 & 0 \\ 1 & -1 & 1 \end{pmatrix} \begin{pmatrix} 1 & 0 & 0 \\ 0 & 1 & 1 \\ 0 & 0 & 1 \end{pmatrix} \begin{pmatrix} 1 & 1 & 0 \\ 0 & 1 & 0 \\ 0 & 0 & 1 \end{pmatrix}.$$

Whenever possible, we choose (for decomposition (3.20)) not a swap matrix but an even permutation for the permutation matrix S. Only when this is not possible do we resort to a SWAP gate. Because the latter represents an odd permutation, it needs four gates:

$$\begin{pmatrix} 0 & 1 \\ 1 & 0 \end{pmatrix} = \text{either} \quad \begin{pmatrix} -1 & 0 \\ 0 & 1 \end{pmatrix} \begin{pmatrix} 1 & -1 \\ 0 & 1 \end{pmatrix} \begin{pmatrix} 1 & 0 \\ 1 & 1 \end{pmatrix} \begin{pmatrix} 1 & -1 \\ 0 & 1 \end{pmatrix}$$

$$\text{or} \quad \begin{pmatrix} 1 & 0 \\ 0 & -1 \end{pmatrix} \begin{pmatrix} 1 & 0 \\ -1 & 1 \end{pmatrix} \begin{pmatrix} 1 & 1 \\ 0 & 1 \end{pmatrix} \begin{pmatrix} 1 & 0 \\ -1 & 1 \end{pmatrix}$$

or similar .

In such decompositions, only three blocks are control gates (with lifting coefficients ± 1), with the remaining one being a SCALE gate (with scaling factor -1). See Figure 5.1b, which shows the first decomposition possibility.

Thus, we finally obtain a decomposition similar to (3.21), but with extra gates: one or zero SCALE gates with scaling factors equal to $\det(M)$, and possibly some SCALE gates with scaling factors of -1.

Figure 5.2 summarizes the present section for the case $w = 2$:

$$\begin{pmatrix} M_{11} & M_{12} \\ M_{21} & M_{22} \end{pmatrix} = \begin{pmatrix} 1 & 0 \\ 0 & S \end{pmatrix} \begin{pmatrix} 1 & 0 \\ L_1 & 1 \end{pmatrix} \begin{pmatrix} 1 & L_2 \\ 0 & 1 \end{pmatrix} \begin{pmatrix} 1 & 0 \\ L_3 & 1 \end{pmatrix}, \tag{5.6}$$

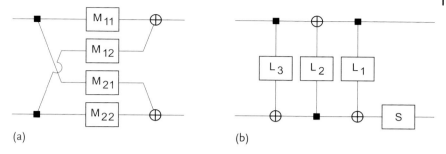

Figure 5.2 A linear transformation of two reals: (a) butterfly scheme, (b) lifting scheme.

with one scaling factor and three lifting coefficients:

$$S = M_{11}M_{22} - M_{12}M_{21}$$
$$L_1 = [M_{22}/(M_{11}M_{22} - M_{12}M_{21}) - 1]/M_{12}$$
$$L_2 = M_{12}$$
$$L_3 = (M_{11} - 1)/M_{12} \,.$$

$$(5.7)$$

Whereas the conventional circuit of Figure 5.2a is called a *butterfly circuit*, Figure 5.2b is sometimes called a *ladder circuit* [66].

When $\det(M) = 1$, this simplifies to

$$S = 1$$
$$L_1 = (M_{22} - 1)/M_{12}$$
$$L_2 = M_{12}$$
$$L_3 = (M_{11} - 1)/M_{12} \,.$$

An important example of such a unit-determinant transformation is the so-called *Givens rotation* (named after the American mathematician Wallace Givens):

$$\begin{pmatrix} \cos(\alpha) & \sin(\alpha) \\ -\sin(\alpha) & \cos(\alpha) \end{pmatrix} = \begin{pmatrix} 1 & 0 \\ \frac{\cos(\alpha)-1}{\sin(\alpha)} & 1 \end{pmatrix} \begin{pmatrix} 1 & \sin(\alpha) \\ 0 & 1 \end{pmatrix} \begin{pmatrix} 1 & 0 \\ \frac{\cos(\alpha)-1}{\sin(\alpha)} & 1 \end{pmatrix} \,.$$

Besides its importance in quantum computing [124, 125], it has a number of classical applications, for example in audio coding [126, 127]. Such decompositions follow a scheme proposed by Oraintara *et al.* [128] after Daubechies and Sweldens [129], following 'a trick' by Buneman [130].

5.3
An Application: the Color Transform

We now describe an application with $w = 3$ taken from everyday life: the transformation from RGB (red–green–blue) color coordinates to XYZ tristimulus val-

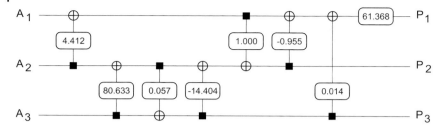

Figure 5.3 Decomposition of a linear reversible circuit into LIFT gates and one SCALE gate.

ues [131]:

$$\begin{pmatrix} P_1 \\ P_2 \\ P_3 \end{pmatrix} = \begin{pmatrix} 2.769 & 1.752 & 1.130 \\ 1.000 & 4.591 & 0.060 \\ 0.000 & 0.057 & 5.594 \end{pmatrix} \begin{pmatrix} A_1 \\ A_2 \\ A_3 \end{pmatrix}.$$

In this example, the determinant is approximately equal to 61.368.

Figure 5.3 shows the decomposition of the color coordinate transform:

$$\begin{pmatrix} 2.769 & 1.752 & 1.130 \\ 1.000 & 4.591 & 0.060 \\ 0.000 & 0.057 & 5.594 \end{pmatrix} =$$

$$\begin{pmatrix} 61.368 & 0 & 0 \\ 0 & 1 & 0 \\ 0 & 0 & 1 \end{pmatrix} \begin{pmatrix} 1 & -0.955 & 0.014 \\ 0 & 1 & 0 \\ 0 & 0 & 1 \end{pmatrix} \begin{pmatrix} 1 & 0 & 0 \\ 1.000 & 1 & -14.404 \\ 0 & 0 & 1 \end{pmatrix}$$

$$\begin{pmatrix} 1 & 0 & 0 \\ 0 & 1 & 0 \\ 0.000 & 0.057 & 1 \end{pmatrix} \begin{pmatrix} 1 & 0 & 0 \\ 0 & 1 & 80.633 \\ 0 & 0 & 1 \end{pmatrix} \begin{pmatrix} 1 & 4.412 & 0 \\ 0 & 1 & 0 \\ 0 & 0 & 1 \end{pmatrix}.$$

We see no permutation matrices in this case.

In Figure 5.3, we have decomposed each control gate into $w - 1$ or less control gates with a single controlling wire. We call such building blocks LIFT gates. They play a role similar to the FEYNMAN gates in Section 3.19. Figure 5.3 displays seven LIFT gates. In general (assuming no permutation matrix is necessary), $w^2 - 1$ or less LIFT gates appear; see Section 3.19.

The following question arises: is the decomposition of an arbitrary element of Σ into $w^2 - 1$ LIFT gates efficient? In order to answer this question, we assume a space of dimension n, to be built with the help of a library of subspaces, each of dimension b. We postulate that L subspaces of dimension b can span the total space of dimension n. Therefore, $(L - 1)b < n$ and $Lb \geq n$, and thus the lower bound

$$L = \left\lceil \frac{n}{b} \right\rceil. \tag{5.8}$$

Comparing (5.8) with (D1), we note that, in an infinite group, the dimensionality plays a similar role to the logarithm of the order of a finite group. This is not surprising. Indeed, if, against better judgement, we treat infinity as an ordinary number, we obtain

$$\frac{\log(N)}{\log(B)} = \frac{\log(\infty^n)}{\log(\infty^b)} = \frac{n\log(\infty)}{b\log(\infty)} = \frac{n}{b} \, .$$

With $n(w) = w^2 - 1$ for $\mathbf{SL}(w, \mathbb{R})$ and $b(w) = 1$ for the LIFT gates, (5.8) becomes

$$L = \left\lceil \frac{w^2 - 1}{1} \right\rceil = w^2 - 1 \, .$$

Thus, our synthesis approach for special linear real transformations is particularly efficient. As synthesis for general linear transformations requires only one extra (SCALE) gate, that synthesis is also very efficient.

5.4
About Determinants

In the previous section, we introduced the subgroup **SL** of the the group **GL**. Whereas the determinant of the matrices of **GL** may have any real value (except 0), the determinant of the matrices of **SL** can only have the value 1. In the finite group $\mathbf{S}_n$, however, we made no similar distinction. Since there are 'special linear groups', why aren't there 'special symmetric groups' too? The reason is the following. Matrix computations happen in a *field*; that is, a set of numbers and two operations (one of which is a kind of addition, and the other a kind of multiplication). In binary computing, the set is $\mathbb{B} = \{0, 1\}$, the addition is XOR, and the multiplication is AND. Such a field is called the 'Galois field' $GF(2)$, after the young French mathematician Évariste Galois, pioneer of the theory of finite groups. In this field, all square matrices have a determinant that is equal to either 0 (singular matrices) or 1 (invertible matrices). Thus: in $GF(2)$, *all* invertible matrices have unit determinants and are thus 'special'. For example,

$$\det \begin{pmatrix} 0 & 1 \\ 1 & 0 \end{pmatrix} = (0 \text{ AND } 0) \text{ XOR} (1 \text{ AND } 1) = 1 \, .$$

If we regard permutation matrices as a subgroup of **GL**, we can compute their determinants in the real field; that is, the field with the number set $\mathbb{R}$ and ordinary addition and multiplication. In that case,

$$\det \begin{pmatrix} 0 & 1 \\ 1 & 0 \end{pmatrix} = (0 \times 0) - (1 \times 1) = -1 \, .$$

Now, in the real field, half of all permutation matrices have determinants equal to $+1$, while the other half have determinants of -1. The former correspond to 'even permutations', and the latter to 'odd permutations'. The even permutations form a subgroup of permutations. Thus, although we have done it by the backdoor route of the real field, we have still discovered a group resembling a 'special symmetric' group. This group has been given the name of *alternating group*. The group $\mathbf{A}_n$ is thus the group of even permutations of n objects or (equivalently) the group of $n \times n$ permutation matrices with determinant 1 in the real field. We have

$$\mathbf{A}_n \subset \mathbf{S}_n , \tag{5.9}$$

and the index of $\mathbf{A}_n$ in $\mathbf{S}_n$ is 2. The order of $\mathbf{A}_n$ is thus $n!/2$.

5.5
LIFT Gates versus SCALE Gates

Whereas the LIFT gates in the analog linear computer are the equivalent of the FEYNMAN gates in the digital linear computer, the SCALE gates have no counterpart in the digital computer. We stress that these SCALE gates behave quite differently from the LIFT gates.

The advantage of the LIFT gates over the SCALE gates is the fact that computing followed by uncomputing is insensitive to errors in the lifting coefficients [66, 67, 128, 132–134]. The inverse of a lifting circuit with lifting coefficient L is a lifting circuit with a lifting coefficient $-L$ (see the template in Figure 5.4a). The inverse circuit can, however, also have the lifting factor L, provided the addition is replaced by a subtraction: see Figure 5.4b. As the Cuccaro subtractor is simply the mirror image of the Cuccaro adder, the inverse circuit of the lifting gate is its mirror image. Well, this is no surprise; see the do-undo structure of Section 3.18. Thus, if the hardware implementation of the multiplier L has limited accuracy, the multiplication will lead to a slightly incorrect product; nevertheless, if we use the same (but mirrored) inaccurate circuit for decomputing, the cascade of computation and uncomputation will be a noncomputation: the two successive inaccuracies cancel each other. Inaccurate multiplication does not prevent perfect reversibility.

The inverse of a SCALE gate with scaling factor S needs a SCALE gate with scaling factor $1/S$. This is illustrated by the template in Figure 5.4c. If S and $1/S$ have

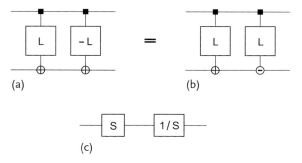

(a)   (b)

(c)

Figure 5.4 Three analog templates: (a) lifting circuit, (b) lifting circuit, and (c) scaling circuit.

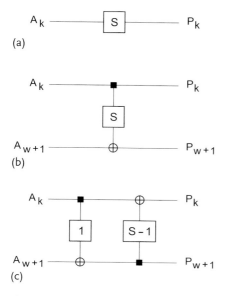

Figure 5.5 Applying an extra line to substitute (a) a SCALE gate with (b) a LIFT gate or (c) two LIFT gates.

limited precision, imperfect inversion can result [66]. In our example of Section 5.3, S equals 61.368. If also $1/S$ is hardwired with a precision of only 10^{-3}, then $1/S$ is approximated by 0.016, leading to imperfect inversion (as 0.016×61.368 is not exactly 1, but 0.981888).

According to Bruekers and van den Enden [66], perfect inversion is only possible if the scaling factor S is a so-called perfect coefficient;[14] that is, it equals $\pm 2^{\pm j}$ for example. If this is not the case, scaling circuits should be avoided for perfect invertibility. We may convert a SCALE gate into a LIFT gate, provided we introduce an extra $(w + 1)$th line with a preset input A_{w+1} and a garbage output P_{w+1}. See for example, Figure 5.5, where A_{w+1} is preset to 0, and where (besides the desired output $S A_k$), we obtain a garbage output equal to A_k:

$$(P_k) = (S)(A_k) \rightarrow \begin{pmatrix} P_k \\ P_{w+1} \end{pmatrix} = \begin{pmatrix} 1 & 0 \\ S & 1 \end{pmatrix} \begin{pmatrix} A_k \\ 0 \end{pmatrix}.$$

If we prefer the desired result $(S A_k)$ to appear at the output P_k and the garbage result (A_k) to appear at the output P_{w+1}, either two liftings (Figure 5.5c) or one lifting and one swap are necessary.

We end this section by discussing a simple example: the $\pm$ circuit, which realizes the linear transformation (3.1). Figure 5.6a shows its icon. Its matrix has the

14) The 'perfect coefficients' of Bruekers and van den Enden form a discrete group (with a denumerable infinity of elements); see the end of Section 2.1.

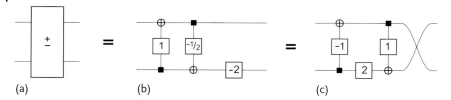

Figure 5.6 Two circuits that implement the $\pm$ block.

determinant

$$\det \begin{pmatrix} 1 & 1 \\ 1 & -1 \end{pmatrix} = -2 \; .$$

Therefore, the synthesis method of Section 5.2 leads to the decomposition

$$\begin{pmatrix} 1 & 1 \\ 1 & -1 \end{pmatrix} = \begin{pmatrix} 1 & 0 \\ 0 & -2 \end{pmatrix} \begin{pmatrix} 1 & 1 \\ -\frac{1}{2} & \frac{1}{2} \end{pmatrix}$$

$$= \begin{pmatrix} 1 & 0 \\ 0 & -2 \end{pmatrix} \begin{pmatrix} 1 & 0 \\ -\frac{1}{2} & 1 \end{pmatrix} \begin{pmatrix} 1 & 1 \\ 0 & 1 \end{pmatrix} \; .$$

Figure 5.6b is the resulting circuit. If we prefer to avoid negative scaling factors, Figure 5.6c gives a possible variant.

5.6
Conclusion

Confronting reversible mappings from $\{0, 1\}^w$ to $\{0, 1\}^w$ with reversible mappings from $\mathbb{R}^w$ to $\mathbb{R}^w$ leads to comparisons between finite groups and infinite groups (i.e., finite-dimensional Lie groups). In the particular case of linear transformations, we have confronted $\mathbf{GL}(w, 2)$ of order $2^{(w-1)w/2}w!_2$ with $\mathbf{GL}(w, \mathbb{R})$ of dimension w^2. Whereas all members of $\mathbf{GL}(w, 2)$ can be generated by control gates and thus by the building block known as the FEYNMAN gate, the members of $\mathbf{GL}(w, \mathbb{R})$ fall into two categories: the members of the special group $\mathbf{SL}(w, \mathbb{R})$, and the others. The former can be generated solely by control gates and thus by the building block known as the LIFT gate; the latter need a second kind of building block: the SCALE gate. These SCALE gates may lead to complications during hardware implementation.

The members of $\mathbf{GL}(w, 2)$ and the members of $\mathbf{GL}(w, \mathbb{R})$ are both represented by $w \times w$ matrices. Nevertheless, the finite group $\mathbf{GL}(w, 2)$ is *not* simply a subgroup of the infinite group $\mathbf{GL}(w, \mathbb{R})$. Suffice it to note that different matrix multiplication tables (i.e., Cayley tables) apply, as is illustrated by (3.14) and (5.5). There is, however, a finite group that is simultaneously a subgroup of $\mathbf{GL}(w, 2)$ and a subgroup of $\mathbf{GL}$ $(w, \mathbb{R})$: the group formed by the $w!$ exchangers. This group is isomorphic to the symmetric group $\mathbf{S}_w$. It is represented by $w \times w$ permutation matrices (see Section 3.7).

5.7
Computations with Complex Numbers

The reasoning of Section 5.1 barely changes if we postulate $A_j \in \mathbb{C}$, $P_j \in \mathbb{C}$, and $M_{jk} \in \mathbb{C}$. Again, we will have LIFT gates like

$$\begin{pmatrix} P_j \\ P_k \end{pmatrix} = \begin{pmatrix} 1 & 0 \\ L & 1 \end{pmatrix} \begin{pmatrix} A_j \\ A_k \end{pmatrix}$$

and SCALE gates like

$$(P_m) = (S)(A_m) \ ,$$

although both the lifting coefficient L and the scaling coefficient S will be complex.

Practical (classical) analog computers use classical physical quantities (such as positions, angles, voltages, currents, ...) to represent numbers. Their information channels can only transport real numbers. Therefore, we must assume that the channel A_j consists of two subwires, each transporting a real number; that is, one with A'_j (the real part of A_j) and the other with A''_j (the imaginary part of A_j). Let us also make similar assumptions for A_k, A_m, P_j, P_k, and P_m. We can then write

$$\begin{pmatrix} P'_j \\ P''_j \\ P'_k \\ P''_k \end{pmatrix} = \begin{pmatrix} 1 & 0 & 0 & 0 \\ 0 & 1 & 0 & 0 \\ L' & -L'' & 1 & 0 \\ L'' & L' & 0 & 1 \end{pmatrix} \begin{pmatrix} A'_j \\ A''_j \\ A'_k \\ A''_k \end{pmatrix}$$

and

$$\begin{pmatrix} P'_m \\ P''_m \end{pmatrix} = \begin{pmatrix} S' & -S'' \\ S'' & S' \end{pmatrix} \begin{pmatrix} A'_m \\ A''_m \end{pmatrix} \ ,$$

with $L = L' + iL''$ and $S = S' + iS''$. According to Section 5.2, we have

$$\begin{pmatrix} 1 & 0 & 0 & 0 \\ 0 & 1 & 0 & 0 \\ L' & -L'' & 1 & 0 \\ L'' & L' & 0 & 1 \end{pmatrix} = \begin{pmatrix} 1 & 0 & 0 & 0 \\ 0 & 1 & 0 & 0 \\ L' & -L'' & 1 & 0 \\ 0 & 0 & 0 & 1 \end{pmatrix} \begin{pmatrix} 1 & 0 & 0 & 0 \\ 0 & 1 & 0 & 0 \\ 0 & 0 & 1 & 0 \\ L'' & L' & 0 & 1 \end{pmatrix}$$

that decomposes the complex LIFT gate into two real LIFT gates, and

$$\begin{pmatrix} S' & -S'' \\ S'' & S' \end{pmatrix} = \begin{pmatrix} S'^2 + S''^2 & 0 \\ 0 & 1 \end{pmatrix} \begin{pmatrix} 1 & \frac{S'-S'^2-S''^2}{(S'^2+S''^2)S''} \\ 0 & 1 \end{pmatrix}$$

$$\times \begin{pmatrix} 1 & 0 \\ S'' & 1 \end{pmatrix} \begin{pmatrix} 1 & \frac{S'-1}{S''} \\ 0 & 1 \end{pmatrix}$$

that decomposes the complex SCALE gate into three real LIFT gates and one real SCALE gate. We obtain exclusively LIFT gates iff the only real scaling coefficient

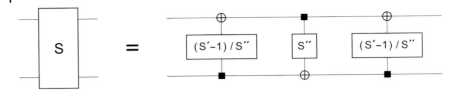

Figure 5.7 Multiplying a complex input number by a unit-magnitude complex multiplier $S = S' + iS''$.

equals 1; that is, if the complex scaling factor S is on the unit circle of the complex plane: $S'^2 + S''^2 = 1$. In that case, we have

$$\begin{pmatrix} S' & -S'' \\ S'' & S' \end{pmatrix} = \begin{pmatrix} 1 & \frac{S'-1}{S''} \\ 0 & 1 \end{pmatrix} \begin{pmatrix} 1 & 0 \\ S'' & 1 \end{pmatrix} \begin{pmatrix} 1 & \frac{S'-1}{S''} \\ 0 & 1 \end{pmatrix} ,$$

a decomposition that is shown in Figure 5.7.

5.8
An Application: the Fourier Transform

One important example of linear relation (5.1) is the discrete Fourier transform (named after the French mathematician Joseph Fourier). It is applied in many a data processor. It is a particularly challenging candidate for reversible computing. After all, the Fourier-transformed data contain the same information as the original data. After all, there is a so-called inverse Fourier transform that allows the original data to be recovered from the Fourier-transformed data. Therefore, such computations really beg for a reversible implementation.

The Fourier transform [135] of the w complex input data $A(0), A(1), \ldots, A(w-1)$ looks like

$$P(k) = \sum_{n=0}^{w-1} A(n)\Omega^{kn} \quad \text{with} \quad 0 \le k \le w - 1 . \tag{5.10}$$

Here, Ω is a complex constant:

$$\Omega = \exp\left(-\frac{2\pi}{w}i\right)$$

called the twiddle factor. Because of the property $\Omega^w = 1$, it is the wth root of unity. The inverse Fourier transform has a similar expression:

$$A(n) = \frac{1}{w} \sum_{k=0}^{w-1} P(k)\Omega^{-kn} .$$

Because the transformed data $P(k)$ contain exactly the same amount of information as the original data $A(n)$, and because the inverse transformation exists, the Fourier transform provides a useful benchmark for reversible computing.

As, in the present book, we count from 1 to w (instead of counting from 0 to $w - 1$), we must first change notation, with $A(n)$ becoming A_{n+1} and $P(k)$ becoming P_{k+1}. Because of (5.10), the matrix elements M_{jk} of (5.1) are

$$M_{jk} = \exp\left[-i\frac{2\pi}{w}(j-1)(k-1)\right] \quad \text{with} \quad 1 \le j \le w \quad \text{and} \quad 1 \le k \le w.$$

For example, for $w = 2$, we have

$$\begin{pmatrix} P_1 \\ P_2 \end{pmatrix} = \begin{pmatrix} \exp(0) & \exp(0) \\ \exp(0) & \exp(-2\pi i/2) \end{pmatrix} \begin{pmatrix} A_1 \\ A_2 \end{pmatrix}$$

$$= \begin{pmatrix} 1 & 1 \\ 1 & -1 \end{pmatrix} \begin{pmatrix} A_1 \\ A_2 \end{pmatrix};$$

that is, the transformation (3.1), also known as the $\pm$ circuit (Section 5.5). For $w = 3$, we have

$$\begin{pmatrix} P_1 \\ P_2 \\ P_3 \end{pmatrix} = \begin{pmatrix} \exp(0) & \exp(0) & \exp(0) \\ \exp(0) & \exp(-2\pi i/3) & \exp(-4\pi i/3) \\ \exp(0) & \exp(-4\pi i/3) & \exp(-8\pi i/3) \end{pmatrix} \begin{pmatrix} A_1 \\ A_2 \\ A_3 \end{pmatrix}$$

$$= \begin{pmatrix} 1 & 1 & 1 \\ 1 & \Omega & \Omega^2 \\ 1 & \Omega^2 & \Omega \end{pmatrix} \begin{pmatrix} A_1 \\ A_2 \\ A_3 \end{pmatrix}.$$

The determinant of the Fourier matrix M is not unity [136, 137]:

$$\det M = \det \begin{pmatrix} \Omega^0 & \Omega^0 & \cdots & \Omega^0 \\ \Omega^0 & \Omega^1 & \cdots & \Omega^{w-1} \\ \cdots & & & \\ \Omega^0 & \Omega^{w-1} & \cdots & \Omega^{(w-1)(w-1)} \end{pmatrix} = w^{w/2} \lambda(w), \quad (5.11)$$

where λ is either 1, i, -1, or $-i$, depending on w.

Because the matrix M has very particular symmetry properties, it is not wise to follow the general-purpose synthesis method of Section 5.2. The so-called fast Fourier transform (FFT) is an efficient way of calculating a Fourier transform when w is a power of 2 by exploiting the special properties of the Fourier matrix. It needs only $\frac{1}{2}w \log_2(w)$ building blocks. Each of these is a circuit with two complex inputs and two complex outputs, called a butterfly:

$$P = A + W B$$
$$Q = A - W B. \quad (5.12)$$

The multiplier W is equal to some Ω^k (with $0 \le k \le w - 1$), and is thus located on the unit circle of the complex plane (i.e., $W'^2 + W''^2 = 1$), a fact that is, according to Section 5.7, very useful in reversible implementation. Figure 5.8 shows how to build the butterfly circuit in a reversible way. Here (again), primed symbols

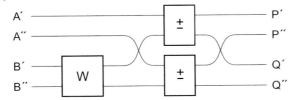

Figure 5.8 The butterfly circuit.

denote real parts and doubly primed symbols denote imaginary parts. The circuit consists of one complex scaling circuit like Figure 5.7 and two real $\pm$ circuits like Figure 5.6, giving a total of nine gates. Most importantly, the circuit does not generate garbage [72].

We note that, thanks to the lifting scheme, an inverse Fourier transform circuit is just the mirror image of the Fourier circuit. Processing the input data $A_1, A_2, \ldots, A_w$ by the Fourier chip and subsequently processing its outputs $P_1, P_2, \ldots, P_w$ by the inverse Fourier chip recovers the original data $A_1, A_2, \ldots, A_w$ exactly. Nevertheless, the data $P_1, P_2, \ldots, P_w$ may not constitute the exact Fourier transform of $A_1, A_2, \ldots, A_w$. Indeed, the limited precisions of both the multipliers W and the products $W B$ of the multiplying blocks (5.12) result in a loss of accuracy. According to Oraintara *et al.* [128], the Fourier transformation is sufficiently accurate provided all multipliers and products inside the circuit have $f(w)$ bits more than the input and output numbers, where f is some complicated function of w that satisfies

$$f(w) < \frac{3}{2} \log_2(w) \, .$$

5.9
Nonlinear Computations

Above, we chose to compare linear reversible gates from the digital world with linear reversible gates from the analog world. We can also make other, similar comparisons. For example, in affine linear transformations, the relationship (5.1) is generalized to

$$\begin{pmatrix} P_1 \\ P_2 \\ \cdots \\ P_w \end{pmatrix} = \begin{pmatrix} V_1 \\ V_2 \\ \cdots \\ V_w \end{pmatrix} + \begin{pmatrix} M_{11} & M_{12} & \cdots & M_{1w} \\ M_{21} & M_{22} & \cdots & M_{2w} \\ \cdots & & & \\ M_{w1} & M_{w2} & \cdots & M_{ww} \end{pmatrix} \begin{pmatrix} A_1 \\ A_2 \\ \cdots \\ A_w \end{pmatrix} \, .$$

If both kinds of parameters (i.e., the vector elements V_j and the matrix elements M_{jk}) are members of $\{0, 1\}$, then we have the finite affine general linear group of Section 3.6; that is, $\mathbf{AGL}(w, 2)$ with order $2^{w(w+1)/2} w!_2$. If, on the contrary, both kinds of parameters (V_j and M_{jk}) are elements of $\mathbb{R}$, then we have the infinite affine general linear group $\mathbf{AGL}(w, \mathbb{R})$ with dimension $w^2 + w$.

One could also envisage investigating analog reversible circuits where the outputs are neither linear nor affine linear functions of the inputs. Let us, for example, look at control gates. In the Boolean case, there are $2^{2^{w-1}}$ possible functions f for the relationship

$$P_w = f(A_1, A_2, \ldots, A_{w-1}) \oplus A_w .$$

Their Reed–Muller expansions are a kind of binary polynomials, with the degree of the polynomial ranging from 0 (if $f = 0$) to $w - 1$ (if the Reed–Muller expansion contains the term $A_1 A_2 \ldots A_{w-1}$). In the real case

$$P_w = f(A_1, A_2, \ldots, A_{w-1}) + A_w ,$$

even if we restrict ourselves to polynomial functions f, we already have an infinite number of coefficients in the polynomial. Thus the dimensionality is infinite. The order of the group of such polynomial control gates is

$$\infty^\infty ,$$

where the lower infinity is a nondenumerable one (∞ being the cardinality of the reals), whereas the upper infinity is a denumerable one (∞ being the cardinality of the rationals; that is, $\aleph_0$). If we drop the polynomial restriction (that is, if we accept arbitrary control functions), the upper infinity is not denumerable anymore. Applying the notation proposed by Wheeler and Penrose [138], the size of the space is then

$$\infty^{\infty^{\infty^{w-1}}} .$$

In a final step, if we drop the restriction to only use control gates, we find that the total number of ways to reversibly transform w reals into w reals is

$$\infty^{w \infty^w} .$$

We now discuss two examples for $w = 1$. Thus, there are ∞^∞ different computations with one real input A and one real output P. Figure 5.9a shows a simple example:

$$P = A^3 .$$

Its inverse exists and is

$$P = \sqrt[3]{A} .$$

Here we assume that $\sqrt[3]{A}$ denotes the real and positive cube root if A is positive, and is minus the positive real cube root of $-A$ if A is negative (e.g., $\sqrt[3]{27}$ represents 3 and $\sqrt[3]{-27}$ denotes -3). Figure 5.9b shows a more tricky example:

$$P = A^3 - 3A .$$

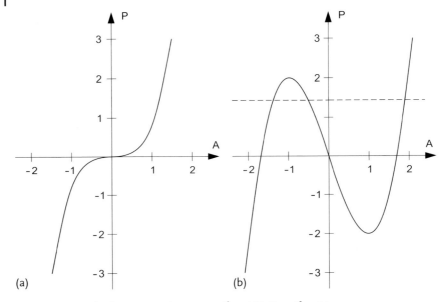

Figure 5.9 Two cubic functions $P(A)$: (a) $P = A^3$ and (b) $P = A^3 - 3A$.

Its inverse does not exist. This is because the function $A^3 - 3A$ is not injective; that is, $A^3 - 3A = A'^3 - 3A'$ does not necessarily imply $A = A'$.

In order to see that $A^3 - 3A$ is not injective, let us consider the cubic equation

$$x^3 - 3x - y = 0 ,$$

where y is a given real parameter. If y is in the range $-2 < y < 2$, then the equation has three different real solutions x. Following Cardano's method (named after the Italian physician/mathematician Girolamo Cardano), these are

$$x = \sqrt[3]{\frac{y}{2} \pm \sqrt{\frac{y^2}{4} - 1}} + \frac{1}{\sqrt[3]{\frac{y}{2} \pm \sqrt{\frac{y^2}{4} - 1}}} .$$

If, for example, $y = \sqrt{2}$ (indicated by the dashed line in Figure 5.9b), then we find (after some trigonometric manipulations) that the three solutions are $x = -\sqrt{2} \approx -1.41$, $x = -(\sqrt{6} - \sqrt{2})/2 \approx -0.52$, and $x = (\sqrt{6} + \sqrt{2})/2 \approx 1.93$. This situation is reminiscent of Figure 3.1. Here, we have an analog calculator with input A and output $A^3 - 3A$; see Figure 5.10. The computer is irreversible because, if we forget the input value $(-\sqrt{2})$, knowledge of the output value $(\sqrt{2})$ is not sufficient to recover the input. For example, $\sqrt{2}$ could equally well have been generated by $-(\sqrt{6} - \sqrt{2})/2$ or by $(\sqrt{6} + \sqrt{2})/2$.

There are two different ways to make an irreversible computation $P = f(A)$ reversible. The first approach requires a second wire and applies the general lifting

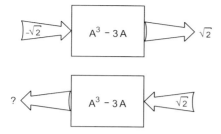

Figure 5.10 An irreversible analog calculator.

scheme:

$$P = A$$
$$Q = B + f(A)$$

where $f(A)$ is an arbitrary (i.e., not necessarily injective) function. Here, $f(A)$ is the function $A^3 - 3A$. If we apply the preset $B = 0$, then Q is the desired result (i.e., $A^3 - 3A$), whereas P is the garbage (equal to A itself). The calculator has two real inputs and two real outputs. It is reversible. Of course it is: we can recover the input A from the output values because we simply have remembered it as the output P. The inverse circuit, by the way, is:

$$P = A$$
$$Q = B - f(A) \, .$$

The second approach makes use of the fact that the value of $A^3 - 3A$ is sufficient to recover the value of A provided we know whether A is in the range $(-\infty, -1)$, in the range $(-1, 1)$, or in the range $(1, +\infty)$. Thus, it is not necessary to 'remember' A; it is sufficient to remember the sign of $A - (-1)$ and the sign of $A - 1$. We then construct a calculator with three outputs:

$$P = A^3 - 3A$$
$$Q = \text{sign}(A + 1)$$
$$R = \text{sign}(A - 1) \, .$$

This leads to two garbage outputs (i.e., Q and R). However, both are 'small' garbage outputs, as they are merely Boolean numbers that can take only two values (i.e., either -1 or 1). Thus, whereas the desired output P is a real, the garbage only consists of two bits, and two bits contain far less information than a real number – after all, a real number needs a (countable) infinity of bits to be represented. For this reason, the outputs Q and R may be considered to represent a very small overhead; we can call them garbiginoes.

5.10
Exercises for Chapter 5

Exercise 5.1
Prove (5.7).

Exercise 5.2
If M_{12} equals 0, then (5.7) cannot be the solution of (5.6). What should we do in this case?

Exercise 5.3
Compute the determinant of the Fourier matrix explicitly in the cases $w = 1$, $w = 2$, $w = 3$, and $w = 4$. Compare your results with (5.11).

Exercise 5.4
What are the values of the line sums of the Fourier matrix?

6
Computing in Modulo 2^b

In Chapter 3 we performed computations with numbers from $\mathbb{B}$; in Chapter 5 we performed computations with numbers from $\mathbb{R}$ (and from $\mathbb{C}$). However, there are choices in-between the cases $\{0, 1\}$ and $\mathbb{R}$, such as the number system where the numbers A_j and the numbers P_j are elements of $\mathbb{Z}$; that is, the infinite set of integers. Reversible integer transformations are important, for example, in signal processing [67, 128, 132, 133], and find multiple applications in video coding [139–142].

In the present chapter we will discuss computations with integers from a finite set, in other words the n members of

$$\mathbb{Z}_n = \left\{ -\frac{n}{2}, -\frac{n}{2} + 1, \ldots, -1, 0, 1, \ldots, \frac{n}{2} - 1 \right\} .$$

Here, of course, n is even. In most computers, n is a power of 2, say 2^b. Thus numbers are registers of b bits. We call b the *word length*. As one of these bits is a sign bit, integers run from -2^{b-1} to $2^{b-1} - 1$. Reversible computing in $\mathbb{Z}_{2^b}$ (especially in $\mathbb{Z}_{16}$ and $\mathbb{Z}_{32}$) has been discussed by Yokoyama *et al.* [1, 37].

6.1
Addition in Modulo 2^b

In fact, we have already discussed circuits that perform the addition of integer numbers with a limited range in Sections 3.21 and 3.22:

$$P = A$$
$$Q = A + B .$$

There, we tacitly assumed that A and B belong to $\{0, 1, \ldots, 2^n - 1\}$. In Figure 3.43, all input numbers are from $\{0, 1, \ldots, 15\}$; in Figure 4.12, all input numbers are from $\{0, 1, \ldots, 255\}$.

Reversible Computing. Alexis De Vos
Copyright © 2010 WILEY-VCH Verlag GmbH & Co. KGaA, Weinheim
ISBN: 978-3-527-40992-1

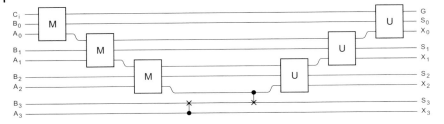

Figure 6.1 Four-bit reversible ripple adder with majority and unmajority circuits.

Table 6.1 Reversible n-bit adder with $n-1$ majority and $n-1$ unmajority circuits.

Gate cost	Logic depth	Logic width	Switch cost
$4n - 2$	$3n$	$2n + 1$	$24n - 16$

In the present chapter, however, A is the binary number $A_{b-1}A_{b-2}A_{b-3}\ldots A_0$, with

- A_{b-1} as the sign bit (either 0 for the $+$ sign or 1 for the $-$ sign),
- A_{b-2} as the most significant bit,
- $\ldots$, and
- A_0 as the least significant bit,

and so A belongs to $\mathbb{Z}_{2^b} = \{-2^{b-1}, -2^{b-1}+1, \ldots, -1, 0, 1, \ldots, 2^{b-1}-1\}$, and similarly for B, P, and Q. In order to obtain Q in modulo 2^b, we drop the possibility of the single carry-over bit C_o mentioned in Section 3.22. This allows for a small simplification of the circuit such that we modify Figure 3.43b to Figure 6.1. Table 6.1 gives the properties of the new circuit (to be compared with the numbers in Table 4.3b). The single carry-in bit C_i cannot be deleted and may be considered a preset. In normal operation it is preset to 0.

If, for any input vector of Figure 6.1, we calculate the corresponding output vector, this analysis results in the full truth table. As the width w of the circuit is $2n + 1 = 9$, the table has $2w = 18$ columns and $2^w = 512$ rows. Table 6.2a shows part of the table (i.e., only 12 rows). Table 6.2b shows the same table in decimal notation; any number N satisfies

$$N = N_2 \times 4 + N_1 \times 2 + N_0$$

if its sign bit (i.e., N_3) is equal to zero.

Negative numbers, however, are more tricky. Indeed, in case $N_3 = 1$, we do *not* have

$$N = -(N_2 \times 4 + N_1 \times 2 + N_0) \, . \tag{6.1}$$

Table 6.2 Four-bit adder: (a) in binary notation; (b) in decimal notation.

$A_3 A_2 A_1 A_0$	$B_3 B_2 B_1 B_0$	C_i	$X_3 X_2 X_1 X_0$	$S_3 S_2 S_1 S_0$	G
0 0 0 0	0 0 0 0	0	0 0 0 0	0 0 0 0	0
0 0 0 0	0 0 0 0	1	0 0 0 0	0 0 0 1	1
0 0 0 0	0 0 0 1	0	0 0 0 0	0 0 0 1	0
. . .			. . .		
0 0 1 0	0 1 0 0	0	0 0 1 0	0 1 1 0	0
0 0 1 0	0 1 0 0	1	0 0 1 0	0 1 1 1	1
0 0 1 0	0 1 0 1	0	0 0 1 0	0 1 1 1	0
. . .			. . .		
0 1 0 1	1 1 0 1	0	0 1 0 1	0 0 1 0	0
0 1 0 1	1 1 0 1	1	0 1 0 1	0 0 1 1	1
0 1 0 1	1 1 1 0	0	0 1 0 1	0 0 1 1	0
. . .			. . .		
1 1 1 1	1 1 1 0	1	1 1 1 1	1 1 1 0	1
1 1 1 1	1 1 1 1	0	1 1 1 1	1 1 1 0	0
1 1 1 1	1 1 1 1	1	1 1 1 1	1 1 1 1	1

(a)

A	B	C_i	X	S	G	
0	0	0	0	0	0	
0	0	1	0	1	1	
0	1	0	0	1	0	
. . .			. . .			
2	4	0	2	6	0	
2	4	1	2	7	1	
2	5	0	2	7	0	
. . .			. . .			
5	−3	0	5	2	0	⇐
5	−3	1	5	3	1	
5	−2	0	5	3	0	
. . .			. . .			
−1	−2	1	−1	−2	1	
−1	−1	0	−1	−2	0	
−1	−1	1	−1	−1	1	

(b)

The reason is as follows. From the upper half of Table 6.2 (where all numbers are positive), we see that

$$S = A + B + C_i$$
$$X = A$$
$$G = C_i ,$$

as expected. Solving these equations for A, B, and C_i, we obtain the reverse, expressions:

$$A = X$$
$$B = S - X - G$$
$$C_i = G .$$

Using Table 6.2b in reverse, with $G = 0$ and $X > S$, yields some negative number $B = S - X$. For example, the row with an arrow says that $S - X = 2 - 5$ is $B = -3$. The corresponding value $B_3 B_2 B_1 B_0 = 1101$ in the same row of Table 6.2a denotes the correct value -3 for B, iff it represents B in the so-called *two's complement* notation [143]:

$$B = -(\overline{B}_2 \times 4 + \overline{B}_1 \times 2 + \overline{B}_0) - 1$$

instead of the 'naive' notation (6.1). Table 6.3 shows the correspondence table between the two's complement notation and the conventional decimal notation for the case $b = 4$.

Table 6.3 Two's complement notation.

-8	1000
-7	1001
-6	1010
-5	1011
-4	1100
-3	1101
-2	1110
-1	1111
0	0000
1	0001
2	0010
3	0011
4	0100
5	0101
6	0110
7	0111

Thus, the modulo 2^b adder of Cuccaro *et al.* functions correctly in both directions for both positive and negative integers provided that we adopt the two's complement convention. Therefore, we will follow this convention below for other computations too.

6.2
Multiplication by a Constant

Assume that we want to multiply a (variable) integer number $A \in \mathbb{Z}_{2^b}$ by a constant real number X, resulting in a new number $P \in \mathbb{Z}_{2^b}$. It is clear that, for most values of X, we must content ourselves with an approximate result. Table 6.4b gives a straightforward truth table for $b = 4$ and $X = \sqrt{2}$, albeit incomplete. In order to complete the table, we must embed it in a larger (reversible) table. Table 6.4c gives a candidate truth table, where the numbers from Table 6.4b are presented in boldface.

It is not obvious how we can reconcile accuracy and reversibility. Inspired by the results of Chapter 5, we will make a distinction between the case where X is a lifting multiplier and the case where X is a scaling multiplier.

Table 6.4 Multiplying by $\sqrt{2}$: (a) in $\mathbb{R}$, (b) in $\mathbb{Z}_{16}$ irreversibly, and (c) in $\mathbb{Z}_{16}$ reversibly.

A	$\sqrt{2}\,A$
-8	$-11.313\ldots$
-7	$-9.899\ldots$
-6	$-8.485\ldots$
-5	$-7.071\ldots$
-4	$-5.656\ldots$
-3	$-4.242\ldots$
-2	$-2.828\ldots$
-1	$-1.414\ldots$
0	$0.000\ldots$
1	$1.414\ldots$
2	$2.828\ldots$
3	$4.242\ldots$
4	$5.656\ldots$
5	$7.071\ldots$
6	$8.485\ldots$
7	$9.899\ldots$

(a)

A	P
-6	-8
-5	-7
-4	-6
-3	-4
-2	-3
-1	-1
0	0
1	1
2	3
3	4
4	6
5	7

(b)

A	P
-8	-3
-7	-2
-6	-8
-5	-7
-4	-6
-3	-4
-2	-3
-1	-1
0	0
1	1
2	3
3	4
4	6
5	7
6	0
7	2

(c)

For scaling multipliers, we will restrict ourselves to the so-called *perfect* scaling factors $\pm 2^{\pm j}$ of Bruekers and van Enden (see Section 5.5). To implement these, it is sufficient to have a 'scaling by −1 block' (which is its own inverse) and a 'scaling by 2 block' (and its inverse, i.e., the 'scaling by 1/2 block'). We discuss those building blocks below, in Sections 6.3 and 6.4. Whenever nonideal scaling is necessary, we rely on extra wires and a lifting procedure (see Figure 5.5). Lifting multipliers are discussed below, in Section 6.5.

6.3
Scaling by −1

We now discuss the multiplication by −1 block (which is its own inverse); see Table 6.5. Computing in two's complement makes multiplying by −1 a difficult task: we cannot simply invert the sign bit. First, we note that Table 6.5a (with $b = 4$) is reversible but has only $2^b - 1$ rows instead of 2^b rows. Therefore, we must embed it in a larger table by adding an extra row; see Tables 6.5b and c. Inspection of the latter table leads to the conclusion that the implementation is a Sylow circuit (see

Table 6.5 Reversibly multiplying by −1 in $\mathbb{Z}_{16}$: (a) incomplete, (b) complete, and (c) complete, in binary form.

A	P
−7	7
−6	6
−5	5
−4	4
−3	3
−2	2
−1	1
0	0
1	−1
2	−2
3	−3
4	−4
5	−5
6	−6
7	−7

(a)

A	P
−8	−8
−7	7
−6	6
−5	5
−4	4
−3	3
−2	2
−1	1
0	0
1	−1
2	−2
3	−3
4	−4
5	−5
6	−6
7	−7

(b)

$A_3 A_2 A_1 A_0$	$P_3 P_2 P_1 P_0$
1 0 0 0	1 0 0 0
1 0 0 1	0 1 1 1
1 0 1 0	0 1 1 0
1 0 1 1	0 1 0 1
1 1 0 0	0 1 0 0
1 1 0 1	0 0 1 1
1 1 1 0	0 0 1 0
1 1 1 1	0 0 0 1
0 0 0 0	0 0 0 0
0 0 0 1	1 1 1 1
0 0 1 0	1 1 1 0
0 0 1 1	1 1 0 1
0 1 0 0	1 1 0 0
0 1 0 1	1 0 1 1
0 1 1 0	1 0 1 0
0 1 1 1	1 0 0 1

(c)

Section 3.11) with OR control functions:

$$P_0 = A_0$$
$$P_k = (A_0 \text{ OR } A_1 \text{ OR} \ldots \text{OR } A_{k-1}) \oplus A_k \quad \text{for} \quad 1 \le k \le b - 1 .$$

We conclude that multiplying by -1 is expensive: both the gate cost and the logic depth are equal to $w - 1 = b - 1$.

6.4
Scaling by 1/2 or by 2

In conventional computers (i.e., irreversible computers), dividing and multiplying an integer $A = A_{w-1}A_{w-2}A_{w-3}\ldots A_2A_1A_0$ by 2 are simple operations. Indeed, $P = A/2$ is found by

- Preserving the sign bit,
- Shifting the remaining one bit to the right, and
- Copying the sign bit into the most significant bit:

$$P_{w-1} P_{w-2} P_{w-3} \ldots P_2 P_1 P_0 = A_{w-1}A_{w-1}A_{w-2}A_{w-3}\ldots A_2A_1 .$$

Analogously, $P = 2A$ is found by preserving the sign bit, shifting the remaining one bit to the left, and writing 0 into the least significant bit:

$$P_{w-1} P_{w-2} P_{w-3} \ldots P_2 P_1 P_0 = A_{w-1}A_{w-3}A_{w-4}\ldots A_2A_1A_00 .$$

It is clear that both operations are irreversible: in the former case, the information relating to the bit A_0 is thrown away; in the latter case, the information relating to the bit A_{w-2} is thrown away.

There are various ways to define a reversible variant for 'division by 2' in order to implement a scaling factor equal to 1/2. Table 6.6 illustrates one of them, for the case $n = 2^b = 2^4 = 16$. It is clear that Table 6.6a is an irreversible truth table;

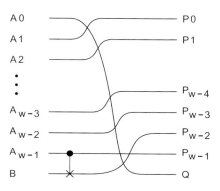

Figure 6.2 Reversible division by 2.

Table 6.6 Dividing by 2 in $\mathbb{Z}_{16}$: (a) irreversibly, (b) reversibly, and (c) in binary form.

A	P
-8	-4
-7	-4
-6	-3
-5	-3
-4	-2
-3	-2
-2	-1
-1	-1
0	0
1	0
2	1
3	1
4	2
5	2
6	3
7	3

(a)

A	B	P	Q		$A_3 A_2 A_1 A_0$	B	$P_3 P_2 P_1 P_0$	Q
-8	0	-4	0		1 0 0 0	0	1 1 0 0	0
-7	0	-4	1		1 0 0 1	0	1 1 0 0	1
-6	0	-3	0		1 0 1 0	0	1 1 0 1	0
-5	0	-3	1		1 0 1 1	0	1 1 0 1	1
-4	0	-2	0		1 1 0 0	0	1 1 1 0	0
-3	0	-2	1		1 1 0 1	0	1 1 1 0	1
-2	0	-1	0		1 1 1 0	0	1 1 1 1	0
-1	0	-1	1		1 1 1 1	0	1 1 1 1	1
0	0	0	0		0 0 0 0	0	0 0 0 0	0
1	0	0	1		0 0 0 1	0	0 0 0 0	1
2	0	1	0		0 0 1 0	0	0 0 0 1	0
3	0	1	1		0 0 1 1	0	0 0 0 1	1
4	0	2	0		0 1 0 0	0	0 0 1 0	0
5	0	2	1		0 1 0 1	0	0 0 1 0	1
6	0	3	0		0 1 1 0	0	0 0 1 1	0
7	0	3	1		0 1 1 1	0	0 0 1 1	1
-8	1	-8	0		1 0 0 0	1	1 0 0 0	0
-7	1	-8	1		1 0 0 1	1	1 0 0 0	1
-6	1	-7	0		1 0 1 0	1	1 0 0 1	0
-5	1	-7	1		1 0 1 1	1	1 0 0 1	1
-4	1	-6	0		1 1 0 0	1	1 0 1 0	0
-3	1	-6	1		1 1 0 1	1	1 0 1 0	1
-2	1	-5	0		1 1 1 0	1	1 0 1 1	0
-1	1	-5	1		1 1 1 1	1	1 0 1 1	1
0	1	4	0		0 0 0 0	1	0 1 0 0	0
1	1	4	1		0 0 0 1	1	0 1 0 0	1
2	1	5	0		0 0 1 0	1	0 1 0 1	0
3	1	5	1		0 0 1 1	1	0 1 0 1	1
4	1	6	0		0 1 0 0	1	0 1 1 0	0
5	1	6	1		0 1 0 1	1	0 1 1 0	1
6	1	7	0		0 1 1 0	1	0 1 1 1	0
7	1	7	1		0 1 1 1	1	0 1 1 1	1

(b)   (c)

note that, for example, -4 appears twice in the output column. In order to make it reversible, we embed it in a larger, reversible table. We choose Table 6.6b, where the numbers from Table 6.6a are repeated in boldface. We have added a one-bit input B, as well as a one-bit output Q. Finally, Table 6.6b is repeated, in two's complement notation, in Table 6.6c. The latter table (where $w = b + 1 = 5$) leads to the Boolean relationships

$$P_k = A_{k+1} \quad \text{for} \quad 0 \leq k \leq w - 3$$
$$P_{w-2} = A_{w-1} \oplus B$$
$$P_{w-1} = A_{w-1}$$
$$Q = A_0 \,,$$

which in turn lead to the implementation shown in Figure 6.2: one FEYNMAN gate and one exchange circuit. We conclude that dividing by 2 is cheap: both the gate cost and the logic depth are equal to 1.

For a 'scaling by 2' module, the reader should read Table 6.6 and Figure 6.2 once again, but this time from right to left.

6.5
Lifting

We now discuss multiplication by an arbitrary constant X by means of lifting coefficients. To do this, we design a building block

$$P = A$$
$$Q = XA + B \,. \tag{6.2}$$

LIFT gates (in contrast to SCALE gates) may profit from the fact a weight factor can be decomposed as the sum of simple parts; for example, $382.25 = 2^8 + 2^7 - 2 + 2^{-2}$ (see also Figure 6.3). Therefore, a LIFT can be built as a cascade of subsequent LIFTs, each with a perfect lifting coefficient. This is not the case with the SCALE gate, because two subsequent scaling factors multiply rather than add together; see the templates in Figure 6.4.

The real number X, just like the integer numbers A and B, is represented by b bits. If we assume that $2^x < X < 2^{x-1}$, then X is approximated with an accuracy of 2^{x-b+1}. For example, for a positive multiplier ($X_{b-1} = 0$), we have

$$X \approx X_{b-2}\, 2^{x-1} + X_{b-3}\, 2^{x-2} + \cdots + X_0\, 2^{x-b+1} \,.$$

For $b = 4$, we have for example $382.25 \approx 1 \times 2^8 + 1 \times 2^7 + 0 \times 2^6$. Thus, the most significant bit is the coefficient of 2^{x-1}, whereas the least significant bit is the coefficient of 2^{x-b+1}.

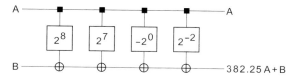

Figure 6.3 Decomposed lifting.

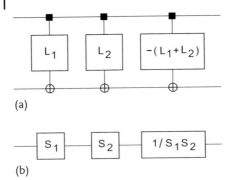

(a)

(b)

Figure 6.4 Two analog templates: (a) LIFT gates; (b) SCALE gates.

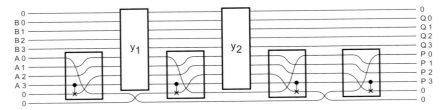

Figure 6.5 Performing a multiplication.

We implement the circuit by applying the decomposition

$$B + XA = \left(\dots \left(\left(B + X_{b-2} \left(2^{x-1} A \right) \right) + X_{b-3} \left(2^{x-2} A \right) \right) + \dots \right.$$
$$\left. + X_0 \left(2^{x-b+1} A \right) \right),$$

where all multipliers X_j take the values of either 0, 1 or -1; thus, $X_j \in \{0, 1, -1\}$. This automatically leads to a circuit like Figure 6.5, an example where $x = 0$. Actually, when we (i.e., humans) perform multiplication 'in our heads', we proceed in a very similar (but decimal) way, where all successive multipliers X_j are in $\{0, 1, 2, \dots, 9\}$. Sometimes we also use the multiplier -1. If, for example, we have to multiply 1768 by $X = 999$, we don't apply $999 = 9 \times 10^2 + 9 \times 10^1 + 9 \times 10^0$, but instead we note that $999 = 10^3 - 10^0$, leading to the fast computation $1768 \times 999 = 1\,768\,000 - 1768 = 1\,766\,232$.

In the figure, we see an equal number of division by 2 blocks, Y blocks, and multiplication by 2 blocks. A block Y_j is either:

- An adder (when the bit X_j equals 1), or
- A follower (when $X_j = 0$), or
- A subtractor (when the bit X_j equals -1).

The bad news is the large width of the circuit: $w = 3n - 1$. We need $n - 1$ inputs preset to 0. At the output, this yields $n - 1$ garbage bits. Fortunately, they all automatically equal 0, meaning that they can be *recycled*; that is, applied as a preset input for a subsequent circuit. We call such lines (which enter as constants and exit as constants) *ancilla lines*, in accordance with standard nomenclature in the quantum computing community [144, 145].

6.6
Exercises for Chapter 6

Exercise 6.1
What is the switch cost of the Sylow circuit described in Section 6.3?

7
Quantum Computing

There is a vast amount of literature on quantum computing. Excellent introductions can be found in [38, 39, 146–149]. Detailed discussions are provided by Nielsen and Chuang [150]. In contrast, (classical) reversible computing is a subject that has been paid much less attention, and even less has been published on the relationship between these two computing methods – usually all that is stated in this regard is that classical reversible computing is a subset of quantum computing. In the present chapter, we demonstrate the relationship between the two architectures, based on group theory [151].

7.1
Doubly Stochastic Matrices

A *doubly stochastic matrix* [152] is an $n \times n$ square matrix m such that

- All entries m_{jk} are real numbers satisfying $0 \le m_{jk} \le 1$,
- All row sums equal unity: $\sum_{k=1}^{n} m_{jk} = 1$, and
- All column sums equal unity: $\sum_{j=1}^{n} m_{jk} = 1$.

The last two conditions are often merged into a single statement: all line sums equal unity (see also Section 4.1). Doubly stochastic matrices constitute a generalization of permutation matrices: a permutation matrix is a doubly stochastic matrix where all m_{jk} are equal to either 0 or 1.

The term 'doubly stochastic' derives from the fact that the matrix entries look like probabilities, and each row and column looks like a probability distribution. Therefore, these matrices are strongly related to the classical scattering matrices (or S-matrices) of statistical physics. The matrix elements are indeed transition probabilities [153, 154]. If

$$
\begin{pmatrix} p_1 \\ p_2 \\ \dots \\ p_n \end{pmatrix} = \begin{pmatrix} m_{11} & m_{12} & \dots & m_{1n} \\ m_{21} & m_{22} & \dots & m_{2n} \\ \dots & & & \\ m_{n1} & m_{n2} & \dots & m_{nn} \end{pmatrix} \begin{pmatrix} a_1 \\ a_2 \\ \dots \\ a_n \end{pmatrix} ,
$$

Reversible Computing. Alexis De Vos
Copyright © 2010 WILEY-VCH Verlag GmbH & Co. KGaA, Weinheim
ISBN: 978-3-527-40992-1

then the doubly stochastic matrix conserves the total probability because

$$\sum_j p_j = \sum_j \sum_k m_{jk} a_k = \sum_k a_k \sum_j m_{jk} = \sum_k a_k .$$

The condition $\sum_j a_j = 1$ automatically implies $\sum_j p_j = 1$. Thus, if the a_j are interpreted as probabilities, then the p_j can also be interpreted as probabilities. However, in contrast to the particular case of permutation matrices (see Section 4.2), an arbitrary doubly stochastic matrix does not lead to $\sum_j \Phi(p_j) = \sum_j \Phi(a_j)$ for an arbitrary function Φ. Therefore, for example, entropy is not conserved.

In passing, we will note that in Appendix E we encounter a $q \times q$ 'flow matrix' F with all entries equal to a positive or zero integer, and all line sums equal to the same integer p. In fact, such matrices are sometimes called 'integer doubly stochastic matrices' [155]. The matrix $\frac{1}{p} F$ has all of its line sums equal to 1 and is thus a doubly stochastic matrix, albeit with the peculiarity that all entries are rational.

Doubly stochastic matrices do *not* form a group. It is true that the product of two doubly stochastic matrices is itself doubly stochastic. It is also true that the identity element (the unit matrix) is doubly stochastic. However, the inverse of a doubly stochastic matrix is usually not a doubly stochastic matrix. Consider an example for $n = 2$. Any 2×2 doubly stochastic matrix has the form

$$\begin{pmatrix} 1 - a & a \\ a & 1 - a \end{pmatrix} ,$$

where a is an arbitrary real number that satisfies $0 \leq a \leq 1$. Its inverse is

$$\begin{pmatrix} 1 - a & a \\ a & 1 - a \end{pmatrix}^{-1} = \begin{pmatrix} \frac{1-a}{1-2a} & \frac{-a}{1-2a} \\ \frac{-a}{1-2a} & \frac{1-a}{1-2a} \end{pmatrix} .$$

If $0 < a < 1$, we have either

- a in the interval $(0, \frac{1}{2})$, but then $\frac{1-a}{1-2a}$ is greater than 1 and $\frac{-a}{1-2a}$ is lower than 0;
  or
- a in the interval $(\frac{1}{2}, 1)$, but then $\frac{1-a}{1-2a}$ is lower than 0 and $\frac{-a}{1-2a}$ is greater than 1.

The fact that doubly stochastic matrices neither form a group nor conserve entropy illustrates that they are a poor description of nature. Indeed, despite the huge merits of statistical mechanics, the basic laws of nature are reversible. Thus, there is need for a more faithful model of nature. This is provided by quantum mechanics. Quantum mechanics is described not by doubly stochastic matrices, but by unitary matrices.

7.2
Unitary Matrices

Whereas classical reversible computing manipulates bits, quantum computers manipulate *qubits*. One bit can have two different values: either 0 or 1. However, we can also write

$$\text{either} \quad \begin{pmatrix} 1 \\ 0 \end{pmatrix} \quad \text{or} \quad \begin{pmatrix} 0 \\ 1 \end{pmatrix}. \tag{7.1}$$

This notation makes comparison with a qubit easier. Indeed, there are an infinite number of values that a qubit can take:

$$\begin{pmatrix} a_1 \\ a_2 \end{pmatrix}, \tag{7.2}$$

where both a_1 and a_2 are arbitrary complex numbers, although $a_1 \bar{a}_1 + a_2 \bar{a}_2 = 1$ must be obeyed. Here, $\bar{X}$ denotes the complex conjugate of the complex number X. It should not be confused with the notation for $\text{NOT}(X)$; that is, the inverse of the Boolean number X, as used in previous chapters.

Whereas a bit can have only two different values, a qubit can have ∞^3 different values, where ∞ represents the number of different real numbers (i.e., the cardinality of $\mathbb{R}$). Note that a_1 contributes two degrees of freedom, a_2 contributes two degrees of freedom, while the restriction $a_1 \bar{a}_1 + a_2 \bar{a}_2 = 1$ removes one degree of freedom. Also note that a bit is a special kind of qubit: both of the vectors in (7.1) take the form of (7.2), and both $1 \times \bar{1} + 0 \times \bar{0}$ and $0 \times \bar{0} + 1 \times \bar{1}$ equal 1 (because $\bar{1} = 1$ and $\bar{0} = 0$).

A set of w (qu)bits is represented by the vector

$$\begin{pmatrix} a_1 \\ a_2 \\ \dots \\ a_{2^w} \end{pmatrix}.$$

In the classical world, all a_j equal 0, except for one $a_k = 1$. Therefore, a set of w bits can have only 2^w different values. In the quantum world, all a_j are in $\mathbb{C}$, with the only restriction being $a_1 \bar{a}_1 + a_2 \bar{a}_2 + \cdots + a_{2^w} \bar{a}_{2^w} = 1$. Therefore, w qubits can have $\infty^{2^{w+1}-1}$ different values.

Whereas classical reversible computing is based on $2^w \times 2^w$ permutation matrices, quantum computing is based on $2^w \times 2^w$ unitary matrices. A matrix m is a unitary matrix iff the matrix product $m m^\dagger$ equals the unit matrix. Here $m^\dagger$ is the *conjugate transpose* of m, otherwise known as the adjoint matrix or Hermitian transpose (after the French mathematician Charles Hermite):

$$(m^\dagger)_{jk} = \bar{m}_{kj}.$$

For example, a 3×3 matrix m is unitary iff

$$\begin{pmatrix} m_{11} & m_{12} & m_{13} \\ m_{21} & m_{22} & m_{23} \\ m_{31} & m_{32} & m_{33} \end{pmatrix} \begin{pmatrix} \bar{m}_{11} & \bar{m}_{21} & \bar{m}_{31} \\ \bar{m}_{12} & \bar{m}_{22} & \bar{m}_{32} \\ \bar{m}_{13} & \bar{m}_{23} & \bar{m}_{33} \end{pmatrix} = \begin{pmatrix} 1 & 0 & 0 \\ 0 & 1 & 0 \\ 0 & 0 & 1 \end{pmatrix}.$$

The unitary $n \times n$ matrices form a Lie group that is called the unitary group and denoted $U(n)$. The reader is invited to verify that permutation matrices are a particular kind of unitary matrix. In fact, the finite group $\mathbf{S}_n$ of $n \times n$ permutation matrices forms a subgroup of the Lie group $U(n)$:

$$\mathbf{S}_n \subset U(n) \, .$$

Whereas a permutation matrix:

- Has a determinant equal to 1 or -1, and
- Has all of its line sums equal to 1,

a unitary matrix:

- Has determinant on the unit circle of the complex plane, and
- Does not necessarily have equal line sums (but if it does, then these identical line sums are on the unit circle).

In spite of these differences, similar (but not identical) synthesis methods can be applied to build a reversible classical circuit and a quantum circuit.

Figure 7.1 shows an example of a quantum circuit: a full adder [42, 43] realized from six elementary quantum gates: two controlled NOTs (i.e., FEYNMANs) and four so-called 'controlled square roots of NOT' (see Section 7.10 for more details regarding this gate). Of course, the circuits of Figures 3.42a and 4.11a are equally valid in a quantum computer. After all, permutation matrices are unitary. However, whereas the circuit in Figure 4.11a contains a three-(qu)bit gate, and the circuit in Figure 3.42a has a three-(qu)bit gate and a four-(qu)bit gate, the alternative circuit of Figure 7.1 is a cascade of exclusively two-qubit gates. This is an illustration of a general (and powerful) quantum circuit theorem [125, 156]:

Any quantum circuit can be decomposed into a cascade of

- Uncontrolled one-qubit gates, and
- One-qubit gates controlled by a single controlling qubit.

The former gates are a generalization of one-bit inverters; the latter are a generalization of two-bit FEYNMAN gates. Figure 7.2 gives another example of this amazing theorem: the three-qubit TOFFOLI gate may be replaced by an appropriate cascade of two-qubit quantum gates [156, 157]. In classical reversible computing, it is *not* possible to build an arbitrary reversible circuit exclusively from inverters and FEYNMAN gates; we need three-bit building blocks at least (see Section 3.6 and Appendix C). For example, the three-bit TOFFOLI gate cannot be decomposed into a cascade of classical two-bit gates.

Just as any w-bit classical reversible circuit is represented by a $2^w \times 2^w$ permutation matrix, any w-qubit quantum circuit is represented by a $2^w \times 2^w$ unitary matrix. When we fill in an $n \times n$ square matrix m with n^2 entries $m_{jk}(\in \mathbb{C})$, each entry gives us two degrees of freedom (one for the real part and one for the imaginary

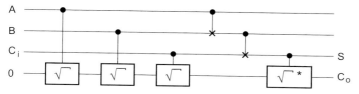

Figure 7.1 A quantum full adder.

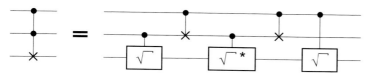

Figure 7.2 Quantum decomposition of a TOFFOLI gate.

Table 7.1 The number R of different classical reversible circuits and the number U of different quantum circuits as functions of the circuit width w.

w	R	U
1	2	∞^4
2	24	∞^{16}
3	40 320	∞^{64}
4	20 922 789 888 000	∞^{256}

part). Thus, there are $2n^2$ degrees of freedom. The unitarity condition ($mm^\dagger$ equals the unit matrix) leads to n^2 restrictions. This leaves us with only n^2 degrees of freedom. Therefore, there are ∞^{n^2} elements in the unitary group $U(n)$. As $n = 2^w$, this yields the group orders of Table 7.1, where ∞ stands for the cardinality of the reals. Whereas the number of different classical reversible circuits $R(w)$ grows very quickly with w (the number of bits), the number of different unitary circuits $U(w)$ grows very, very quickly with w, the number of qubits.

7.3
Entropy in the Quantum World

Whereas we have $\sum p_j = \sum a_j = 1$ for permutation matrices (Section 4.2), and thus the a_j as well as the p_j can be interpreted as probabilities, we have $\sum p_j \overline{p}_j = \sum a_j \overline{a}_j = 1$ for unitary matrices, such that the $a_j \overline{a}_j = |a_j|^2$ and the $p_j \overline{p}_j = |p_j|^2$ play the role of probabilities. The quantities a_j and p_j are complex numbers and play the role of amplitudes.

A set of w qubits can be in a state $\sum a_j \Psi_j$, where the Ψ_j are its 2^w eigenstates $00\ldots00$, $00\ldots01$, $00\ldots10$, $\ldots$, $11\ldots10$, and $11\ldots11$. The 2^w complex coefficients a_j are the amplitudes. In quantum computing they can take any value as long as

$\sum a_j \bar{a}_j = 1$. If all $a_j = 0$ except for $a_k = 1$, then the circuit input is in the eigenstate Ψ_k (corresponding to the classical input bit string corresponding to the binary number $k - 1$). In all other cases, the input is in a quantum-mechanical superposition (corresponding to no classical input).

Although $\sum a_j \bar{a}_j$ is conserved by a unitary transformation, $\sum \Phi(a_j \bar{a}_j)$ (where Φ denotes an arbitrary function) is not conserved. In particular, the quantity

$$\sum -p_j \bar{p}_j \log(p_j \bar{p}_j)$$

is not equal to

$$\sum -a_j \bar{a}_j \log(a_j \bar{a}_j) . \tag{7.3}$$

Does this mean that a unitary transformation changes entropy? No: the expression (7.3) is *not* the entropy associated with the quantum state $(a_1, a_2, \ldots, a_{2^w})$.

We must be careful not to confuse a 'quantum superposition' and a 'quantum mixture' [158, 159]. Although the state $(a_1, a_2, \ldots, a_{2^w})$ is a superposition of the 2^w states $000\ldots00, 000\ldots01, \ldots$, and $111\ldots11$, it is nevertheless a pure quantum state. Therefore, its entropy is zero [160]. Analogously, the output of the unitary circuit; that is, the state $(p_1, p_2, \ldots, p_{2^w})$, is a pure state and has zero entropy. Thus, the unitary transformation conserves entropy: $0 = 0$.

A mixed quantum state contains uncertainty: we have a probability π_1 that the system is in state $(^1a_1, {}^1a_2, \ldots, {}^1a_{2^w})$, a probability π_2 that the system is in state $(^2a_1, {}^2a_2, \ldots, {}^2a_{2^w})$, $\ldots$, and a probability π_k that the system is in state $(^ka_1, {}^ka_2, \ldots, {}^ka_{2^w})$. The entropy of such a mixture is relatively classical; it equals

$$\sum_{j=1}^{k} -\pi_j \log(\pi_j) ,$$

a quantity that is perfectly conserved during unitary transformation.

7.4
Entanglement

The phenomenon of mixing should not be confused with the typical quantum phenomenon of *entanglement*. Two bits may be entangled but can still be in a pure state (a_1, a_2, a_3, a_4). In fact, most pure states are entangled. States that are not entangled are termed 'separable'. A two-qubit state is separable iff it is possible to write the two-qubit vector $(a_1, a_2, a_3, a_4)^T$ as a so-called tensor product of two one-qubit vectors; that is, if the equation

$$\begin{pmatrix} a_1 \\ a_2 \\ a_3 \\ a_4 \end{pmatrix} = \begin{pmatrix} b_1 \begin{pmatrix} c_1 \\ c_2 \end{pmatrix} \\ b_2 \begin{pmatrix} c_1 \\ c_2 \end{pmatrix} \end{pmatrix}$$

has a solution b_1, b_2, c_1, c_2 (that satisfies both $b_1\bar{b}_1 + b_2\bar{b}_2 = 1$ and $c_1\bar{c}_1 + c_2\bar{c}_2 = 1$). Here, the tensor product is defined as:

$$\begin{pmatrix} b_1 \\ b_2 \end{pmatrix} \otimes \begin{pmatrix} c_1 \\ c_2 \end{pmatrix} = \begin{pmatrix} b_1 \begin{pmatrix} c_1 \\ c_2 \end{pmatrix} \\ b_2 \begin{pmatrix} c_1 \\ c_2 \end{pmatrix} \end{pmatrix} = \begin{pmatrix} b_1 c_1 \\ b_1 c_2 \\ b_2 c_1 \\ b_2 c_2 \end{pmatrix}.$$

Of course, classical states are separable. For a two-bit circuit, only four classical input patterns are possible:

$$\begin{pmatrix} 1 \\ 0 \\ 0 \\ 0 \end{pmatrix}, \quad \begin{pmatrix} 0 \\ 1 \\ 0 \\ 0 \end{pmatrix}, \quad \begin{pmatrix} 0 \\ 0 \\ 1 \\ 0 \end{pmatrix}, \quad \text{and} \quad \begin{pmatrix} 0 \\ 0 \\ 0 \\ 1 \end{pmatrix},$$

each of which can be written as a tensor product of two one-bit vectors; for example,

$$\begin{pmatrix} 1 \\ 0 \\ 0 \\ 0 \end{pmatrix} = \begin{pmatrix} 1 \begin{pmatrix} 1 \\ 0 \end{pmatrix} \\ 0 \begin{pmatrix} 1 \\ 0 \end{pmatrix} \end{pmatrix} = \begin{pmatrix} 1 \\ 0 \end{pmatrix} \otimes \begin{pmatrix} 1 \\ 0 \end{pmatrix}.$$

7.5
Control Circuits and Control Gates

Assume a circuit of width w; that is, a circuit with w inputs $A_1, A_2, \ldots, A_w$, and w outputs $P_1, P_2, \ldots, P_w$ (either classical or quantum) – see Figure 3.4. The outputs are calculated from the inputs by means of a linear transformation described by a $2^w \times 2^w$ matrix.

We will consider a special class of circuits where $w = u + v$. We have $P_1 = A_1, P_2 = A_2, \ldots, P_u = A_u$; these (qu)bits will be called the controlling (qu)bits. The remaining v outputs $P_{u+1}, P_{u+2}, \ldots, P_{u+v}$ (called the controlled (qu)bits) are calculated from the corresponding inputs $A_{u+1}, A_{u+2}, \ldots, A_{u+v}$ by means of a transformation described by a $2^v \times 2^v$ matrix. However, that matrix is chosen according to the value of the vector $(A_1, A_2, \ldots, A_u)$. Because the latter vector has 2^u eigenstates, there are 2^u different $2^v \times 2^v$ matrices involved. The overall transformation is described by a $2^w \times 2^w$ matrix built from 2^u blocks, each of size $2^v \times 2^v$, situated on the diagonal. All matrices and submatrices involved are either permutation matrices (classical reversible computing) or unitary matrices (quantum computing).

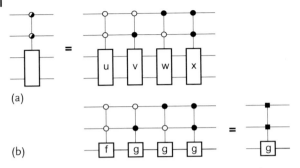

Figure 7.3 Icons for (a) a control circuit and (b) a control gate.

For example, for the case $u = 2$ and $v = 1$ (and thus $w = 3$), the unitary $2^w \times 2^w = 8 \times 8$ matrix looks like

$$
C = \begin{pmatrix}
U_{11} & U_{12} & 0 & 0 & 0 & 0 & 0 & 0 \\
U_{21} & U_{22} & 0 & 0 & 0 & 0 & 0 & 0 \\
0 & 0 & V_{11} & V_{12} & 0 & 0 & 0 & 0 \\
0 & 0 & V_{21} & V_{22} & 0 & 0 & 0 & 0 \\
0 & 0 & 0 & 0 & W_{11} & W_{12} & 0 & 0 \\
0 & 0 & 0 & 0 & W_{21} & W_{22} & 0 & 0 \\
0 & 0 & 0 & 0 & 0 & 0 & X_{11} & X_{12} \\
0 & 0 & 0 & 0 & 0 & 0 & X_{21} & X_{22}
\end{pmatrix}
$$

with $2^u = 4$ submatrices, each of size $2^v \times 2^v = 2 \times 2$. Thus, if $(A_1, A_2) = (0,0)$, matrix U is applied to A_3; if $(A_1, A_2) = (0,1)$, matrix V is applied to A_3; etc. Figure 7.3a shows an example for $u = v = 2$ (and thus $w = 4$). Here we follow the graphical notation by Möttönen et al. [161, 162].

In some cases, only two different submatrices F and G are present, and one of them (i.e., F) is the $2^v \times 2^v$ unit matrix. Figure 7.3b shows an example:

$$
C = \begin{pmatrix}
1 & 0 & 0 & 0 & 0 & 0 & 0 & 0 \\
0 & 1 & 0 & 0 & 0 & 0 & 0 & 0 \\
0 & 0 & G_{11} & G_{12} & 0 & 0 & 0 & 0 \\
0 & 0 & G_{21} & G_{22} & 0 & 0 & 0 & 0 \\
0 & 0 & 0 & 0 & G_{11} & G_{12} & 0 & 0 \\
0 & 0 & 0 & 0 & G_{21} & G_{22} & 0 & 0 \\
0 & 0 & 0 & 0 & 0 & 0 & G_{11} & G_{12} \\
0 & 0 & 0 & 0 & 0 & 0 & G_{21} & G_{22}
\end{pmatrix}. \tag{7.4}
$$

In this case, the gate g of width v is applied to the controlled (qu)bits iff a particular Boolean function $\varphi(A_1, A_2, \ldots, A_u)$ of the controlling (qu)bits equals 1. This special control circuit is called a *control gate* [52]. The function φ is called the *control function*. In the example of Figure 7.3b and (7.4), we have $\varphi(A_1, A_2) = A_1 \text{ OR } A_2$. We have already encountered some control gates with $u = v = 1$ (and thus $w = 2$)

in Figures 7.1 and 7.2:

$$
\begin{pmatrix} 1 & 0 & 0 & 0 \\ 0 & 1 & 0 & 0 \\ 0 & 0 & \frac{1+i}{2} & \frac{1-i}{2} \\ 0 & 0 & \frac{1-i}{2} & \frac{1+i}{2} \end{pmatrix},
\begin{pmatrix} 1 & 0 & 0 & 0 \\ 0 & 1 & 0 & 0 \\ 0 & 0 & 0 & 1 \\ 0 & 0 & 1 & 0 \end{pmatrix}, \text{ and }
\begin{pmatrix} 1 & 0 & 0 & 0 \\ 0 & 1 & 0 & 0 \\ 0 & 0 & \frac{1-i}{2} & \frac{1+i}{2} \\ 0 & 0 & \frac{1+i}{2} & \frac{1-i}{2} \end{pmatrix}.
$$

Control gates are particularly important in classical reversible computing, as there exist only two different 2×2 permutation matrices, one representing the follower, the other representing the inverter. Thus, a classical reversible control circuit with $v = 1$ always simplifies to a control gate. In quantum computing, even when v is as small as 1, as many as ∞^4 different 2×2 unitary matrices are allowed; the probability that two of these 2×2 blocks in a control circuit matrix will be equal is infinitesimally small.

7.6
Synthesis

Section 3.16 describes the synthesis of an arbitrary classical reversible circuit of width w. The resulting cascade is shown in Figure 3.27e, with an example presented in Figure 3.28a: a cascade of $2w - 1$ control gates. The question then arises as to whether, in a similar way, an arbitrary quantum circuit of width w can be synthesized as a cascade of $2w - 1$ control circuits. In that case, each box in Figure 3.27e would represent a 2×2 unitary matrix (instead of a 2×2 NOT matrix).

In order to answer this question, let us recall why the decomposition works for binary circuits. For the first control gate in the string, there are $2^{2^{w-1}}$ possibilities (because there are that many possible control functions). For the second gate in the string, there are also $2^{2^{w-1}}$ possibilities, etc. Because there are $2w - 1$ control gates, this yields a total of

$$
N = 2^{2^{w-1}} \times 2^{2^{w-1}} \times \ldots \times 2^{2^{w-1}} = \left[2^{2^{w-1}}\right]^{2w-1} = 2^{\left(w - \frac{1}{2}\right)2^w}
$$

possible choices. Now we have that

$$
2^{\left(w - \frac{1}{2}\right)2^w} > 2^{\left[w - \frac{1}{\log(2)}\right]2^w}
$$

for the simple reason that 2 is larger than $\log(2)$. Taking (3.2) into account, we may conclude that

$$
N > (2^w)! = R(w) , \tag{7.5}
$$

where R is the number of reversible circuits (Table 7.1). Thus, the number of potential choices is high enough to synthesize all possible reversible circuits of width w. The reader should note that inequality (7.5) is a necessary condition but not a sufficient condition. The sufficient condition is provided by Birkhoff's theorem (Appendix E).

We now check whether a similar decomposition could also work for quantum computer synthesis. For each control circuit in the string, there are $(\infty^4)^{2^{w-1}} = \infty^{2^{w+1}}$ possibilities. With $2w - 1$ of these blocks, we obtain a total of

$$N = \infty^{2^{w+1}} \times \infty^{2^{w+1}} \times \ldots \times \infty^{2^{w+1}} = \left[\infty^{2^{w+1}}\right]^{2w-1} = \infty^{2(2w-1)2^w}$$

possible combinations. This is far from being sufficient:

$$N < \infty^{(2^w)^2} = U(w) ,$$

where U is the number of quantum circuits (Table 7.1).

Increasing the number of control circuits in the cascade from merely $2w - 1$ to as many as $2^w - 1$ could remedy the problem. In that case,

$$N = \infty^{2^{w+1}} \times \infty^{2^{w+1}} \times \ldots \times \infty^{2^{w+1}} = \left[\infty^{2^{w+1}}\right]^{2^w-1} = \infty^{2^{2w+1}-2^{w+1}} .$$

This new N satisfies

$$N > \infty^{(2^w)^2} = U(w) .$$

However, again, the inequality sign is a necessary but not sufficient condition for the synthesis method to work properly. Is there a theorem about unitary matrices (similar to the Birkhoff theorem for permutation matrices) that provides us with the guarantee that such a decomposition always exists? The answer is yes: the cosine-sine decomposition of unitary matrices comes to our rescue.

7.7
Decomposition

In order to find the synthesis method of a quantum circuit, we decompose its unitary $U(2^w)$-matrix according to Figure 7.4b. For example, for $w = 3$:

$$
\begin{pmatrix}
U_{11} & U_{12} & U_{13} & U_{14} & U_{15} & U_{16} & U_{17} & U_{18} \\
U_{21} & U_{22} & U_{23} & U_{24} & U_{25} & U_{26} & U_{27} & U_{28} \\
U_{31} & U_{32} & U_{33} & U_{34} & U_{35} & U_{36} & U_{37} & U_{38} \\
U_{41} & U_{42} & U_{43} & U_{44} & U_{45} & U_{46} & U_{47} & U_{48} \\
U_{51} & U_{52} & U_{53} & U_{54} & U_{55} & U_{56} & U_{57} & U_{58} \\
U_{61} & U_{62} & U_{63} & U_{64} & U_{65} & U_{66} & U_{67} & U_{68} \\
U_{71} & U_{72} & U_{73} & U_{74} & U_{75} & U_{76} & U_{77} & U_{78} \\
U_{81} & U_{82} & U_{83} & U_{84} & U_{85} & U_{86} & U_{87} & U_{88}
\end{pmatrix}
=
$$

$$
\begin{pmatrix}
L_{11} & L_{12} & L_{13} & L_{14} & 0 & 0 & 0 & 0 \\
L_{21} & L_{22} & L_{23} & L_{24} & 0 & 0 & 0 & 0 \\
L_{31} & L_{32} & L_{33} & L_{34} & 0 & 0 & 0 & 0 \\
L_{41} & L_{42} & L_{43} & L_{44} & 0 & 0 & 0 & 0 \\
0 & 0 & 0 & 0 & L_{55} & L_{56} & L_{57} & L_{58} \\
0 & 0 & 0 & 0 & L_{65} & L_{66} & L_{67} & L_{68} \\
0 & 0 & 0 & 0 & L_{75} & L_{76} & L_{77} & L_{78} \\
0 & 0 & 0 & 0 & L_{85} & L_{86} & L_{87} & L_{88}
\end{pmatrix}
$$

$$\times \begin{pmatrix} M_{11} & 0 & 0 & 0 & M_{15} & 0 & 0 & 0 \\ 0 & M_{22} & 0 & 0 & 0 & M_{26} & 0 & 0 \\ 0 & 0 & M_{33} & 0 & 0 & 0 & M_{37} & 0 \\ 0 & 0 & 0 & M_{44} & 0 & 0 & 0 & M_{48} \\ M_{51} & 0 & 0 & 0 & M_{55} & 0 & 0 & 0 \\ 0 & M_{62} & 0 & 0 & 0 & M_{66} & 0 & 0 \\ 0 & 0 & M_{73} & 0 & 0 & 0 & M_{77} & 0 \\ 0 & 0 & 0 & M_{84} & 0 & 0 & 0 & M_{88} \end{pmatrix}$$

$$\times \begin{pmatrix} R_{11} & R_{12} & R_{13} & R_{14} & 0 & 0 & 0 & 0 \\ R_{21} & R_{22} & R_{23} & R_{24} & 0 & 0 & 0 & 0 \\ R_{31} & R_{32} & R_{33} & R_{34} & 0 & 0 & 0 & 0 \\ R_{41} & R_{42} & R_{43} & R_{44} & 0 & 0 & 0 & 0 \\ 0 & 0 & 0 & 0 & R_{55} & R_{56} & R_{57} & R_{58} \\ 0 & 0 & 0 & 0 & R_{65} & R_{66} & R_{67} & R_{68} \\ 0 & 0 & 0 & 0 & R_{75} & R_{76} & R_{77} & R_{78} \\ 0 & 0 & 0 & 0 & R_{85} & R_{86} & R_{87} & R_{88} \end{pmatrix} . \tag{7.6}$$

On the right-hand side of the equation, each of the submatrices (that is, the two L-submatrices of size $2^{w-1} \times 2^{w-1}$, the 2^{w-1} M-submatrices, each of size 2×2, and the two R-submatrices of size $2^{w-1} \times 2^{w-1}$) is unitary. In other words, an arbitrary member of $U(2^w)$ is decomposed into two members of $U(2^{w-1})^2$ and one member of $U(2)^{2^{w-1}}$.

The above decomposition is always possible, and is even far from unique. Whereas the matrix on the left-hand side of (7.6) is an arbitrary member of $U(8)$, each of the three matrices on the right-hand side is member of a subgroup of $U(8)$; two are members of the same subgroup isomorphic to $U(4)^2$, and the middle one is a member of a subgroup isomorphic to $U(2)^4$. Figure 7.4b shows the resulting three-part circuit. Note that the middle matrix M represents a control circuit with the first qubit controlled. Applying such a decomposition $w - 1$ times (Figure 7.4), we can demonstrate that this eventually leads to a synthesis consisting of a cascade of exactly $L(w) = 2^w - 1$ control circuits (Figure 7.4d). Figure 7.4 has to be confronted with Figure 7.5, which basically repeats Figure 3.27. We arrive at the surprising result that the efficient classical synthesis method of Section 3.16 is not applicable to quantum computing, while the inefficient classical synthesis method of Section 3.15 comes to our rescue.

The above quantum synthesis is rather efficient, as one can prove that no synthesis is possible with fewer than 2^{w-1} control circuits. Indeed, any synthesis method [53, 68] leads to a cascades of depth L satisfying

$$L \geq \left\lceil \frac{n}{b} \right\rceil . \tag{7.7}$$

See Section 5.3. With the dimensions $n = (2^w)^2 = 2^{2w}$ and $b = 4 \times 2^{w-1}$, this yields

$$L \geq \left\lceil \frac{2^{2w}}{2^{w+1}} \right\rceil = 2^{w-1} .$$

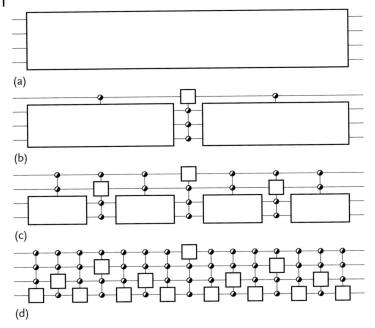

(a)

(b)

(c)

(d)

Figure 7.4 Step-by-step decomposition of a quantum circuit of width $w = 4$: (a) original logic circuit, (b) and (c) intermediate steps, (d) final decomposition.

We conclude that the synthesis (which has a depth of $2^w - 1$) is overkill by a factor of approximately 2. It is thus no surprise that we are allowed to choose the matrices M from a (small) subgroup of $U(2)^{2^w/2}$. We can choose a controlled ROTATOR as control circuit. Each of the 2×2 blocks within the M-matrix then takes the form

$$
\begin{pmatrix} M_{j,j} & M_{j,j+m} \\ M_{j+m,j} & M_{j+m,j+m} \end{pmatrix} = C(\theta_j) = \begin{pmatrix} \cos(\theta_j) & \sin(\theta_j) \\ -\sin(\theta_j) & \cos(\theta_j) \end{pmatrix} , \tag{7.8}
$$

where m is a shorthand notation for 2^{w-1}. Such matrices form a well-known one-dimensional subgroup of the four-dimensional group $U(2)$. As a result, decomposition (7.6) is the well-known *cosine–sine decomposition* [163]. The cosine–sine decomposition has been applied for quantum circuit synthesis [161, 164, 165]. The attentive reader will also recognize the Givens transformation of Section 5.2 in (7.8).

7.8
Discussion

The above sections have been summarized in a table that compares classical reversible computing with quantum computing; see Table 7.2. An additional distinction between classical reversible logic and quantum logic is the fact that many clas-

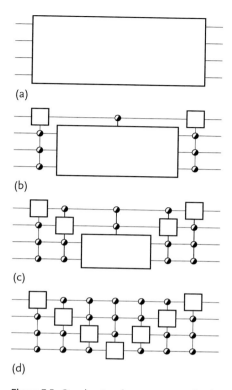

(a)

(b)

(c)

(d)

Figure 7.5 Step-by-step decomposition of a classical reversible logic circuit of width $w = 4$: (a) original logic circuit, (b) and (c) intermediate steps, (d) final decomposition.

Table 7.2 Classical reversible computing versus quantum computing.

Classical reversible computing	Quantum computing
Numbers $\in \{0, 1\} = \mathbb{B}$	Numbers $\in \mathbb{C}$
Finite groups	Infinite groups
w bits $\rightarrow$ symmetric group S_{2^w}	w qubits $\rightarrow$ unitary group $U(2^w)$
Birkhoff's decomposition theorem	The cosine-sine decomposition theorem
$\rightarrow 2w - 1$ blocks from subgroups $S_2^{2^{w-1}}$	$\rightarrow 2^w - 1$ blocks from subgroups $U(2)^{2^{w-1}}$

sical fabrication technologies are available (see Section 4.5), whereas quantum logic technology is unfortunately still missing.

The differences between classical and quantum computing may be explained as follows. If n is an even integer, then:

- For *any* factorization $n = p \times q$, an arbitrary member a of the symmetric group S_n can be decomposed as the product $b_1 c b_2$, where both b_1 and b_2 are mem-

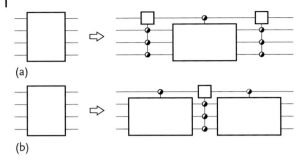

(a)

(b)

Figure 7.6 Decomposition of a circuit into three parts: (a) a member of $\mathbf{S}_{16}$ into two members of $\mathbf{S}_2^8$ and one member of $\mathbf{S}_8^2$, and (b) a member of $U(16)$ into two members of $U(8)^2$ and one member of $U(2)^8$.

bers of the same Young subgroup $\mathbf{S}_p^q$, and c is a member of the dual Young subgroup $\mathbf{S}_q^p$. We make use of this freedom of choice by choosing the most efficient factorization; that is, $n = p \times q = 2 \times \frac{n}{2}$.

- An arbitrary member a of the unitary group $U(n)$ can *only* be decomposed as the product $b_1 c b_2$ (where both b_1 and b_2 are members of a same subgroup $U(p)^q$, and c is a member of the dual subgroup $U(q)^p$) for the factorization $n = p \times q = \frac{n}{2} \times 2$.

This leads to two different decompositions of an arbitrary circuit into three simpler circuits; see Figure 7.6.

7.9
Bottom-Up and Top-Down

Reversible logic circuits, acting on w bits, form a group isomorphic to the symmetric group $\mathbf{S}_n$ of degree n and order $n!$, where n is a shorthand notation for 2^w. Quantum circuits, acting on w qubits, form a group isomorphic to the unitary group $U(n)$. Whereas $\mathbf{S}_n$ is finite, $U(n)$ is an infinite group; that is, a Lie group (with a nondenumerable order; in other words, ∞^{n^2}) with dimension n^2.

Although $\mathbf{S}_n$ is a subgroup of $U(n)$, it is a giant step from $\mathbf{S}_n$ to $U(n)$. Therefore, the question of whether there are groups X that are simultaneously a subgroup of $U(n)$ and a supergroup of $\mathbf{S}_n$ arises; i.e.,

$$\mathbf{S}_n \subset \mathrm{X} \subset U(n) \,. \tag{7.9}$$

Such group may be either:

- A finite group with order $> n!$, or
- A discrete group with a countable infinity $\aleph_0$ as order, or
- A Lie group with dimension $< n^2$.

Each of these possibilities deserves our attention. The larger the group X, the more difficult it is to implement it in hardware, but the more powerful the resulting computer. Assuming that the quantum computer based on the whole group $U(n)$ is overkill for a lot of interesting problems, we must look for a satisfactory compromise between simplicity (found close to $\mathbf{S}_n$) and computational power (found close to $U(n)$). Such a computer can be referred to as 'reversible plus' or 'quantum light'.

We can tackle this problem in two ways: either bottom-up or top-down. If we consider it bottom-up, we start from the symmetric group and add some extra group generators. If we take the top-down approach, we start from the unitary group and impose some restrictions.

7.10
Bottom-Up Approach

In the bottom-up approach, we take the finite group $\mathbf{S}_n$ (with $n = 2^w$) and one or more extra generators $\{g_1, g_2, \ldots\}$. These generators, together with the elements of $\mathbf{S}_n$, generate a new group $\mathbf{G}$, which is called the closure of $\mathbf{S}_n$ and $\{g_1, g_2, \ldots\}$. It is automatically a supergroup of $\mathbf{S}_n$. Below we provide two examples: we add either one (g_1) or two $(g_1$ and $g_2)$ generators and consider how much the order G of $\mathbf{G}$ exceeds order$(\mathbf{S}_n) = n!$.

7.10.1
One-(Qu)bit Calculations

A single qubit is in a state $a_1 \Psi_1 + a_2 \Psi_2$, where Ψ_1 and Ψ_2 are its two eigenstates and where $a_1 \bar{a}_1 + a_2 \bar{a}_2 = 1$. If $a_1 = 1$ and $a_2 = 0$, then the input is in the eigenstate Ψ_1 (corresponding to a classical input bit equal to 0). If $a_1 = 0$ and $a_2 = 1$, then the input is in the eigenstate Ψ_2 (corresponding to a classical input bit equal to 1). In all other cases, the input is in a quantum-mechanical superposition of 0 and 1.

We introduce the 2×2 unitary matrix

$$\sigma = \frac{1}{2} \begin{pmatrix} 1 + i & 1 - i \\ 1 - i & 1 + i \end{pmatrix}.$$

This satisfies $\sigma^2 = \nu$, where ν is the inverter or NOT gate:

$$\nu = \begin{pmatrix} 0 & 1 \\ 1 & 0 \end{pmatrix}.$$

Thus, σ is the notorious square root of NOT [166–169]; see Figure 7.7. It plays the role of the extra generator g_1, generating a matrix group of order 4 with elements

$$\varphi = \begin{pmatrix} 1 & 0 \\ 0 & 1 \end{pmatrix}, \quad \sigma = \begin{pmatrix} \omega & \bar{\omega} \\ \bar{\omega} & \omega \end{pmatrix}, \quad \nu = \begin{pmatrix} 0 & 1 \\ 1 & 0 \end{pmatrix}, \quad \text{and} \quad \bar{\sigma} = \begin{pmatrix} \bar{\omega} & \omega \\ \omega & \bar{\omega} \end{pmatrix},$$

Figure 7.7 Two square roots of NOT give one NOT.

where φ stands for the follower (the identity gate), ω is the complex number given by

$$\omega = \frac{1}{2} + i\frac{1}{2}$$

and $\overline{\omega}$ is its complex conjugate:

$$\overline{\omega} = \frac{1}{2} - i\frac{1}{2}.$$

The matrix $\overline{\sigma}$ obeys $\overline{\sigma}^2 = \nu$ and is thus the 'other' square root of NOT. Together, the four matrices form a group with respect to the operation of ordinary matrix multiplication that is isomorphic to the cyclic group of order 4; that is, to $\mathbf{Z}_4$ (Section 2.8). We have $\sigma^1 = \sigma$, $\sigma^2 = \nu$, $\sigma^3 = \overline{\sigma}$, and $\sigma^4 = \varphi$. Therefore, we have found a group X that satisfies (7.9). Indeed,

$$\mathbf{S}_2 \subset \mathbf{Z}_4 \subset U(2)$$

with orders

$$2 < 4 < \infty^4.$$

Any one of the four matrices transforms the input state $a_1 \Psi_1 + a_2 \Psi_2$ into an output state $p_1 \Psi_1 + p_2 \Psi_2$:

$$\begin{pmatrix} p_1 \\ p_2 \end{pmatrix} = \begin{pmatrix} U_{11} & U_{12} \\ U_{21} & U_{22} \end{pmatrix} \begin{pmatrix} a_1 \\ a_2 \end{pmatrix}.$$

Because the matrix U is unitary, we automatically have $p_1\overline{p}_1 + p_2\overline{p}_2 = 1$. If the input is in an eigenstate (either $(a_1, a_2) = (1, 0)$ or $(a_1, a_2) = (0, 1)$), then the output is in a quantum superposition. For example,

$$\begin{pmatrix} p_1 \\ p_2 \end{pmatrix} = \begin{pmatrix} \omega & \overline{\omega} \\ \overline{\omega} & \omega \end{pmatrix} \begin{pmatrix} 1 \\ 0 \end{pmatrix} = \begin{pmatrix} \omega \\ \overline{\omega} \end{pmatrix}. \tag{7.10}$$

However, as the output of one circuit may be the input of a subsequent circuit, we have to consider the possibility that (a_1, a_2) is in such a superposition. In fact, we must consider all possible values of (a_1, a_2) and (p_1, p_2), which may be transformed into one another. These values are found to be either a column or a row of one of the four matrices. Thus, in total, four and only four states need to be considered: $(1, 0)$, $(0, 1)$, $(\omega, \overline{\omega})$, and $(\overline{\omega}, \omega)$. Such an object that may be in four different states is intermediate between a bit (which can be in only two different states) and a qubit (which may be in as many as ∞^3 different states).

Table 7.3 displays how each of the four matrices acts on the column matrix $(a_1, a_2)^T$. The tables constitute the truth tables of the four reversible transformations. Each of these tables expresses a permutation of the four objects $(1, 0)$, $(0, 1)$, $(\omega, \overline{\omega})$, and $(\overline{\omega}, \omega)$. Thus, together they form a permutation group that is a subgroup of the symmetric group $\mathbf{S}_4$, and we have $\mathbf{Z}_4 \subset \mathbf{S}_4$.

Table 7.3 The four members of the group with $w = 1$: (a) follower, (b) square root of NOT, (c) NOT, and (d) square root of NOT.

$a_1 a_2$	$p_1 p_2$		$a_1 a_2$	$p_1 p_2$		$a_1 a_2$	$p_1 p_2$		$a_1 a_2$	$p_1 p_2$
1 0	1 0		1 0	$\omega\ \overline{\omega}$		1 0	0 1		1 0	$\overline{\omega}\ \omega$
0 1	0 1		0 1	$\overline{\omega}\ \omega$		0 1	1 0		0 1	$\omega\ \overline{\omega}$
$\omega\ \overline{\omega}$	$\omega\ \overline{\omega}$		$\omega\ \overline{\omega}$	0 1		$\omega\ \overline{\omega}$	$\overline{\omega}\ \omega$		$\omega\ \overline{\omega}$	1 0
$\overline{\omega}\ \omega$	$\overline{\omega}\ \omega$		$\overline{\omega}\ \omega$	1 0		$\overline{\omega}\ \omega$	$\omega\ \overline{\omega}$		$\overline{\omega}\ \omega$	0 1
(a)			(b)			(c)			(d)	

7.10.2
Two-(Qu)bit Calculations

Two qubits exist in a superposition $a_1 \Psi_1 + a_2 \Psi_2 + a_3 \Psi_3 + a_4 \Psi_4$ with $\sum a_k \bar{a}_k = 1$. The eigenstates Ψ_1, Ψ_2, Ψ_3, and Ψ_4 correspond to the classical bit values (A_1, A_2) of $(0, 0)$, $(0, 1)$, $(1, 0)$, and $(1, 1)$, respectively, whereas the other (i.e., superposition) states have no classical equivalent.

The subset of two-qubit circuits that we investigate [170] must comprise the circuit that calculates the square root of NOT of qubit #2. This circuit is represented by the matrix

$$\sigma_2 = \begin{pmatrix} \omega & \overline{\omega} & 0 & 0 \\ \overline{\omega} & \omega & 0 & 0 \\ 0 & 0 & \omega & \overline{\omega} \\ 0 & 0 & \overline{\omega} & \omega \end{pmatrix}. \tag{7.11}$$

The required set of two-qubit circuits should also contain all classical reversible two-bit circuits. These are generated by two generators:

$$a = \begin{pmatrix} 0 & 1 & 0 & 0 \\ 1 & 0 & 0 & 0 \\ 0 & 0 & 1 & 0 \\ 0 & 0 & 0 & 1 \end{pmatrix} \quad \text{and} \quad b = \begin{pmatrix} 0 & 1 & 0 & 0 \\ 0 & 0 & 1 & 0 \\ 0 & 0 & 0 & 1 \\ 1 & 0 & 0 & 0 \end{pmatrix}, \tag{7.12}$$

which generate a group isomorphic to $\mathbf{S}_4$ (according to Section 2.4).

Straightforward calculations (performed with the aid of the algebra software package GAP of Section 2.4) reveal that the group generated by the three generators $\{\sigma_2, a, b\}$ has an order equal to 192. Note that the number 192 is an common order. Indeed, according to Conway et al. [171], there are 6013 different groups with orders smaller than 200. Among these, no less than 1543 (i.e., about 26% of them) have orders that are precisely equal to 192. The group constitutes the closure of the group (isomorphic to $\mathbf{Z}_4$) generated by the first generator and the

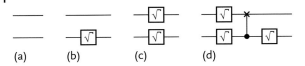

Figure 7.8 Four representative circuits: (a) follower, (b) square root of NOT, (c) double square root of NOT, and (d) a more complicated circuit.

group (isomorphic to S_4) generated by the two other generators. Let us call this closure Υ. All 192 different 4×4 unitary matrices of Υ have entries from the set $\{0, 1, \overline{\omega}, \omega, -\frac{1}{2}, \frac{1}{2}, -\frac{i}{2}, \frac{i}{2}\}$. We have:

- 24 matrices with entries from $\{0, 1\}$,
- 72 matrices with entries from $\{0, \overline{\omega}, \omega\}$,
- 72 matrices with entries from $\{\frac{1}{2}, -\frac{i}{2}, \frac{i}{2}\}$, and
- 24 matrices with entries from $\{-\frac{1}{2}, \frac{1}{2}\}$.

The four classes of matrices are the four double cosets in which the group Υ is partitioned by its S_4 subgroup. Representatives of these double cosets are, for example,

$$
\begin{pmatrix} 1 & 0 & 0 & 0 \\ 0 & 1 & 0 & 0 \\ 0 & 0 & 1 & 0 \\ 0 & 0 & 0 & 1 \end{pmatrix}, \quad
\begin{pmatrix} \omega & \overline{\omega} & 0 & 0 \\ \overline{\omega} & \omega & 0 & 0 \\ 0 & 0 & \omega & \overline{\omega} \\ 0 & 0 & \overline{\omega} & \omega \end{pmatrix},
$$

$$
\frac{1}{2}\begin{pmatrix} i & 1 & 1 & -i \\ 1 & i & -i & 1 \\ 1 & -i & i & 1 \\ -i & 1 & 1 & i \end{pmatrix}, \quad \text{and} \quad
\frac{1}{2}\begin{pmatrix} -1 & 1 & 1 & 1 \\ 1 & 1 & 1 & -1 \\ 1 & 1 & -1 & 1 \\ 1 & -1 & 1 & 1 \end{pmatrix}.
$$

Figure 7.8 shows the four representative circuits. The group Υ satisfies (7.9):

$$S_4 \subset \Upsilon \subset U(4)$$

with orders

$$24 < 192 < \infty^{16} .$$

It is worth noting that a matrix like

$$
c = \begin{pmatrix} 1 & 0 & 0 & 0 \\ 0 & 1 & 0 & 0 \\ 0 & 0 & \omega & \overline{\omega} \\ 0 & 0 & \overline{\omega} & \omega \end{pmatrix}, \tag{7.13}
$$

which may be interpreted as a 'controlled square root of NOT' (or as a 'square root of controlled NOT'), is *not* a member of the group Υ. In contrast, the 'controlled NOT;'

that is,

$$\begin{pmatrix} 1 & 0 & 0 & 0 \\ 0 & 1 & 0 & 0 \\ 0 & 0 & 0 & 1 \\ 0 & 0 & 1 & 0 \end{pmatrix},$$

is a member. The circuit that calculates the square root of NOT of qubit #1:

$$\sigma_1 = \begin{pmatrix} \omega & 0 & \overline{\omega} & 0 \\ 0 & \omega & 0 & \overline{\omega} \\ \overline{\omega} & 0 & \omega & 0 \\ 0 & \overline{\omega} & 0 & \omega \end{pmatrix}$$

is also automatically a member.

If we add the matrix (7.13) as a fourth generator, the group Υ is enlarged into a new group Ω (i.e., the closure of Υ and c), which surprisingly has infinite order. We can prove this [170] by investigating one particular element of Ω:

$$y = abc = \begin{pmatrix} 0 & 0 & \omega & \overline{\omega} \\ 0 & 1 & 0 & 0 \\ 0 & 0 & \overline{\omega} & \omega \\ 1 & 0 & 0 & 0 \end{pmatrix}.$$

The theory of the Z-transform tells us that the matrix sequence $\{y, y^2, y^3, \ldots\}$ is not periodic; see Appendix G. In other words, all matrices $y, y^2, y^3, \ldots$ are different. Therefore, the order of the group element y is infinite, which means that the order of the group Ω itself is also infinite; see Section 2.8. One can additionally prove [170] that order(Ω) is denumerable. Thus, we can finally conclude that order(Ω) equals $\aleph_0$:

$$S_4 \subset \Omega \subset U(4) \quad \text{with}$$
$$24 < \aleph_0 < \infty^{16} .$$

7.10.3
Three- and Multi-(Qu)bit Calculations

Using two 8×8 matrices, in an analogous manner to (7.12), we generate the group of all classical reversible circuits of width 3. Adding the single quantum matrix

$$\sigma_3 = \begin{pmatrix} \omega & \overline{\omega} & 0 & 0 & 0 & 0 & 0 & 0 \\ \overline{\omega} & \omega & 0 & 0 & 0 & 0 & 0 & 0 \\ 0 & 0 & \omega & \overline{\omega} & 0 & 0 & 0 & 0 \\ 0 & 0 & \overline{\omega} & \omega & 0 & 0 & 0 & 0 \\ 0 & 0 & 0 & 0 & \omega & \overline{\omega} & 0 & 0 \\ 0 & 0 & 0 & 0 & \overline{\omega} & \omega & 0 & 0 \\ 0 & 0 & 0 & 0 & 0 & 0 & \omega & \overline{\omega} \\ 0 & 0 & 0 & 0 & 0 & 0 & \overline{\omega} & \omega \end{pmatrix}$$

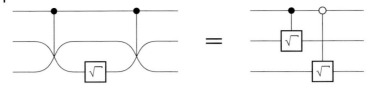

Figure 7.9 Fabricating two controlled $\sqrt{\text{NOT}}$ gates from a single $\sqrt{\text{NOT}}$ gate.

Table 7.4 The number of different reversible circuits, as a function of the circuit width w, if we do not allow square roots of NOT, if we allow square roots of NOT, or if we allow controlled square roots of NOT.

w	Classical	Classical plus $\sqrt{\text{NOT}}$	Classical plus controlled $\sqrt{\text{NOT}}$
1	2	4	not applicable
2	24	192	$\aleph_0$
3	40 320	$\aleph_0$	$\aleph_0$
4	20 922 789 888 000	$\aleph_0$	$\aleph_0$

(the square root of NOT of qubit #3) as an extra generator allows us to convert the finite group into a group of infinite order. Thus, in the case $w = 3$, we do not even need to introduce a controlled square root of NOT in order to obtain an infinite group. Figure 7.9 explains why. From the group of classical circuits, we take two FREDKIN gates and combine them with a single square root of NOT, thus realizing Figure 7.9a. The reader will easily verify that this circuit is equivalent to Figure 7.9b. Subsequent application of Section 7.10.2 to the first and second qubits proves the infiniteness of the generated group.

As circuits of width 3 form a subgroup of circuits of width n (where n is any integer larger than 3), the same conclusion holds for any width larger than 3. Table 7.4 summarizes the results.

7.11
Top-Down Approach

In the top-down approach, we start from U(n) and impose restrictions. All unitary matrices have a determinant on the unit circle. A subgroup is found, for example, by imposing that the determinant equals 1. The resulting group is called the special unitary group, a Lie group of dimension $n^2 - 1$, denoted as SU(n):

$$\text{SU}(n) \subset \text{U}(n) \, ,$$

which is quite similar to (5.4) and (5.9).

For another example, we draw inspiration from permutation matrices by noting that all of them have all of their line sums equal to 1. Indeed, all unitary matrices with line sums equal to 1 form a Lie group of dimension $(n - 1)^2$. Special unitary matrices with line sums equal to 1 form a Lie group of dimension $(n - 1)^2 - 1$.

The three subgroups above have dimensions of the form $n^2 - an - b$, a number barely smaller than n^2, the dimension of $U(n)$ itself. This is not completely a surprise, as many well-known subgroups [15, 123] of $U(n)$ have dimensions of the form $An^2 + Bn + C$.

The hunt for appropriate Lie groups, subgroups of $U(n)$, with dimensions that are substantially smaller than n^2 (e.g., of the order $n \log(n)$ or n or $\log(n)$) that nevertheless allow powerful quantum computing is ongoing. We will give an example for $n = 2$ (i.e., a one-qubit example). The one-dimensional matrix group

$$\frac{1}{2} \begin{pmatrix} 1 + \exp(i\theta) & 1 - \exp(i\theta) \\ 1 - \exp(i\theta) & 1 + \exp(i\theta) \end{pmatrix}$$

is both a subgroup of the four-dimensional unitary group $U(2)$ and a supergroup of the symmetric group $\mathbf{S}_2$. Once again, we find a group X that satisfies (7.9)

$$\mathbf{S}_2 \subset X \subset U(2) \ ,$$

this time with orders

$$2 < \infty^1 < \infty^4 \ .$$

The two elements of $\mathbf{S}_2$ (the one-bit follower and the one-bit inverter) are represented by the above matrix for $\theta = 0$ and $\theta = \pi$, respectively. The two square roots of NOT correspond to $\theta = \pi/2$ and $\theta = 3\pi/2$. The matrix with $\theta = \pi/k$ represents the kth root of NOT.

7.12
An Application: the Quantum Fourier Transform

Quantum computers are particularly powerful. Their computing power is well illustrated by considering the quantum Fourier transformation [40, 146, 172, 173]. Using only w input qubits and w output qubits, it performs a Fourier transformation on 2^w complex data. In contrast, the classical Fourier transformation of width w transforms only w complex numbers (Section 5.8). The classical Fourier transformer realizes the linear transformation

$$\begin{pmatrix} P_1 \\ P_2 \\ \dots \\ P_w \end{pmatrix} = \begin{pmatrix} \exp(0) & \exp(0) & \dots & \exp(0) \\ \exp(0) & \exp(-2\pi i/w) & \dots & \exp(-2(w-1)\pi i/w) \\ \dots & & & \\ \exp(0) & \exp(-2(w-1)\pi i/w) & \dots & \exp(-2(w-1)(w-1)\pi i/w) \end{pmatrix} \begin{pmatrix} A_1 \\ A_2 \\ \dots \\ A_w \end{pmatrix}.$$

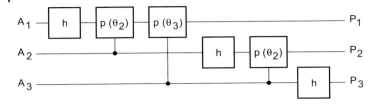

Figure 7.10 A three-qubit Fourier transform circuit.

The quantum Fourier transformer realizes the matrix transformation

$$
\begin{pmatrix} p_1 \\ p_2 \\ \cdots \\ p_{2^w} \end{pmatrix} = \frac{1}{\sqrt{2^w}}
$$

$$
\times \begin{pmatrix} \exp(0) & \exp(0) & \cdots & \exp(0) \\ \exp(0) & \exp(-2\pi i/2^w) & \cdots & \exp(-2(2^w-1)\pi i/2^w) \\ \cdots & & & \\ \exp(0) & \exp(-2(2^w-1)\pi i/2^w) & \cdots & \exp(-2(2^w-1)(2^w-1)\pi i/2^w) \end{pmatrix} \begin{pmatrix} a_1 \\ a_2 \\ \cdots \\ a_{2^w} \end{pmatrix}.
$$

$$(7.14)$$

The transformation matrix is thus of size $2^w \times 2^w$ (instead of merely $w \times w$). More-over, a normalizing factor $1/\sqrt{2^w}$ is applied in order to make the matrix unitary. We refer to it as the *unitary Fourier transform*. Its determinant is a power of i.

Just as in Section 5.8, it is unwise to apply general-purpose decomposition meth-ods (e.g., the cosine-sine decomposition of Section 7.7) here. Indeed, there is a par-ticularly efficient decomposition based on two simple matrices h and p. The former matrix, the 2×2 unitary matrix

$$
h = \frac{1}{\sqrt{2}} \begin{pmatrix} 1 & 1 \\ 1 & -1 \end{pmatrix},
$$

represents a one-qubit gate, and is known as the HADAMARD gate [40, 168] (named after the French mathematician Jacques Hadamard). It equals the two-point unitary Fourier transform matrix (i.e., matrix (7.14) with $w = 1$). The latter matrix, the 4×4 unitary matrix

$$
p(\theta) = \begin{pmatrix} 1 & 0 & 0 & 0 \\ 0 & 1 & 0 & 0 \\ 0 & 0 & 1 & 0 \\ 0 & 0 & 0 & \exp(i\theta) \end{pmatrix},
$$

$$(7.15)$$

represents a two-qubit circuit; that is, the control gate known as the 'controlled PHASE' [168].

Figure 7.10 shows an example [173] of a Fourier circuit for $w = 3$. Here, the phase angles θ_k take the value $2\pi/k$. For an arbitrary w, the quantum circuit con-sists of w HADAMARD gates and $(w-1)w/2$ PHASE gates. The total gate count thus

Figure 7.11 Icons for two different controlled Z gates.

amounts to $w(w + 1)/2$. Note that this number is significantly smaller than the logic depth $2^w - 1$ obtained in Section 7.7 for an arbitrary quantum circuit. The reason for this is clear: the Fourier matrix is far from an arbitrary unitary matrix: it shows many remarkable symmetries. It is thus no surprise that we need far fewer than $2^w - 1$ gates to implement it. Next, we compare the cost $w(w + 1)/2$ with the number of (complex) LIFT gates needed in the classical 2^w-point Fourier transform circuit (Section 5.8), i.e.,

$$9 \times \frac{1}{2} 2^w \log_2(2^w) = \frac{9}{2} w 2^w .$$

We note that the gate

$$p(\theta_2) = p(\pi) = \begin{pmatrix} 1 & 0 & 0 & 0 \\ 0 & 1 & 0 & 0 \\ 0 & 0 & 1 & 0 \\ 0 & 0 & 0 & -1 \end{pmatrix} \tag{7.16}$$

is called the 'controlled Z gate'. Its symbol is presented in Figure 7.11a [47, 165, 174, 175], and it should not be confused with the icon of the SWAP gate (see Figure 3.6b). In an analogous manner to the use of open circles in Figure 3.12c, we can generalize the notation of Figure 7.11a. For example, Figure 7.11b represents the unitary transformation

$$\begin{pmatrix} 1 & 0 & 0 & 0 \\ 0 & -1 & 0 & 0 \\ 0 & 0 & 1 & 0 \\ 0 & 0 & 0 & 1 \end{pmatrix} . \tag{7.17}$$

We close this chapter by noting that the gates (7.15)–(7.17) are special cases of the unitary transformation

$$\begin{pmatrix} \exp(i\alpha) & 0 & 0 & 0 \\ 0 & \exp(i\beta) & 0 & 0 \\ 0 & 0 & \exp(i\gamma) & 0 \\ 0 & 0 & 0 & \exp(i\delta) \end{pmatrix} .$$

Figure 7.12 gives two different interpretations of this circuit: a one-qubit gate acting on qubit #2, controlled by qubit #1; and a one-qubit gate acting on qubit #1,

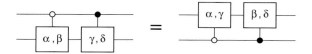

Figure 7.12 Two different representations of the same quantum circuit.

controlled by qubit #2, respectively. The former view is based on the decomposition

$$
\begin{pmatrix}
\exp(i\alpha) & 0 & 0 & 0 \\
0 & \exp(i\beta) & 0 & 0 \\
0 & 0 & 1 & 0 \\
0 & 0 & 0 & 1
\end{pmatrix}
\begin{pmatrix}
1 & 0 & 0 & 0 \\
0 & 1 & 0 & 0 \\
0 & 0 & \exp(i\gamma) & 0 \\
0 & 0 & 0 & \exp(i\delta)
\end{pmatrix},
$$

while the latter view is based on the decomposition

$$
\begin{pmatrix}
\exp(i\alpha) & 0 & 0 & 0 \\
0 & 1 & 0 & 0 \\
0 & 0 & \exp(i\gamma) & 0 \\
0 & 0 & 0 & 1
\end{pmatrix}
\begin{pmatrix}
1 & 0 & 0 & 0 \\
0 & \exp(i\beta) & 0 & 0 \\
0 & 0 & 1 & 0 \\
0 & 0 & 0 & \exp(i\delta)
\end{pmatrix}.
$$

This illustrates yet another property that distinguishes quantum circuits from classical reversible circuits: the ambiguity of controlling and controlled qubits [148]. In quantum circuits it is not always clear who is controlling whom (after all, in the quantum world, little is certain!).

7.13
Nonlinear Computations

In Chapter 5 (on classical analog computers), we first investigated the case where the outputs $P_1, P_2, \ldots, P_w$ were linear functions of the inputs $A_1, A_2, \ldots, A_w$ (Sections 5.1 to 5.8). We then considered the case where those w outputs were nonlinear functions of the w inputs (Section 5.9).

In the present chapter, we have studied quantum computers where the outputs $p_1, p_2, \ldots, p_{2^w}$ are linear functions of the inputs $a_1, a_2, \ldots, a_{2^w}$. The question then arises of whether we must now study quantum computers where the 2^w outputs are nonlinear functions of the 2^w inputs. The answer is no. The laws of quantum physics are linear. Our quantum-mechanical universe obeys linear (and unitary) transformations, and so any event can be described by a matrix multiplication. However, the matrices involved are of size $2^w \times 2^w$, not size $w \times w$. We do not have to investigate a nonlinear case; we do not even have to investigate the affine linear case.

7.14
Exercises for Chapter 7

Exercise 7.1
Check the equality in Figure 7.2 by straightforward matrix multiplication.

Exercise 7.2
In order to demonstrate that most two-qubit states (a_1, a_2, a_3, a_4) are entangled, prove that nonentanglement requires that $a_1 a_4 - a_3 a_2 = 0$. Is this condition also sufficient?

Exercise 7.3
In general, a 2×2 matrix with complex entries – that is, an arbitrary element of $\mathbf{GL}(2, \mathbb{C})$ – has eight degrees of freedom:

$$\begin{pmatrix} a \exp(i\alpha) & b \exp(i\beta) \\ c \exp(i\gamma) & d \exp(i\delta) \end{pmatrix},$$

where each of the eight parameters a, α, b, β, c, γ, d, and δ is real. Show that introducing the unitarity condition reduces the number of degrees of freedom to four, and that a possible representation is

$$\begin{pmatrix} \cos(\theta) \exp(i\alpha) & \sin(\theta) \exp(i\beta) \\ -\sin(\theta) \exp(i\gamma) & \cos(\theta) \exp(-i\alpha + i\beta + i\gamma) \end{pmatrix}. \tag{7.18}$$

What is the determinant of this unitary matrix? For what values of θ, α, β, and γ is this matrix is a permutation matrix?

Exercise 7.4
Apply the cosine-sine decomposition to (7.18).

Exercise 7.5
Prove that the 2×2 NOT matrix has four and only four square roots. Check that they are all unitary.

Exercise 7.6
Prove that the 2×2 identity matrix has an infinite number of square roots.

Exercise 7.7
Check that result (7.10) – in other words, $\begin{pmatrix} p_1 \\ p_2 \end{pmatrix} = \begin{pmatrix} \omega \\ \omega \end{pmatrix}$ – fulfils $p_1 \overline{p}_1 + p_2 \overline{p}_2 = 1$.

Exercise 7.8
What is the 4×4 matrix that represents the square root of the SWAP gate?

Exercise 7.9

Consider the group $\mathbf{S}_2$, which is represented by the two matrices $\varphi = \begin{pmatrix} 1 & 0 \\ 0 & 1 \end{pmatrix}$ and $\nu = \begin{pmatrix} 0 & 1 \\ 1 & 0 \end{pmatrix}$. Add two extra generators: the Pauli matrices $y = \begin{pmatrix} 0 & -i \\ i & 0 \end{pmatrix}$ and $z = \begin{pmatrix} 1 & 0 \\ 0 & -1 \end{pmatrix}$, named after the Austrian physicist Wolfgang Pauli, in order to generate the so-called Pauli group. What is the order of this group?

8
Reversible Programming Languages

In the previous chapters, we discussed computer circuits; in other words, computer hardware. Any survey of computer science would not, however, be complete without also treating the subject of computer software, such as programming languages. Programming languages that can be run both forwards and backwards were actually first developed quite some time ago [176]; one of them is known as Janus [177]. Below, we follow ideas developed by Yokoyama *et al.* [1, 134, 178, 179].

Let us assume that x_1, x_2, x_3, and x_4 are the names of four registers. Then, for a reversible computation like (5.3), the software code uses the following assignment:

$$x\_4 \; := \; x\_4 \; + \; f(x\_1, \; x\_2, \; x\_3) \, , \tag{8.1}$$

where f stands for an arbitrary function. Note that, according to tradition, we do not explicitly write down the assignments

```
x_1:= x_1 ;
x_2:= x_2 ;
x_3:= x_3 .
```

An expression like (8.1) is called either a *reversible assignment* [180] or a *reversible update* [1, 134]. The inverse assignment of (8.1) is of course

$$x\_4 \; := \; x\_4 \; - \; f(x\_1, \; x\_2, \; x\_3) \, . \tag{8.2}$$

Besides the operations + and −, Yokoyama *et al.* [1, 178] also consider the operator ^, which stands for "bitwise XOR" operation. This operation is its own inverse.

As an example, we can translate Figure 5.3 into computer code:

```
A_1:= A_1 + 4.412 * A_2 ;
A_2:= A_2 + 80.633 * A_3 ;
A_3:= A_3 + 0.057 * A_2 ;
A_2:= A_2 - 14.404 * A_3 ;
A_2:= A_2 + A_1 ;
A_1:= A_1 - 0.955 * A_2 + 0.014 * A_3 ;
A_1:= 61.368 * A_1 .
```

Reversible Computing. Alexis De Vos
Copyright © 2010 WILEY-VCH Verlag GmbH & Co. KGaA, Weinheim
ISBN: 978-3-527-40992-1

Such translations are quite straightforward. However, a computer language should contain more than mere assignments. In order to achieve a structured computer language, we need some extra structures: control structures like conditionals and loops.

8.1
The if-then-else Structure

The conventional conditional (or `if-then-else`) statement consists of two parts: a test, and one or two sequences of assignments; see Figure 8.1a. The reversible jump structure, however, consists of three parts: a test, one or two sequences of assignments, and an assertion; see Figure 8.1b. The corresponding computer code looks like:

$$\text{if } e_1 \text{ then } s_1 \text{ else } s_2 \text{ fi } e_2 \,, \tag{8.3}$$

where e_1 is the expression to be tested, s_1 and s_2 are the assignment sequences (one of which must be executed), and e_2 is the expression to be asserted.

As an example, we consider the following computation that needs to be programmed. We must compute two unknown variables P and Q from two known (real) variables A and B. If $A < 0$, then we must apply the linear transforma-

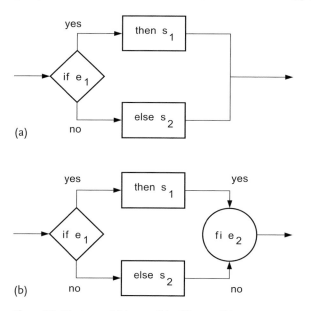

Figure 8.1 The jump: (a) irreversible; (b) reversible.

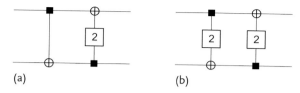

(a)   (b)

Figure 8.2 Two different lifting schemes.

tion

$$P = 3A + 2B$$
$$Q = A + B .$$
(8.4)

Otherwise, we must apply another linear transformation:

$$P = 5A + 2B$$
$$Q = 2A + B .$$
(8.5)

Figure 8.2 shows how both transformations can be hardwired by a lifting scheme. For the software implementation, we assume two registers: x and y, that initially contain the values A and B, respectively, but end up containing the results P and Q, respectively, when the computation is finished. The reversible program is as follows:

```
if (x < 0)       then { y := y + x ;
                        x := x + 2*y }
                 else { y := y + 2*x ;
                        x := x + 2*y }
fi (x-2*y < 0),
```

where the appropriate expression e_2 was found by solving either the set (8.4) or the set (8.5) for A:

$$A = P - 2Q .$$

In the inverse of (8.3), the assertion becomes the test and the test becomes the assertion, and all assignments are inverted:

```
if e₂ then s₁⁻¹ else s₂⁻¹ fi e₁
```

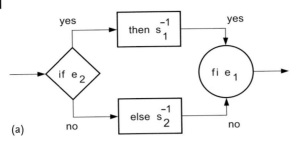

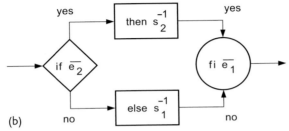

Figure 8.3 Two different ways of reversing Figure 8.1b.

(see Figure 8.3a). For our example, this yields:

```
if (x-2*y < 0)      then { x := x - 2*y ;
                            y := y - x }
                    else { x := x - 2*y ;
                            y := y - 2*x }
fi (x < 0).
```

Note that in s_1^{-1}, for example, the order of the assignments is reversed, but $+$ signs must become $-$ signs too. In order to get an inverse code that looks even more like the forward code read from bottom to top, we can apply

$$\text{if NOT}(e_2) \text{ then } s_2^{-1} \text{ else } s_1^{-1} \text{ fi NOT}(e_1)$$

(see Figure 8.3b). For our example, this yields:

```
if (x-2*y >= 0)     then { x := x - 2*y ;
                            y := y - 2*x }
                    else { x := x - 2*y ;
                            y := y - x }
fi (x >= 0).
```

The reader should, however, note that there is a pitfall: the fact that both s_1 and s_2 are reversible statements is *not* sufficient to conclude that the statement (8.3) is invertible. As an illustration, let us consider the computation

$$P = A + 3 \quad \text{if} \quad A < 3 \tag{8.6}$$

$$= 2A - 2 \quad \text{if} \quad A \geq 3 . \tag{8.7}$$

Both s_1 (x := x + 3) and s_2 (x := 2*x - 2) are invertible (the inverses s_1^{-1} and s_2^{-1} are x := x - 3 and x := (1/2)*x + 1, respectively). Nevertheless, (8.6), (8.7) is not invertible, as any value of P in the interval $4 \leq P < 6$ cannot be traced back to an unambiguous origin A. For example, $P = 5$ may equally well result from $A = 2$ as from $A = 7/2$; see Figure 8.4a. A garbigino (see Section 5.9) can come to our rescue here.

In contrast to (8.6) and (8.7), the computation

$$P = A + 3 \quad \text{if} \quad A < 5 \tag{8.8}$$

$$= 2A - 2 \quad \text{if} \quad A \geq 5 \tag{8.9}$$

is perfectly reversible (Figure 8.4b). The computer code for this looks like

```
if (x < 5)    then { x :=    x + 3 }
              else { x := 2*x - 2 }
fi (x < 8).
```

Of course, the computer that reads the program cannot look at figures in order to decide whether the program is reversible or not. So how does it see a fundamental difference between (8.6) and (8.7) and (8.8) and (8.9)? Solving the equation in (8.8) for A and substituting the result into the inequality in (8.8) yields $P < 8$; solving the equation in (8.9) for A and substituting the result into the inequality in (8.9) yields the dual result $P \geq 8$. In contrast, solving the equation in (8.6) for A and substituting the result into the inequality of (8.6) yields $P < 8$; solving the equation

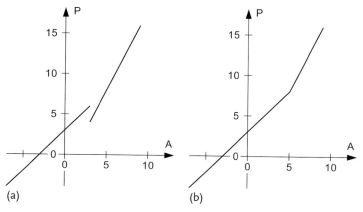

(a)   (b)

Figure 8.4 Two piecewise affine linear functions $P(A)$: (a) an irreversible one; (b) a reversible one.

in (8.7) for A and substituting the result into the inequality of (8.7) yields the result $P \geq 4$. Problems arise from the fact that the two conditions $P < 8$ and $P \geq 4$ overlap. Proving the presence or absence of such a conflict, however, only works when the statements are simple. Finding and checking assertions in the general case is a difficult task, if it is possible at all.

The story above is reminiscent of reversible hardware; see the twin circuit in Figure 3.22 of Section 3.14. Assume a reversible logic circuit of the form

$$\text{if } f_1 \text{ then } g_1 \text{ else } g_2 \, ,$$

where f_1 is an arbitrary Boolean function of n binary variables, and both g_1 and g_2 are reversible Boolean transformations; see, for example, Table 8.1 with $n = 3$.

The hardware implementation is straightforward provided that we allow an extra wire with a zero preset and garbage output; see Figure 8.5, where the logic width is thus $w = n + 1$. Because the circuit contains exclusively reversible building blocks, it is reversible, and so there is an inverse circuit such as its mirror image. However, an inverse circuit of the form

$$\text{if } f_2 \text{ then } g_1^{-1} \text{ else } g_2^{-2}$$

only exists provided f_1, g_1, and g_2 are such that the $f_1 = 1$ output rows P, Q, R of the g_1 table do not overlap with the $f_1 = 0$ output rows P, Q, R of the g_2 table; that is, if the 2^n words in boldface in Table 8.1 are different.

In that case, the circuit of Figure 8.5 can be supplemented by a second control gate; see Figure 8.6. The extra gate does not affect the output values P, Q, and R. It does however change the $n + 1$ th output bit into 0; that is, into its original input value. We have termed such a garbage bit that has a value that is always its preset input value an 'ancilla bit' (Section 6.5).

Table 8.1 One Boolean function f_1 and two reversible circuits g_1 and g_2, all with $n = 3$ variables.

ABC	f_1		ABC	PQR		ABC	PQR
0 0 0	1		0 0 0	**0 0 0**		0 0 0	1 0 0
0 0 1	1		0 0 1	**0 1 0**		0 0 1	1 1 1
0 1 0	0		0 1 0	1 0 1		0 1 0	**1 1 0**
0 1 1	1		0 1 1	**1 1 1**		0 1 1	0 0 1
1 0 0	1		1 0 0	**1 0 0**		1 0 0	0 0 0
1 0 1	0		1 0 1	1 1 0		1 0 1	**1 0 1**
1 1 0	1		1 1 0	**0 0 1**		1 1 0	0 1 0
1 1 1	0		1 1 1	0 1 1		1 1 1	**0 1 1**

| (a) | | (b) | | (c) |

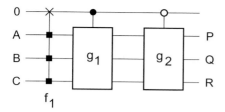

Figure 8.5 A controlled twin circuit of width 4: if $f_1(A, B, C) = 1$ then apply g_1, else apply g_2.

The reader could argue that any reversible circuit of width $w = n + 1$ can be decomposed as in Figure 8.6. That was exactly the point made in Section 3.16 (Figure 3.23b). However, here we have an extra property: whatever the values of $A, B, \ldots$, an input of zero for the uppermost wire leads to a zero at its output (and an input of 1 leads to an output of 1).

8.2
The do-until Structure

The conventional loop (or do-until) structure consists of two parts: a test, and a sequence of assignments; see Figure 8.7a. The reversible loop structure, however, consists of three parts: an assertion, one or two sequences of assignments, and a test; see Figure 8.7b. The corresponding computer code looks like

$$\text{from } e_1 \text{ do } s_1 \text{ loop } s_2 \text{ until } e_2 ,$$

where e_1 is the assertion, s_1 and s_2 are the assignment sequences, and e_2 is the expression to be tested.

As an example, we will calculate the n th Fibonacci number F_n (named after the Italian mathematician Leonardo Fibonacci Pisano), by applying the linear transformation

$$P = B$$
$$Q = A + B$$

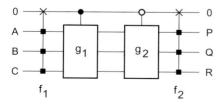

Figure 8.6 A symmetric controlled twin circuit of width 4: (a) if $f_1(A, B, C) = 1$ then apply g_1, else apply g_2; (b) if $f_2(P, Q, R) = 1$ then apply g_1^{-1}, else apply g_2^{-1}.

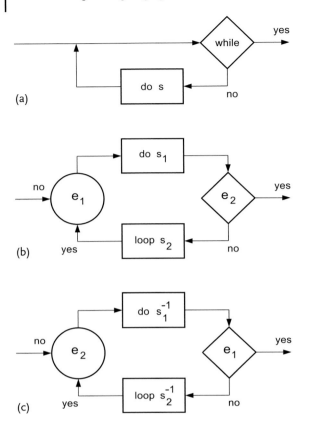

Figure 8.7 Loops: (a) irreversible, (b) reversible, (c) reversed.

$n - 1$ times. The forward reversible computer code looks like

```
from (j = 2) do    { y := y + x ;
                     x := x - y ;
                     x := -x        }
            loop { j := j + 1      }
  until (j = n),
```

where we have applied a lift factor of 1, a lift factor of -1, and a scale factor of -1. If the registers x, y, and j initially contain the numbers a, b, and 1, then, after running the program, they contain $a F_{n-2} + b F_{n-1}$, $a F_{n-1} + b F_n$, and n. If, in particular, we preset a to be equal to the Fibonacci number $F_0 = 0$, and b to be equal to the Fibonacci number $F_1 = 1$, then we ultimately obtain F_{n-1} in register x (the garbage) and F_n in register y (the result).

A possible inverse code (Figure 8.7c) is:

```
from (j = n) do    { x := -x ;
                     x := x + y ;
                     y := y - x      }
              loop { j := j - 1     }
until (j = 2).
```

8.3
Exercises for Chapter 8

Exercise 8.1

A pocket calculator has to compute your tax T to be paid on your yearly income I, where both I and T can be considered to be positive real numbers. The (fair) tax system is as follows: the part of I up to 1000 euros is charged at 10%, the part between 1000 and 10 000 euros is charged at 30%, and any part above 10 000 euros is charged at 50%. Write a reversible program that computes $T(I)$. Check that the program is able to calculate your income from the tax you pay.

Appendix A
The Number of Linear Reversible Circuits

There are 2^w different linear functions $P(A_1, A_2, \ldots, A_w)$ of w Boolean variables. Therefore, the number L of different linear reversible circuits of width w can be determined as follows:

- For the first linear function, $P_1(A_1, A_2, \ldots, A_w)$, all linear functions are eligible with one exception: the constant function 0. Therefore, we count:

$$2^w - 1 .$$

- For the second linear function, $P_2(A_1, A_2, \ldots, A_w)$, all linear functions are eligible except the functions 0 and P_1. Therefore, we count:

$$2^w - 2 = 2(2^{w-1} - 1) .$$

- For the third linear function, $P_3(A_1, A_2, \ldots, A_w)$, all linear functions are eligible except the functions 0, P_1, P_2, and $P_1 \oplus P_2$. Therefore, we count:

$$2^w - 4 = 2^2 \, (2^{w-2} - 1) .$$

- $\ldots$
- For the jth linear function, $P_j(A_1, A_2, \ldots, A_w)$, we count

$$2^w - \left[1 + \binom{j-1}{1} + \binom{j-1}{2} + \cdots + \binom{j-1}{j-1}\right] = 2^w - (1+1)^{j-1}$$
$$= 2^{j-1}(2^{w-j+1} - 1)$$

eligible functions.

Thus, the total number of allowed combinations is:

$$L = (2^w - 1) \cdot 2(2^{w-1} - 1) \cdot 2^2(2^{w-2} - 1) \cdot \ldots \cdot 2^{w-1}(2^1 - 1)$$
$$= 2^{0+1+2+\cdots+(w-1)}(2 - 1)(2^2 - 1)(2^3 - 1) \ldots (2^w - 1)$$
$$= 2^{(w-1)w/2} \prod_{j=1}^{w} (2^j - 1)$$
$$= 2^{(w-1)w/2} w!_2 .$$

Reversible Computing. Alexis De Vos
Copyright © 2010 WILEY-VCH Verlag GmbH & Co. KGaA, Weinheim
ISBN: 978-3-527-40992-1

Appendix B
Bounds for the q-Factorial

For $w > 1$, the q-factorial of w, in other words

$$w!_q = 1(1 + q)(1 + q + q^2)\ldots(1 + q + \cdots + q^{w-1}) \,,$$

may be written as follows:

$$w!_q = \frac{q^2 - 1}{q - 1} \frac{q^3 - 1}{q - 1} \cdots \frac{q^w - 1}{q - 1} \,.$$

This leads to

$$w!_q = \frac{1}{(q - 1)^{w-1}} \prod_{k=2}^{w} q^k \prod_{k=2}^{w} \left(1 - \frac{1}{q^k}\right) \,.$$

We first calculate the middle factor of the right-hand side:

$$\prod_{k=2}^{w} q^k = q^{w^2/2 + w/2 - 1} \,.$$

We then investigate the logarithm of the last factor (denoted X):

$$\log(X) = \log\left(\prod_{k=2}^{w} \left(1 - \frac{1}{q^k}\right)\right) = \sum_{k=2}^{w} \log\left(1 - \frac{1}{q^k}\right) \,.$$

For any x satisfying $0 < x \le a < 1$, we have

$$\frac{\log(1 - a)}{a} x \le \log(1 - x) < 0 \,.$$

Choosing a equal to $\frac{1}{q^2}$ and x equal to $\frac{1}{q^2}, \frac{1}{q^3}, \ldots$, etc. successively, we obtain

$$-q^2 \log\left(\frac{q^2}{q^2 - 1}\right) \frac{q^{w-1} - 1}{q^w(q - 1)} < \log(X) < 0$$

and therefore

$$-\frac{q}{q - 1} \log\left(\frac{q^2}{q^2 - 1}\right) < \log(X) < 0 \,.$$

Reversible Computing. Alexis De Vos
Copyright © 2010 WILEY-VCH Verlag GmbH & Co. KGaA, Weinheim
ISBN: 978-3-527-40992-1

For the bifactorial ($q = 2$), this yields

$$-2\log\left(\frac{4}{3}\right) < \log(X) < 0$$

and thus

$$\frac{9}{16} < X < 1 \,.$$

We finally obtain

$$\frac{9}{16} 2^{w^2/2 + w/2 - 1} < w!_2 \leq 2^{w^2/2 + w/2 - 1} \,,$$

where an equality sign is introduced in order to incorporate the case $w = 1$.
   As a result, the order $2^{(w-1)w/2} w!_2$ of $\mathbf{GL}(w, 2)$ satisfies

$$\frac{9}{32} 2^{w^2} < 2^{(w-1)w/2} w!_2 \leq \frac{1}{2} 2^{w^2} \,.$$

The total number of $w \times w$ matrices with all w^2 entries equal to either 0 or 1 is 2^{w^2}. Thus, the fraction of them with nonzero determinants (i.e., with determinants equal to 1) is between 27% and 50%. Using numerical computation, we can verify that this fraction is about 29% for large values of w.

Appendix C
A Theorem about Universal Reversible Gates

C.1
Universality in Conventional Logic Circuits

Assume that we want to build a logic circuit that can calculate an arbitrary Boolean function. Such a logic circuit (either conventional or reversible) can be built from the combination of smaller circuits, all chosen from a small set of different building blocks. The combination is called a synthesis and the small set is called the library of the synthesis. The members of this set are called gates. Thus, in practice, gates are 'simple' small circuits. A logic gate is said to be universal if it is sufficient to synthesize the arbitrary function. In other words, the set consisting of this single gate can act as a library.

In order to be a universal building block, a gate needs to fulfil some requirements. These conditions are different for conventional logic circuits and reversible logic circuits. It is well known that the NAND gate (with two bits of input and one bit of output; see Section 1.2) is a universal building block for conventional binary logic. So is the NOR gate. Their universality is a rather exceptional property. For example, the NOT, the AND, the OR, the XOR, and the XAND gates are not universal. Figure C.1a illustrates the universality of the NAND gate by synthesizing the example function

$$f(A_1, A_2, A_3) = \overline{A_1} A_2 + A_1 A_3 \, . \tag{C1}$$

It is clear that neither the NAND nor the NOR gate can function as the universal reversible building block of a reversible circuit, as they are not reversible in the first place. For reversible circuits, we thus have to search for new universal gates; that is, reversible ones. To find out which reversible circuits are universal and which are not, we start from a well-established theorem of conventional circuits and modify it, step by step, to deduce a new theorem of reversible circuits.

We rely on a theorem published by both Glushkov [181] (it is called Theorem 5 in Chapter II of his book) and Mukhopadhyay [182] (it is called Theorem 3.3 in his paper). It is related to conventional (i.e., not necessarily reversible) logic circuits:

Reversible Computing. Alexis De Vos
Copyright © 2010 WILEY-VCH Verlag GmbH & Co. KGaA, Weinheim
ISBN: 978-3-527-40992-1

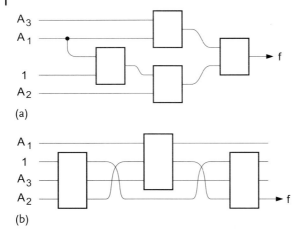

(a)

(b)

Figure C.1 Synthesis of the same Boolean function (a) by NAND gates, and (b) by TOFFOLI gates.

Theorem C.1

A logic gate is universal iff it is neither affine linear nor monotonic.

For the definition of affine linear circuits and monotonic circuits, the reader is referred to Sections 3.6 and 3.4, respectively.

C.2
Preliminary Concepts

The Hamming distance, named after the American mathematician Richard Hamming, between two binary vectors $(X_1, X_2, \ldots, X_n)$ and $(Y_1, Y_2, \ldots, Y_n)$ is the number of 1s in the vector $(X_1 \text{ XOR } Y_1, X_2 \text{ XOR } Y_2, \ldots, X_n \text{ XOR } Y_n)$; that is, the number of places where X_k differs from Y_k. Thus, the Hamming distance is an integer between 0 and n. The Hamming weight of a vector $(X_1, X_2, \ldots, X_n)$ is defined as its Hamming distance from the zero vector $(0, 0, \ldots, 0)$; that is, the number of 1s in the vector X.

We consider a logic gate with w binary inputs A_j and w binary outputs P_j. We use the different values of the input $(A_1, A_2, \ldots, A_w)$ as the coordinates of a w-dimensional hypercube. This solid has 2^w corners (or vertices) and $w2^{w-1}$ edges. We note that each corner of the hypercube (with Hamming weight p) is connected by edges to its w neighbors (of which p have weight $p - 1$ and $w - p$ have weight $p + 1$).

We can represent a truth table by giving each corner of the hypercube a label $(P_1, P_2, \ldots, P_w)$. If the truth table is reversible, all 2^w labels are different. Then two labels have a Hamming distance of at least 1.

Note that all corners $(A_1, A_2, \ldots, A_w)$ with the same Hamming weight p lie in the same hyperplane $A_1 + A_2 + \cdots + A_w = p$, perpendicular to the vector $(1, 1, \ldots, 1)$; that is, the hypercube's diagonal.

We define a 'climbing path' as a path that travels, along the hypercube's edges, from point $(0, 0, \ldots, 0)$ to point $(1, 1, \ldots, 1)$ by consecutive steps that each increase a single coordinate A_j from 0 to 1 (Section 1.6). A climbing path thus consists of a sequence of w edges. There are $w!$ different climbing paths.

C.3
No-Fan-Out Theorem and Its Consequences

Theorem C.1 is valid for conventional logic circuits, where fan-out is allowed (see Figure 3.39a). Because fan-out is forbidden in reversible circuits, we are not allowed to apply Theorem C.1 without modification. The interdiction of fan-outs in reversible circuits needs to be circumvented by using a reversible gate with the so-called duplicating property and applying at least one constant input to that gate; see Section 3.20.1. Figure 3.39 illustrates the duplicating property of Tables 3.8b and 3.8c. In a reversible circuit, a fan-out like that in Figure 3.39a needs to be replaced with a reversible gate, such as those in Figure 3.39b or in Figure 3.39c. Thus, in order to be universal, a reversible gate needs this duplicating property; whenever necessary, it must be able to provide the copying function. This means that Theorem C.1 has to be amended for reversible circuits:

Theorem C.2

A reversible logic gate is universal iff it is neither affine linear nor monotonic, but is able to provide the copying function.

So, which reversible circuits have this duplicating property? A reversible circuit of width w has a duplicating property iff there is a sequence of $w - 1$ Boolean constants $c_1, c_2, \ldots, c_{j-1}, c_{j+1}, \ldots, c_w$ and two outputs $P_k(A_1, A_2, \ldots, A_w)$ and $P_l(A_1, A_2, \ldots, A_w)$ such that

$$\begin{aligned}
\text{either} \quad & P_k(c_1, c_2, \ldots, c_{j-1}, A_j, c_{j+1}, \ldots, c_w) = A_j \quad \text{and} \\
& P_l(c_1, c_2, \ldots, c_{j-1}, A_j, c_{j+1}, \ldots, c_w) = A_j, \\
\text{or} \quad & P_k(c_1, c_2, \ldots, c_{j-1}, A_j, c_{j+1}, \ldots, c_w) = \overline{A_j} \quad \text{and} \\
& P_l(c_1, c_2, \ldots, c_{j-1}, A_j, c_{j+1}, \ldots, c_w) = \overline{A_j}, \\
\text{or} \quad & P_k(c_1, c_2, \ldots, c_{j-1}, A_j, c_{j+1}, \ldots, c_w) = A_j \quad \text{and} \\
& P_l(c_1, c_2, \ldots, c_{j-1}, A_j, c_{j+1}, \ldots, c_w) = \overline{A_j}.
\end{aligned}$$

See Table C.1 for the case where $k < l$. As a consequence, a reversible gate has the duplicating property iff its truth table contains two rows such that

Table C.1 Two rows from the truth tables of three different reversible circuits with the duplicating property.

(a)

$A_1 A_2 \ldots A_j \ldots A_w$	$P_1 P_2 \ldots P_k \ldots P_l \ldots P_w$
0	0 0
1	1 1

(b)

$A_1 A_2 \ldots A_j \ldots A_w$	$P_1 P_2 \ldots P_k \ldots P_l \ldots P_w$
0	1 1
1	0 0

(c)

$A_1 A_2 \ldots A_j \ldots A_w$	$P_1 P_2 \ldots P_k \ldots P_l \ldots P_w$
0	0 1
1	1 0

- The Hamming distance between the two input vectors $(A_1, A_2, \ldots, A_w)$ is 1, and
- The Hamming distance between the two output vectors $(P_1, P_2, \ldots, P_w)$ is at least 2.

Note that in the second example of Section 3.20.1, w equals 3, $j = 1$, $k = 2$, and $l = 3$. Table 3.8c is of the type shown in Table C.1a. The two rows in Table C.1a correspond to the fourth and eighth rows in Table 3.8c.

We have the following theorem:

Theorem C.3

A reversible gate has the duplicating property iff it is not an affine exchanger.

The proof of this is as follows. We assume that the reversible gate does *not* have the duplicating property. Therefore, the Hamming distance between the labels of any pair of neighboring corners has to be equal to 1. We construct the circuit by applying labels $(P_1, P_2, \ldots, P_w)$ in hyperplanes of ever-increasing Hamming weight:

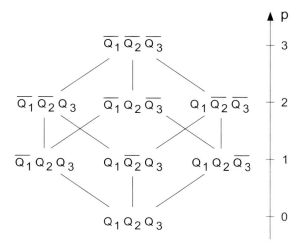

Figure C.2 Cube with labels representing a reversible circuit of width 3 without the duplicating property.

- For $p = 0$, we have full freedom: we attach an arbitrary label $(Q_1, Q_2, \ldots, Q_w)$ to the corner $(A_1, A_2, \ldots, A_w) = (0, 0, \ldots, 0)$. There are 2^w ways to do this.
- For $p = 1$, we can distribute the w labels $(\overline{Q}_1, Q_2, Q_3, \ldots, Q_w)$, $(Q_1, \overline{Q}_2, Q_3, \ldots, Q_w)$, $\ldots$, $(Q_1, Q_2, \ldots, Q_{w-1}, \overline{Q}_w)$ freely among the w corners. This yields $w!$ possibilities.
- For $p = 2$, there is no freedom: as each corner of weight 2 is connected (by means of two edges) to two corners of weight 1, its label is determined by the two labels downstream.
- ...
- For an arbitrary p (with $2 \leq p \leq w$), there is again no freedom: as each corner of weight p is connected (by means of $p!$ different paths) to p different corners of weight 1, its label is completely determined by the p labels of weight 1.

See the example in Figure C.2, with $w = 3$. We conclude that there are only $w!2^w$ different reversible circuits without the duplicating property.

On the other hand, we can easily check that all affine exchangers lack the duplicating property. As there are exactly $w!2^w$ different affine exchangers (Section 3.9), we must conclude that all reversible gates that lack the duplicating property are affine exchangers. This proves Theorem C.3.

Combining the above Theorems C.2, C.3, we obtain the following conclusion:

Theorem C.4

A reversible logic gate is universal iff it is neither affine linear nor monotonic nor an affine exchanger.

C.4
Final Theorem

We will now add a new theorem:

Theorem C.5

A reversible logic gate is monotonic iff it is an exchanger.

If the truth table is reversible, at each step of a climbing path at least one of the label numbers $P_1, P_2, \ldots, P_w$ must change. Such a change can only be from 0 to 1 if all the functions $P_1(A_1, A_2, \ldots, A_w)$, $P_2(A_1, A_2, \ldots, A_w)$, etc., are monotonic. Because there are w steps, exactly one of the numbers $P_1, P_2, \ldots, P_w$ must increase from 0 to 1 at each step. This reasoning demonstrates that, along a climbing path of a monotonic reversible gate, both the Hamming weight of $(A_1, A_2, \ldots, A_w)$ and the Hamming weight of $(P_1, P_2, \ldots, P_w)$ increase in unit steps from 0 to w. We can conclude that, in each corner, the weight of $(P_1, P_2, \ldots, P_w)$ equals the weight p of $(A_1, A_2, \ldots, A_w)$. In other words, monotonic reversible gates conserve weight. Thus, all monotonic reversible circuits are conservative reversible circuits. The opposite, however, is not true.

We construct a monotonic reversible gate by applying labels $(P_1, P_2, \ldots, P_w)$ in hyperplanes of ever-increasing Hamming weight:

- For $p = 0$, there is no freedom: we have to attach the label $(P_1, P_2, \ldots, P_w) = (0, 0, \ldots, 0)$ to the corner $(A_1, A_2, \ldots, A_w) = (0, 0, \ldots, 0)$.
- For $p = 1$, we can distribute the w labels $(1, 0, 0, \ldots, 0)$, $(0, 1, 0, 0, \ldots, 0)$, $\ldots$, $(0, 0, \ldots, 0, 1)$ freely among the w corners. This yields $w!$ possibilities.
- For $p = 2$, there is again no freedom: as each corner of weight 2 is connected (by means of two edges) to two corners of weight 1, its label is determined by the two labels downstream.
- $\ldots$
- For an arbitrary p (with $2 \leq p \leq w$), there is again no freedom: as each corner of weight p is connected (by means of $p!$ different paths) to p different corners of weight 1, its label of weight p is completely determined by the p labels of weight 1.

See the example in Figure C.3, with $w = 4$. We conclude that there are only $w!$ different monotonic reversible circuits.

We now remark that all exchangers are monotonic, and that the number of different exchangers equals $w!$. As the number of exchangers equals the number of monotonic reversible circuits, and as all exchangers are monotonic, this leads unavoidably to the conclusion that the only monotonic reversible circuits that exist are the exchangers. This proves Theorem C.5. Table 3.3b is an example: this monotonic reversible circuit is indeed an exchanger: $P_1 = A_3$, $P_2 = A_1$, and $P_3 = A_2$.

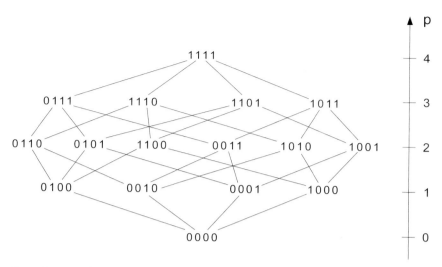

Figure C.3 Four-dimensional hypercube with labels representing a monotonic reversible circuit of width 4.

Taking Theorem C.5 into account, Theorem C.4 can be simplified:

Theorem C.6

A reversible logic gate is universal iff it is neither affine linear nor an affine exchanger.

Noting that all affine exchangers are affine linear, Theorem C.6 can be simplified further:

Theorem C.7

A reversible logic gate is universal iff it is not affine linear.

C.5
Discussion

Because the two reversible circuits of width 1 and all 24 reversible circuits of width 2 are affine linear, none of them can act as a universal primitive. We need a width of at least three. Among the $8! = 40\,320$ different reversible circuits of $w = 3$, only 1344 are affine linear (see Table 3.2). All the other 38 976 circuits can be used as a universal building block. The TOFFOLI gate ($P_1 = A_1$, $P_2 = A_2$, $P_3 = A_1 A_2 \oplus A_3$) is often put forward, but any other choice is equally good. Figure C.1b provides an example: the function f of (C1) realized exclusively with the TOFFOLI gate. However, 38 975 other circuits of width $w = 3$ can do the job too.

Table C.2 The number R of different reversible gates and the number U of different universal reversible gates as functions of the gate width w.

w	R	U	$\frac{U}{R}$ (in %)
1	2	0	0
2	24	0	0
3	40 320	38 976	96.7
4	20 922 789 888 000	20 922 789 565 440	99.999 998 5

For general width, we denote the total number of reversible circuits by $R(w)$ and the number of affine linear reversible circuits by $AL(w)$; see Table 3.2. For $w \geq 3$, as many as $U(w) = R(w) - AL(w) = (2^w)! - 2^{(w+1)w/2} w!_2$ circuits can play the role of the universal building block. Table C.2 shows that they form the vast majority. They do *not* form a subgroup of the group **R** of reversible circuits. Recall Lagrange's theorem and observe that the number U is not a divisor of the number R, the order of **R**.

C.6
Exercises for Appendix C

Exercise C.1
Check that both circuits in Figure C.1 do indeed provide the function in (C1).

Appendix D
Synthesis Efficiency

In this appendix, we follow the reasoning method introduced by Even *et al.* [183], Maslov and Dueck [44], and Patel *et al.* [31]. Let us assume a set of N circuits that are to be synthesized with the help of a library of B different building blocks (a subset of the former set, including the trivial identity gate). We build all possible cascades of length l. We call $m(l)$ the number of different circuits that can be synthesized by these cascades. Note that these m circuits automatically include all circuits synthesized by a shorter cascade, because we have included the identity building block in the library.

The question then arises: what cascade length L is needed to guarantee that these cascades contain the synthesis of all N given circuits; that is, to guarantee that $m(L) \geq N$? A hypothetical 'most efficient' library (where all different cascades yield different circuits) would realize $m(l) = B^l$. Therefore, $B^{L-1} < N$ and $B^L \geq N$, and thus

$$L = \left\lceil \frac{\log(N)}{\log(B)} \right\rceil . \tag{D1}$$

Here $\lceil x \rceil$ stands for the *ceiling* of x; that is, the smallest integer larger than or equal to x. We now apply this general result to five different cases:

1. In a first application, N is the total number of reversible circuits of width w, and B is the number of controlled NOT gates of width w (with an arbitrary controlled wire). Thus,

$$N = (2^w)!$$
$$B = w(2^{2^{w-1}} - 1) + 1 ,$$

where (in the latter equation) we have taken care to avoid multiple counting of the identity gate (see Section 3.10). Using Stirling's inequalities (3.2), we obtain

$$N > 2^{[w - \frac{1}{\log(2)}]2^w}$$
$$B \leq w2^{2^{w-1}}$$

Reversible Computing. Alexis De Vos
Copyright © 2010 WILEY-VCH Verlag GmbH & Co. KGaA, Weinheim
ISBN: 978-3-527-40992-1

and finally conclude that

$$L > \frac{\left[w - \frac{1}{\log(2)} \right] 2^w}{2^{w-1} + \frac{\log w}{\log(2)}} > 2w - 4 \ .$$

Therefore, our decomposition in Section 3.16 (with length $2w - 1$) is close to optimal.

2. If we keep $N = (2^w)!$, but choose B to be the number of controlled SWAP gates of width w, then B is somewhat smaller:

$$B = \frac{w(w-1)}{2} (2^{2^{w-2}} - 1) + 1 \ ,$$

leading to

$$L > 4w - 10 \ .$$

This proves that the synthesis method of Section 3.16 cannot work with $2w - 1$ controlled SWAP gates. The reader is kindly invited to verify that this (negative) result does *not* conflict with the theorem of Appendix E for n equal to a multiple of 4 and $p = 4$ and $q = \frac{n}{4}$.

3. If we apply the general result (D1) to the decomposition of controlled NOT gates into TOFFOLI gates, we have

$$N = 2^{2^{w-1}}$$
$$B = 3^{w-1}$$

and thus obtain

$$L > \frac{\log(2)}{2\log(3)} \frac{2^w}{w} \ .$$

Therefore, the Reed–Muller decomposition, which needs a cascade of up to $\frac{1}{2} 2^w$ building blocks (Section 3.16.3), is not optimal.

4. We consider all the linear Boolean reversible circuits (w wide): $N = a2^{w^2}$ with $a \approx 0.29$, after Section 3.5. For the building blocks, we choose the linear controlled NOTs (with an arbitrary controlled wire): $B = w(2^{w-1} - 1) + 1 \approx w2^{w-1}$. Thus, (D1) yields

$$L \approx \frac{\log(2) \, w^2}{\log(2) \, w} = w \ .$$

5. We now consider the same N but apply a smaller library: only FEYNMAN gates. Applying (D1) again, this time with $B = w(w-1) + 1$, yields

$$L \approx \frac{\log(2) \, w^2}{2\log(w)} = \frac{\log(2)}{2} \frac{w^2}{\log(w)} \ .$$

D.1
Exercises for Appendix D

Exercise D.1

We want to build an arbitrary exchange gate (of width w) from a library of all possible SWAP gates. What are the values of N and B? What is the lower bound L of the maximum cascade length?

Appendix E
Birkhoff's Theorem

Let n be an integer; that is, the number of objects in the set $\{1,2,\ldots,n\}$. Let p be a divisor of n; in other words we have $n = pq$, where both p and q are integers. We arrange the n objects into q rows, each of p objects, in an arrangement called a Young tableau [184]. We consider an arbitrary permutation a of the n objects. During such a permutation, the q subsets exchange q^2 flows F_{ij}. These F_{ij} form a $q \times q$ matrix F with all matrix elements equal to $0, 1, 2, \ldots$, or p. The matrix element F_{ij} denotes the number of objects that move from row $\#i$ to row $\#j$:

$$F_{ij} = \sum_{k=1}^{p} \sum_{m=1}^{p} P_{(i-1)p+k,(j-1)p+m} \, ,$$

where P is the $n \times n$ permutation matrix representing the original permutation a. The matrix F has $2q$ properties:

$$\sum_{j} F_{ij} = p$$

$$\sum_{i} F_{ij} = p \, ,$$

of which $2q - 1$ are independent. As an example, we consider an arbitrary permutation a of the 35 objects $\{1,2,\ldots,35\}$. Figure E.1a shows the permutation a as a mapping in the Young tableau for $n = 35$, $p = 7$, and $q = 5$. The tableau consists of the five sets $\{1,2,\ldots,7\}$, $\{8,9,\ldots,14\}$, $\ldots$, and $\{29,30,\ldots,35\}$. These sets exchange a number of objects according to the flow matrix

$$F = \begin{pmatrix} 6 & 0 & 0 & 1 & 0 \\ 1 & 5 & 0 & 0 & 1 \\ 0 & 1 & 5 & 0 & 1 \\ 0 & 0 & 0 & 6 & 1 \\ 0 & 1 & 2 & 0 & 4 \end{pmatrix} \, ,$$

where, for example, $F_{53} = 2$ expresses that in Figure E.1a two objects are mapped from the fifth row $\{29,30,\ldots,35\}$ to the third row $\{15,16,\ldots,21\}$. We can indeed see an arrow pointing from case 31 to case 18, and another from case 35 to

Reversible Computing. Alexis De Vos
Copyright © 2010 WILEY-VCH Verlag GmbH & Co. KGaA, Weinheim
ISBN: 978-3-527-40992-1

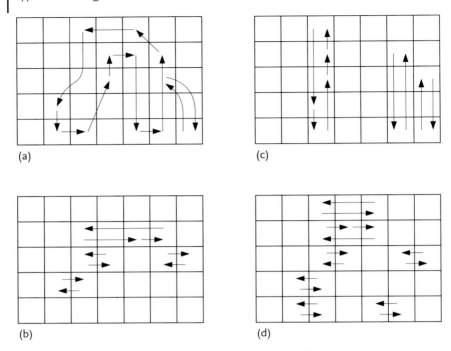

Figure E.1 Decomposition of (a) an arbitrary permutation of 35 objects into (b) a first 'horizontal' permutation, (c) a 'vertical' permutation, and (d) a second 'horizontal' permutation.

case 20. The reader is invited to verify that, for this 5×5 matrix F, all row sums and all column sums (in short: all line sums) are equal to $p = 7$.

Note that the $q \times q$ flow matrix F contains incomplete information on the permutation a. Complete information on a is given by the $n \times n = 35 \times 35$ permutation matrix P.

Theorem E.1

Each permutation a can be decomposed as

$$a = h_1 v h_2 \, ,$$

where both h_1 and h_2 only permute objects within rows of the Young tableau, and where v only permutes objects within columns of the tableau.

Figures E.1b–d show the permutations h_1, v, and h_2 that are to be performed successively:

- The vertical permutation v (Figure E.1c) is found as follows: the cycles of a are projected onto columns, yielding one or more vertical cycles.

- The horizontal permutation h_1 (Figure E.1b) merely consists of horizontal arrows that map the arrow tails of the vertical and oblique arrows in Figure E.1a to the corresponding arrow tails of Figure E.1c. Subsequently, additional horizontal arrows are added to form closed horizontal cycles.
- Finally, the horizontal permutation h_2 (Figure E.1d) simply equals $v^{-1}h_1^{-1}a$.

The fact that it is always possible to construct an appropriate vertical permutation v is a direct consequence of either Birkhoff's theorem [163, 185] (also known as the Birkhoff–von Neumann theorem after the American mathematician Garrett Birkhoff and the Hungarian/American mathematician John von Neumann), Hall's marriage theorem (after the English mathematician Philip Hall), König's theorem (after the Hungarian mathematician Dénes König), or the maximum-flow theorem; all of these well-known theorems in combinatorics are equivalent [186]. As an example, one of the formulations of the Birkhoff theorem says: any matrix of size $q \times q$ and line sum p can be decomposed as the sum of p matrices of the same size and unit line sum [187]. In other words, any flow matrix with a line sum of p can be decomposed as the sum of p permutation matrices. For example, the above matrix F of size 5×5 with a line sum of 7 can be decomposed as the following sum of seven permutation matrices:

$$
F = 4 \begin{pmatrix} 1 & 0 & 0 & 0 & 0 \\ 0 & 1 & 0 & 0 & 0 \\ 0 & 0 & 1 & 0 & 0 \\ 0 & 0 & 0 & 1 & 0 \\ 0 & 0 & 0 & 0 & 1 \end{pmatrix} + \begin{pmatrix} 0 & 0 & 0 & 1 & 0 \\ 1 & 0 & 0 & 0 & 0 \\ 0 & 1 & 0 & 0 & 0 \\ 0 & 0 & 0 & 0 & 1 \\ 0 & 0 & 1 & 0 & 0 \end{pmatrix} + \begin{pmatrix} 1 & 0 & 0 & 0 & 0 \\ 0 & 0 & 0 & 0 & 1 \\ 0 & 0 & 1 & 0 & 0 \\ 0 & 0 & 0 & 1 & 0 \\ 0 & 1 & 0 & 0 & 0 \end{pmatrix}
$$
$$
+ \begin{pmatrix} 1 & 0 & 0 & 0 & 0 \\ 0 & 1 & 0 & 0 & 0 \\ 0 & 0 & 0 & 0 & 1 \\ 0 & 0 & 0 & 1 & 0 \\ 0 & 0 & 1 & 0 & 0 \end{pmatrix} .
$$

We can apply one of these p permutations to each of the p columns of the Young tableau in order to obtain the desired vertical permutation v. In Figure E.1c, we do indeed recognize four empty columns (corresponding to the four identity matrices in the matrix sum) and three columns that are not empty (corresponding to the remaining three matrices in the matrix sum). The Birkhoff decomposition thus gives a precise procedure for what was called the 'projection of permutation a onto the p columns' in the text above.

Thus, the theorem says that one permutation of n objects can be decomposed into:

- A product of q disjoint subpermutations, each of p objects, followed by
- A product of p disjoint subpermutations, each of q objects, and finally
- A second product of q disjoint subpermutations, each of p objects.

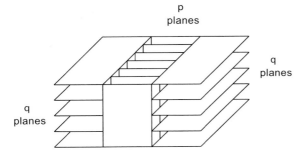

p
planes

q
planes

q
planes

Figure E.2 Symbolic decomposition of an arbitrary permutation of 35 objects into five 'horizontal' subpermutations, seven 'vertical' subpermutations, and five 'horizontal' subpermutations.

This is symbolically depicted in Figure E.2. In brief, one big spaghetti is decomposed into $2q + p$ small permutations. The theorem can be interpreted in terms of group theory; if we define

- **N** as the group of all permutations of the n objects,
- **H** as the group of all 'horizontal permutations' of these objects, and
- **V** as the group of all 'vertical permutations',

then

- **N** is isomorphic to the symmetric group $\mathbf{S}_n$,
- **H** is isomorphic to the Young subgroup $\mathbf{S}_p \times \mathbf{S}_p \times \ldots \times \mathbf{S}_p = \mathbf{S}_p^q$, and
- **V** is isomorphic to the Young subgroup $\mathbf{S}_q \times \mathbf{S}_q \times \ldots \times \mathbf{S}_q = \mathbf{S}_q^p$.

Note that the Young subgroups $\mathbf{S}_p^q$ and $\mathbf{S}_q^p$ are based on two so-called dual partitions of the number n:

$$n = p + p + \cdots + p \quad (q \text{ terms}), \text{ and}$$
$$n = q + q + \cdots + q \quad (p \text{ terms}).$$

Therefore, these two subgroups are referred to as dual Young subgroups. The combinatorial theorem says the following: if the group **N** is partitioned into double cosets by means of the subgroup **H**, then we can choose a representative of each double coset that is a member of **V**. Determining how many double cosets the supergroup **N** is partitioned into by the subgroup **H** is a very difficult problem. We will call this number $X(p, q)$. Fortunately, it is not important to know the value of X, while the fact that (thanks to Birkhoff's theorem) each of the X double cosets contains (at least) one member of **V** is essential.

We now consider the special case where n is even. We distinguish between two special subcases [52]:

- $p = 2$ and thus $q = n/2$.
- $p = n/2$ and thus $q = 2$.

In the latter subcase, the group $\mathbf{S}_n$ is partitioned by the subgroup isomorphic to $\mathbf{S}_{n/2}^2$ into exactly

$$X\left(\frac{n}{2}, 2\right) = \frac{n}{2} + 1$$

double cosets [46]. Such partitioning is applied in Section 3.15. In the former subcase, the number of double cosets into which $\mathbf{S}_n$ is partitioned by the subgroup $\mathbf{S}_2^{n/2}$ is surprisingly complicated [188]:

$$X\left(2, \frac{n}{2}\right) = \frac{\left[\left(\frac{n}{2}\right)!\right]^2}{2^n} \sum_{k=0}^{n/2} \frac{2^k(n - 2k)!}{\left[\left(\frac{n}{2} - k\right)!\right]^2 k!} .$$

This partitioning is applied in Section 3.16.

We end this appendix by noting that the Birkhoff theorem guarantees the existence of a decomposition of the flow matrix into permutation matrices, but that it does not tell us how to find it. An algorithm (for arbitrary p and q) is not straightforward; this algorithm should be computationally efficient (i.e., not an exhaustive search!), and should give results in all cases. The history of this problem involves a lot of failed attempts [189]. Fortunately, fast and reliable algorithms for arbitrary values of q and p based on coloring bipartite graphs [187, 190] have been found. For example, Paredes and Hall [191] perform a decomposition with time complexity $\mathcal{O}(qp \log p)$, whereas Peng *et al.* [192] propose an algorithm with time complexity $\mathcal{O}(qp)$. There are simple and efficient dedicated algorithms for small values of p, as well as for small values of q.

E.1
Exercises for Appendix E

Exercise E.1
If we multiply an $n \times n$ matrix with all line sums equal to a by an $n \times n$ matrix with all line sums equal to b, does this result in an $n \times n$ matrix where all line sums are equal? If the answer is yes, what is the value of this sum?

Exercise E.2
Invent an algorithm to find a Birkhoff decomposition of an arbitrary integer $q \times q$ matrix which has all of its line sums equal to 2. Apply your algorithm to the matrix

$$\begin{pmatrix} 1 & 0 & 1 & 0 & 0 & 0 & 0 \\ 1 & 0 & 0 & 1 & 0 & 0 & 0 \\ 0 & 0 & 0 & 0 & 0 & 2 & 0 \\ 0 & 0 & 0 & 0 & 1 & 0 & 1 \\ 0 & 2 & 0 & 0 & 0 & 0 & 0 \\ 0 & 0 & 1 & 1 & 0 & 0 & 0 \\ 0 & 0 & 0 & 0 & 1 & 0 & 1 \end{pmatrix} .$$

Exercise E.3
Invent an algorithm to find **all** Birkhoff matrix decompositions for the same case with $p = 2$ and arbitrary q. Apply your algorithm to the matrix of the previous exercise.

Exercise E.4
Demonstrate that, in the case $q = 2$, Birkhoff matrix decomposition is both trivial and unique.

Exercise E.5
Invent an algorithm to find a Birkhoff decomposition of an integer 3×3 matrix that has all of its line sums equal to an arbitrary number p. Apply your algorithm to the matrix

$$\begin{pmatrix} 2 & 3 & 4 \\ 1 & 4 & 4 \\ 6 & 2 & 1 \end{pmatrix} .$$

Is the decomposition unique?

Exercise E.6
We have fifteen objects arranged into three rows of five objects, $n = p \times q = 5 \times 3 = 15$:

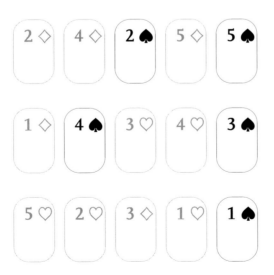

Rearrange the 15 objects such that you obtain the 'standard' arrangement:

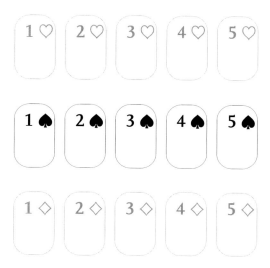

However, you are only allowed to proceed in the 'Birkhoff way':

- First move the cards only in the horizontal direction,
- Then move the cards only in the vertical direction, and
- Finally, move the cards only in the horizontal direction.

Exercise E.7
Convince yourself that the case $p = 2$ is easy. To do this, choose $n = p \times q = 2 \times n/2$ by taking the 13 cards with hearts and the 13 cards with spades. Create an arbitrary arrangement with two rows, such as

K	K	2	7	6	5	2	4	4	9	3	8	3
1	7	Q	8	J	9	5	10	10	J	Q	6	1

The challenge is then to permute the 26 cards in the Birkhoff way in order to arrive at the standard ordering:

1	2	3	4	5	6	7	8	9	10	J	Q	K
1	2	3	4	5	6	7	8	9	10	J	Q	K

Exercise E.8
Amaze your friends by shuffling a full deck of $n = p \times q = 13 \times 4 = 52$ cards and subsequently performing the Birkhoff card permutation. This is a tricky one – don't forget to practice!

Appendix F
Microentropy and Macroentropy

The phase space of a physical system is divided into N parts. Let p_m be the probability that the system is in part #m of the phase space. We have $\sum_{m=1}^{N} p_m = 1$. If k is the Boltzmann constant (see Section 4.1), the entropy of the system is

$$\sigma = -k \sum_{m=1}^{N} p_m \log(p_m) .$$

This is dependent on the number (N) of sections into which the total phase space is divided (and on the way it is divided into these N parts). If we initially apply a coarse graining and divide the phase space into n 'large' parts ($n < N$; usually $n \ll N$), and then apply a fine graining to each of these macroparts (i.e., divide part #1 into n_1 subparts, part #2 into n_2 subparts, ..., part #n into n_n subparts, such that $n_1 + n_2 + \cdots + n_n = N$), then

$$\sigma = -k \sum_{i=1}^{n} \sum_{j=1}^{n_i} p_{ij} \log(p_{ij})$$

can be proven to be exactly the sum of two contributions:

$$\sigma = -k \sum_{i=1}^{n} q_i \log(q_i) - k \sum_{i=1}^{n} q_i \sum_{j=1}^{n_i} \frac{p_{ij}}{q_i} \log\left(\frac{p_{ij}}{q_i}\right) . \tag{F1}$$

Here q_i is a shorthand notation for $\sum_{j=1}^{n_i} p_{ij}$; that is, the probability of being in macrocell #i. The former term in (F1) is called the macroscopic entropy S; the latter term in (F1) is called the microscopic entropy s [193–196]. Thus, however we assemble the microcells of the phase space into larger macrocells (see Figure F.1, where $N = 4 + 6 + 4 + 4 = 18$), we can always write

$$\sigma = S + s .$$

The contribution S is the entropy associated with how the probabilities are distributed *among* the macrocells; the contribution s is the entropy associated with the way probabilities are distributed among the microcells *within* the macrocells.

The phase space of an electronic system consists of all possible positions and velocities of the electrons. Because we assign a logic 1 to a positive voltage over a capacitor and a logic 0 to a negative voltage over the same capacitor, we take a special

Reversible Computing. Alexis De Vos
Copyright © 2010 WILEY-VCH Verlag GmbH & Co. KGaA, Weinheim
ISBN: 978-3-527-40992-1

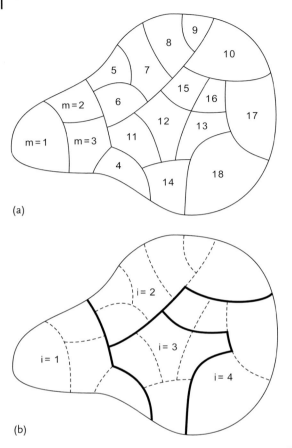

(a)

(b)

Figure F.1 Dividing up a phase space: (a) directly into microcells; (b) into macrocells and then into microcells.

interest in whether the electrons are in the lower or the upper plate of the capacitor. We are not interested in their exact position within the capacitor plate, nor in the velocity or spin of the electrons. This is an example of the coarse graining of phase space. Figure F.1 is, for example, the phase space of an electronic circuit consisting of two capacitors. In Figure F.1a we are interested in all details relating to all of the quantum numbers of all electrons. In Figure F.1b we are only concerned with which two of the four capacitor plates the electrons are located in. In this example, it is clear that the macroscopic entropy S is associated with the two bits of information we can store into the two capacitors. If $q_1 = q_2 = q_3 = q_4 = \frac{1}{4}$, we find that

$$S = -k \sum_{i=1}^{4} q_i \log(q_i) = 2k \log(2) = 2 \, \text{bit} \,.$$

The microscopic entropy s is not associated with information, but with heat. In other words, s is the Boltzmann entropy (named after Ludwig Boltzmann – the same

Boltzmann referred to in Section 4.1), whereas S is the Shannon entropy [197] (named after the same Shannon referred to in Section 1.8). It is important to recognize that the way that we split σ into a macroscopic part S that we associate with information and a microscopic part s that we associate with heat is arbitrary. What we consider a coarse or a fine division of phase space is determined by the technology we choose. Whereas the division of phase space into microcells is based upon the basic principles of physics (e.g., Heisenberg's uncertainty principle, named after the German physicist Werner Heisenberg), its division into macrocells is based upon the available technology.

F.1
Exercises for Appendix F

Exercise F.1
Assume that Table F.1a gives the probabilities p_m of the physical system of Figure F.1. Check that $\sum p_m = 1$. Calculate the microentropy s, the macroentropy S, and the entropy σ separately, and check that σ equals $s + S$.

Table F.1 Two probability distributions.

m	p_m	m	p_m
1	0.01	1	0.01
2	0.02	2	0.02
3	0.03	3	0.03
4	0.04	4	0.04
5	0.01	5	0.00
6	0.01	6	0.02
7	0.01	7	0.01
8	0.01	8	0.01
9	0.10	9	0.10
10	0.05	10	0.05
11	0.02	11	0.02
12	0.01	12	0.01
13	0.01	13	0.01
14	0.01	14	0.01
15	0.15	15	0.15
16	0.16	16	0.16
17	0.17	17	0.17
18	0.18	18	0.18

| (a) | | (b) | |

Exercise F.2

Perform the same exercise for Table F.1b, and explain how to treat

$$-p_5 \log(p_5) = -0 \times (-\infty).$$

Appendix G
Computing the Successive Powers of a Matrix

According to the basic theory of the Z-transform [198], the jth power of a given $n \times n$ matrix y (i.e., the matrix y^j) takes the form:

$$y^j = \sum_{k=1}^{n} c_k z_k^j \,, \tag{G1}$$

where $z_1, z_2, \ldots,$ and z_n are merely complex numbers, not matrices (i.e., they are the n solutions of the eigenvalue equation), and where $c_1, c_2, \ldots,$ and c_n are suitable $n \times n$ matrices (determined from the initial conditions $y, y^2, \ldots,$ and y^n). For $n = 4$, the eigenvalue equation looks like

$$\det \left[y - \begin{pmatrix} z & 0 & 0 & 0 \\ 0 & z & 0 & 0 \\ 0 & 0 & z & 0 \\ 0 & 0 & 0 & z \end{pmatrix} \right] = 0 \,.$$

For

$$y = \begin{pmatrix} 0 & 0 & \omega & \overline{\omega} \\ 0 & 1 & 0 & 0 \\ 0 & 0 & \overline{\omega} & \omega \\ 1 & 0 & 0 & 0 \end{pmatrix} ,$$

this yields

$$\det \begin{pmatrix} -z & 0 & \omega & \overline{\omega} \\ 0 & 1-z & 0 & 0 \\ 0 & 0 & \overline{\omega} - z & \omega \\ 1 & 0 & 0 & -z \end{pmatrix} = 0 \,.$$

Considering that $\omega = (1+i)/2$ and $\overline{\omega} = (1-i)/2$, we then obtain the fourth-degree equation

$$(z - 1)^2(z^2 + \omega z + i) = 0 \,.$$

Reversible Computing. Alexis De Vos
Copyright © 2010 WILEY-VCH Verlag GmbH & Co. KGaA, Weinheim
ISBN: 978-3-527-40992-1

The four solutions of the equation are $z_1 = z_2 = 1$, $z_3 = \frac{\sqrt{7}-1}{4} + i\frac{\sqrt{7}+1}{4}$, and $z_4 = \frac{-\sqrt{7}-1}{4} + i\frac{-\sqrt{7}+1}{4}$. Because one solution has a multiplicity of 2, expression (G1) must be replaced by

$$y^j = c_1 z_1^j + c_2 j z_2^j + c_3 z_3^j + c_4 z_4^j$$

with appropriate matrices c_1, c_2, c_3, and c_4 (again to be determined from the initial conditions y, y^2, y^3, and y^4). Note the factor j in the second term on the right-hand side!

Because y is unitary, its eigenvalues automatically lie on the unit circle of the complex plane: $|z_1| = |z_2| = |z_3| = |z_4| = 1$. Their phase angles are $\theta_1 = \theta_2 = 0$, $\theta_3 = \pi/2 - \theta$, and $\theta_4 = \pi + \theta$, where $\theta = \arccos\left(\frac{\sqrt{7}-1}{4}\right) = \arctan\left(\sqrt{7}\right) - \pi/4 \approx 24°17'43''$. After straightforward but laborious calculations, we obtain the values of the constant matrices c_1, c_2, c_3, and c_4. Their precise values are not important; it is sufficient to note that neither c_3 nor c_4 is the zero matrix.

Neither z_3^j nor z_4^j is periodic, because the angle θ is not a rational multiple of π. Indeed, according to Jahnel [199], the only rational angles (between 0 and 90°) with cosines equal to quadratic irrationals are 30°, 36°, 45°, and 72° (which have cosines equal to $\sqrt{3}/2$, $\sqrt{5}/4 + 1/4$, $\sqrt{2}/2$, and $\sqrt{5}/4 - 1/4$, respectively). Similarly, according to Calcut [200], the only rational angles (between 0 and 90°) with tangents equal to a quadratic irrational are 15°, 22°30′, 30°, 60°, 67°30′, and 75° (which have tangents equal to $2 - \sqrt{3}$, $\sqrt{2} - 1$, $\sqrt{3}/3$, $\sqrt{3}$, $\sqrt{2} + 1$, and $2 + \sqrt{3}$, respectively). Because neither z_3^j nor z_4^j is periodic, the matrix sequence $\{y^j\}$ is not periodic.

G.1
Exercises for Appendix G

Exercise G.1
In the present book, we have encountered a number of 2×2 unitary matrices:

$$\begin{pmatrix} \cos(\theta) & \sin(\theta) \\ -\sin(\theta) & \cos(\theta) \end{pmatrix}, \begin{pmatrix} 1 & 0 \\ 0 & 1 \end{pmatrix}, \begin{pmatrix} \omega & \overline{\omega} \\ \overline{\omega} & \omega \end{pmatrix}, \begin{pmatrix} 0 & 1 \\ 1 & 0 \end{pmatrix}, \begin{pmatrix} \overline{\omega} & \omega \\ \omega & \overline{\omega} \end{pmatrix},$$

$$\frac{1}{2}\begin{pmatrix} 1 + \exp(i\theta) & 1 - \exp(i\theta) \\ 1 - \exp(i\theta) & 1 + \exp(i\theta) \end{pmatrix}, \quad \text{and} \quad \frac{1}{\sqrt{2}}\begin{pmatrix} 1 & 1 \\ 1 & -1 \end{pmatrix}.$$

Compute the eigenvalues of these matrices. For each matrix, check whether the modulus is equal to 1, and compute the phase angle. Deduce the powers and the order of each matrix.

Post Scriptum

Rolf Landauer triggered the emergence of the branch of science known as reversible computing. The present book attempts to demonstrate how rich this subject is. In it, we have computed in different worlds $\mathbb{W}$: $\mathbb{W}$ was successively the world $\mathbb{B}$ of Boolean numbers 0 and 1, the world $\mathbb{Z}$ of integers, the world $\mathbb{Z}_{2^b}$ of integers modulo 2^b, the world $\mathbb{R}$ of real numbers, and the world $\mathbb{C}$ of complex numbers. Besides the numbers in $\mathbb{W}$, we encountered column vectors (in both $\mathbb{W}^w$ and $\mathbb{W}^{2^w}$), as well as square matrices (in both $\mathbb{W}^{w^2}$ and $\mathbb{W}^{2^{2w}}$), where w is the computing width, in either bits or qubits.

We applied group theory with finite and infinite groups, countable and uncountable. We discussed Fourier transforms and Z-transforms. Aside from mathematics, we visited the fields of physics, engineering, and computer science. We investigated energy and entropy.

Finally, we find that the subject also leads to some philosophical musing. What is the difference between forward and backward? What is the difference between forecasting and remembering? Between computing and memorizing? Between left and right? Between future and past? And finally: what is computing? What is thinking? Is it merely permuting objects?

Although we have visited all of these worlds and encountered all of these questions, there is still a lot more to explore – we have merely scratched the surface. Nevertheless, I hope that you enjoyed reading the book as much as I enjoyed writing it.

Reversible Computing. Alexis De Vos
Copyright © 2010 WILEY-VCH Verlag GmbH & Co. KGaA, Weinheim
ISBN: 978-3-527-40992-1

References

1 Yokoyama, T., Axelsen, H., and Glück, R. (2008) *Principles of a reversible programming language.* Proceedings of the Computing Frontiers 2008 Conference, Ischia, May 2008, pp. 43–54.

2 Sasao, T. and Fujita, M. (1996) *Representation of Discrete Functions,* Kluwer Academic Publishers, Boston.

3 Bochmann, D. and Steinbach, B. (1991) *Logikentwurf mit* XBOOLE, Verlag Technik, Berlin.

4 Steinbach, B. and Posthoff, C. (2007) *Extended theory of Boolean normal forms.* Proceedings of the 6th Annual Hawaii International Conference on Statistics, Mathematics and Related Fields, Honolulu, January 2007, pp. 1124–1139.

5 Gaidukov, A. (2002) *Algorithm to derive minimum ESOP for 6-variable function.* Proceedings of the 5th International Workshop on Boolean Problems, Freiberg, September 2002, pp. 141–148.

6 Pogosyan, G., Rosenberg, I., and Takada, S. (2004) *Building minimum ESOPs through redundancy elimination.* Proceedings of the 6th International Workshop on Boolean Problems, Freiberg, September 2004, pp. 201–206.

7 Fidytek, R., Mostowski, A., Somla, R., and Szepietowski, A. (2001) Algorithms counting monotone Boolean functions. *Information Processing Letters,* **79**, 203–209.

8 Bochmann, D., Posthoff, C., Shmerko, V., Stanković, R., Tošić, Ž., and Yanushkevich, S. (2000) *Logic differential calculus as part of switching theory.* Proceedings of the 4th IEEE International Conference on New Information Technologies in Education, Minsk, December 2000, pp. 126–135.

9 Yildiz, B. and Subaşi, M. (2002) An interpreter for the Boolean derivative. *Applied Mathematics and Computation,* **129**, 43–54.

10 Scott, W. (1964) *Group Theory,* Dover Publications, New York.

11 Hall, P. (1968) *The Theory of Groups,* AMS Chelsea Publishing, Providence.

12 Cameron, P. (1999) *Permutation Groups,* Cambridge University Press, Cambridge.

13 Hall, B. (2003) *Lie Groups, Lie Algebras, and Representations, an Elementary Introduction,* Springer Verlag, New York.

14 Baker, A. (2007) *Matrix Groups, an Introduction to Lie Group Theory,* Springer Verlag, London.

15 Stillwell, J. (2008) *Naive Lie Theory,* Springer, New York.

16 Kaplansky, I. (1971) *Infinite Abelian Groups,* University of Michigan Press, Ann Arbor.

17 Bosma, W., Cannon, J., and Playoust, C. (1997) The Magma algebra system I: the user language. *Journal of Symbolic Computation,* **23**, 459–484.

18 Computational Algebra Group, University of Sydney (2008) MAGMA computational algebra system. http://magma.maths.usyd.edu.au/magma/.

19 Cannon, J. (1984) An introduction to the group theory language `Cayley`, in *Computational Group Theory*, (ed. M. Atkinson), Academic Press, London, pp. 145–183.

20 Schönert, M. (1992) `GAP`. *Computer Algebra Nederland Nieuwsbrief*, **9**, 19–28.

21 van Leeuwen, M., Cohen, A., and Lisser, B. (1991) `LiE`, a package for Lie group computations. *Computer Algebra Nederland Nieuwsbrief*, **7**, 34–35.

22 van Leeuwen, M. (2007) `LiE`, a software package for Lie group computations. http://www-math.univ-poitiers.fr/~maavl/LiE.

23 De Vos, A. and Van Rentergem, Y. (2005) *Reversible computing: from mathematical group theory to electronical circuit experiment*. Proceedings of the Computing Frontiers 2005 Conference, Ischia, May 2005, pp. 35–44.

24 Kerber, A. (1970) Representations of permutation groups I. *Lecture Notes in Mathematics*, Vol. 240, Springer Verlag, Berlin, pp. 17–23.

25 James, G. and Kerber, A. (1981) The representation theory of the symmetric group. *Encyclopedia of Mathematics and its Applications*, **16**, 15–33.

26 Jones, A. (1996) A combinatorial approach to the double cosets of the symmetric group with respect to Young subgroups. *European Journal of Combinatorics*, **17**, 647–655.

27 Courant, R. (1970) *Differential and Integral Calculus*, Blackie & Son Limited, London, p. 361.

28 Sasao, T. and Kinoshita, K. (1979) Conservative logic elements and their universality. *IEEE Transactions on Computers*, **28**, 682–685.

29 Fredkin, E. and Toffoli, T. (1982) Conservative logic. *International Journal of Theoretical Physics*, **21**, 219–253.

30 Cattaneo, G., Leporati, A., and Leporini, R. (2002) Fredkin gates for finite-valued reversible and conservative logics. *Journal of Physics A: Mathematical and General*, **35**, 9755–9785.

31 Patel, K., Markov, I., and Hayes, J. (2004) *Optimal synthesis of linear reversible circuits*. Proceedings of the 13th International Workshop on Logic and Synthesis, Temecula, June 2004, pp. 470–477.

32 Kerntopf, P. (2002) *On universality of binary reversible logic gates*. Proceedings of the 5th International Workshop on Boolean Problems, Freiberg, September 2002, pp. 47–52.

33 De Vos, A. and Storme, L. (2004) *All non-linear reversible logic gates are r-universal*. Proceedings of the 6th International Workshop on Boolean Problems, Freiberg, September 2004, pp. 25–31.

34 De Vos, A. and Storme, L. (2004) r-Universal reversible logic gates. *Journal of Physics A: Mathematical and General*, **37**, 5815–5824.

35 De Vos, A., Raa, B., and Storme, L. (2002) Generating the group of reversible logic gates. *Journal of Physics A: Mathematical and General*, **35**, 7063–7078.

36 Miller, D. and Dueck, G. (2003) *Spectral techniques for reversible logic synthesis*. Proceedings of the 6th International Symposium on Representations and Methodology of Future Computing Technologies, Trier, March 2003, pp. 56–62.

37 Thomsen, M. (2009) Design and simulation of a simple reversible microprocessor (M.Sc. thesis). Københavns Universitet, København.

38 Feynman, R. (1985) Quantum mechanical computers. *Optics News*, **11**, 11–20.

39 Feynman, R. (1996) *Feynman Lectures on Computation*, Addison–Wesley Publishing, Reading.

40 Beth, T. and Rötteler, M. (2001) Quantum algorithms: applicable algebra and quantum physics, in *Quantum Information* (eds. Alber, G., Beth, T., Horodecki, M., Horodecki, P., Horodecki, R., Rötteler, M., Weinfurter, H., Werner, R., and Zeilinger, A.), Springer Verlag, Berlin, pp. 96–150.

41 Van Rentergem, Y., De Vos, A., and De Keyser, K. (2007) Six synthesis methods for reversible logic. *Open Systems & Information Dynamics*, **14**, 91–116.

42 Wille, R. and Drechsler, R. (2009) *Effect of BDD optimalization on synthesis of* *reversible and quantum logic*. Proceedings of the Workshop on Reversible Computation, York, March 2009, pp. 33–45.

43 Wille, R. and Drechsler, R. (2009) *BDD-based synthesis of reversible logic for large functions*. Proceedings of the Design Automation Conference, San Francisco, July 2009, pp. 270–275.

44 Maslov, D. and Dueck, G. (2004) Reversible cascades with minimal garbage. *IEEE Transactions on Computer-Aided Design of Integrated Circuits and Systems*, 23, 1497–1509.

45 Van Rentergem, Y., De Vos, A., and De Keyser, K. (2006) *Using group theory in reversible computing*. Proceedings of the IEEE World Congress on Computational Intelligence, Vancouver, July 2006, pp. 8566–8573.

46 Van Rentergem, Y., De Vos, A., and Storme, L. (2005) Implementing an arbitrary reversible logic gate. *Journal of Physics A: Mathematical and General*, 38, 3555–3577.

47 Eastin, B. and Flammia, S. (2008) Q-Circuit tutorial. http://info.phys.unm.edu/Qcircuit/.

48 Denayer, H. (2005) Ontwerp van reversibele digitale schakelingen met behulp van Maitrapoorten (M.Sc. thesis). Universiteit Gent, Gent.

49 Bejan, A. (2000) *Shape and Structure, from Engineering to Nature*, Cambridge University Press, Cambridge.

50 De Vos, A. and Van Rentergem, Y. (2007) Synthesis of reversible logic for nanoelectronic circuits. *International Journal of Circuit Theory and Applications*, 35, 325–341.

51 Van Rentergem, Y. and De Vos, A. (2007) *Synthesis and optimization of reversible circuits*. Proceedings of the Reed–Muller 2007 Workshop, Oslo, May 2007, pp. 67–75.

52 De Vos, A. and Van Rentergem, Y. (2008) Young subgroups for reversible computers. *Advances in Mathematics of Communications*, 2, 183–200.

53 De Vos, A., and Van Rentergem, Y. (2008) *Networks for reversible logic*. Proceedings of the 8th International Workshop on Boolean Problems, Freiberg, September 2008, pp. 41–47.

54 Clos, C. (1953) A study of non-blocking switching networks. *Bell Systems Technical Journal*, 32, 406–424.

55 Hwang, F. (1983) Control algorithms for rearrangeable Clos networks. *IEEE Transactions on Communications*, 31, 952–954.

56 Hui, J. (1990) *Switching and Traffic Theory for Integrated Broadband Networks*, Kluwer Academic Publishers, Boston, pp. 53–138.

57 Chao, J., Jing, Z., and Liew, S. (2003) Matching algorithms for three-stage bufferless Clos network switches. *IEEE Communications Magazine*, 41, 46–54.

58 Jajszczyk, A. (2003) Nonblocking, repackable, and rearrangeable Clos networks: fifty years of the theory evolution. *IEEE Communications Magazine*, 41, 28–33.

59 Maslov, D., Dueck, G., and Miller, D. (2003) *Templates for Toffoli networks synthesis*. Proceedings of the 12th International Workshop on Logic and Synthesis, Laguna Beach, May 2003, pp. 320–325.

60 Maslov, D., Dueck, G., and Miller, D. (2003) *Simplification of Toffoli networks via templates*. Proceedings of the 16th Symposium on Integrated Circuits and System Design, São Paulo, September 2003, pp. 53–58.

61 Maslov, D., Dueck, G., and Miller, D. (2005) Toffoli network synthesis with templates. *IEEE Transactions on Computer-Aided Design of Integrated Circuits and Systems*, 24, 807–817.

62 Maslov, D., Dueck, G., and Miller, D. (2003) *Fredkin/Toffoli templates for reversible logic synthesis*. Proceedings of the International Conference on CAD, San Jose, November 2003, pp. 256–261.

63 Maslov, D., Dueck, G., and Miller, D. (2005) Synthesis of Fredkin–Toffoli reversible networks. *IEEE Transactions on Very Large Scale Integration Systems*, 13, 765–769.

64 Dick, J., Dueck, G., and Maslov, D. (2004) *Toffoli templates with 8 gates*. Proceedings of the 6th International Workshop on Boolean Problems, Freiberg, September 2004, pp. 41–47.

65 Van Rentergem, Y. (2008) Ontwerp van digitale reversibele schakelingen (Ph.D.

thesis). Universiteit Gent, Gent, pp. 153–170.

66 Bruekers, F. and van den Enden, A. (1992) New networks for perfect inversion and perfect reconstruction. *IEEE Journal on Selected Areas in Communications*, **10**, 130–137.

67 Hao, P. and Shi, Q. (2001) Matrix factorizations for reversible integer mapping. *IEEE Transactions on Signal Processing*, **49**, 2314–2324.

68 De Vos, A. and De Baerdemaecker, S. (2010) Decomposition of a linear reversible computer: digital versus analog. *International Journal of Unconventional Computing*, **6**, 239–263.

69 Lo, H. (1998) Quantum cryptology, in *Introduction to Quantum Computation and Information* (eds. Lo, H., Popescu, S., and Spiller, T.), World Scientific, Singapore, pp. 76–119.

70 Yang, G., Hung, W., Song, X., and Perkowski, M. (2005) Majority-based reversible logic gate. *Theoretical Computer Science*, **334**, 259–274.

71 Cuccaro, S., Draper, T., Kutin, S., and Moulton, D. (2005) *A new quantum ripple-carry addition circuit*. Proceedings of the 8th Workshop on Quantum Information Processing, Cambridge, June 2005, arXiv:quant-ph/0410184v1.

72 Skoneczny, M., Van Rentergem, Y., and De Vos, A. (2008) *Reversible Fourier transform chip*. Proceedings of the 15th International Conference on Mixed Design of Integrated Circuits and Systems, Poznań, June 2008, pp. 281–286.

73 De Vos, A. (2002) The expectation value of the entropy of a digital message. *Open Systems & Information Dynamics*, **9**, 97–113.

74 Gershenfeld, N. (1996) Signal entropy and the thermodynamics of computation. *IBM Journal of Research and Development*, **35**, 577–586.

75 Markov, I. (2003) *An introduction to reversible circuits*. Proceedings of the 12th International Workshop on Logic and Synthesis, Laguna Beach, May 2003, pp. 318–319.

76 Frank, M. (2005) *Introduction to reversible computing: motivation, progress, and challenges*. Proceedings of the 2005 Comput-

ing Frontiers Conference, Ischia, May 2005, pp. 385–390.

77 De Vos, A. (2003) *Lossless computing*. Proceedings of the IEEE Workshop on Signal Processing, Poznań, October 2003, pp. 7–14.

78 Hayes, B. (2006) Reverse engineering. *American Scientist*, **94**, 107–111.

79 Landauer, R. (1961) Irreversibility and heat generation in the computational process. *IBM Journal of Research and Development*, **5**, 183–191.

80 Keyes, R. and Landauer, R. (1970) Minimal energy dissipation in logic. *IBM Journal of Research and Development*, **14**, 153–157.

81 Bennett, C. (1973) Logical reversibility of computation. *IBM Journal of Research and Development*, **17**, 525–532.

82 Bennett, C. and Landauer, R. (1985) The fundamental physical limits of computation. *Scientific American*, **253**, 38–46.

83 Landauer, R. (1991) Information is physical. *Physics Today*, **44**, 23–29.

84 Nyíri, B. (1991) On the entropy current. *Journal of Non-equilibrium Thermodynamics*, **16**, 179–186.

85 Callen, H. (1960) *Thermodynamics*, John Wiley & Sons, Inc., New York.

86 De Vos, A. (2008) *Thermodynamics of Solar Energy Conversion*, Wiley-VCH, Weinheim.

87 Chuang, I. and Yamamoto, Y. (1996) *The dual-rail quantum bit and quantum error correction*. Proceedings of the 4th Workshop on Physics and Computation, Boston, November 1996, pp. 82–91.

88 Radhakrishnan, D., Whitaker, S., and Maki, G. (1985) Formal design procedures for pass transistor switching circuits. *IEEE Journal of Solid-State Circuits*, **20**, 531–536.

89 Shandrakasan, A., Sheng, S., and Brodersen, R. (1992) Low-power CMOS digital design. *IEEE Journal of Solid-State Circuits*, **27**, 473–484.

90 Zimmermann, R. and Fichtner, W. (1997) Low-power logic styles: CMOS versus pass-transistor logic. *IEEE Journal of Solid-State Circuits*, **32**, 1079–1090.

91 Alioto, M. and Palumbo, G. (2002) Analysis and comparison on full adder block in submicron technology. *IEEE Trans-*

actions on Very Large Scale Integration Systems, **10**, 806–823.

92 Nikolaidis, S. and Nikolaidis, T. (2007) Analysing the operation of the basic pass transistor structure. *International Journal of Circuit Theory and Applications*, **35**, 1–15.

93 Singh, M., Giacomotto, C., Zeydel, B., and Oklobdzija, V. (2007) *Logic style comparison for ultra low power operation in 65 nm technology*. Proceedings of the 17th International Workshop PATMOS, Göteborg, September 2007, pp. 181–190.

94 Desoete, B., De Vos, A., Sibiński, M., and Widerski, T. (1999) *Feynman's reversible logic gates, implemented in silicon*. Proceedings of the 6th International Conference on Mixed Design of Integrated Circuits and Systems, Kraków, June 1999, pp. 497–502.

95 Desoete, B. and De Vos, A. (2002) A reversible carry-look-ahead adder using control gates. *Integration, the VLSI Journal*, **33**, 89–104.

96 De Vos, A. and Beunis, F. (2003) *Optimizing reversible chips*. Proceedings of the 10th International Conference on Mixed Design of Integrated Circuits and Systems, Łódź, June 2003, pp. 263–267.

97 Van Rentergem, Y. and De Vos, A. (2005) Optimal design of a reversible full adder. *International Journal of Unconventional Computing*, **1**, 339–355.

98 Moore, G. (1965) Cramming more components onto integrated circuits. *Electronics*, **38**, 114–117.

99 Bohr, M., Chau, R., Ghani, T., and Mistry, K. (2007) The high-*k* solution. *IEEE Spectrum*, **44**, 23–29.

100 De Vos, A. and Van Rentergem, Y. (2005) *Energy dissipation in reversible logic addressed by a ramp voltage*. Proceedings of the 15th International Workshop PATMOS, Leuven, September 2005, pp. 207–216.

101 Zeitzoff, P. and Chung, J. (2005) A perspective from the 2003 ITRS. *IEEE Circuits & Systems Magazine*, **21**, 4–15.

102 Patra, P. and Fussell, D. (1996) *On efficient adiabatic design of MOS circuits*. Proceedings of the 4th Workshop on Physics and Computation, Boston, November 1996, pp. 260–269.

103 Belleville, M. and Faynot, O. (2001) *Low-power SOI design*. Proceedings of the 11th International Workshop PATMOS, Yverdon, September 2001, pp. 8.1.1–8.1.10.

104 Nagaya, M. (2003) Fully-depleted type SOI device enabling an ultra low-power solar radio wristwatch. *OKI Technical Review*, **70**, 48–51.

105 Mead, C. and Conway, L. (1980) *Introduction to VLSI Systems*, Addison-Wesley, Reading, pp. 333–371.

106 van der Meer, P., van Staveren, A., and van Roermund, A. (2004) *Low-Power Deep Sub-Micron CMOS Logic*, Kluwer, Boston.

107 Desoete, B. and De Vos, A. (1998) *Optimal charging of capacitors*. Proceedings of the 8th International Workshop PATMOS, Lyngby, October 1998, pp. 335–344.

108 De Vos, A. and Desoete, B. (2000) Equipartition principles in finite-time thermodynamics. *Journal of Nonequilibrium Thermodynamics*, **25**, 1–13.

109 Svensson, L. (1999) *Energy-recovery CMOS in the deep-submicron domain*. Proceedings of the 9th International Workshop PATMOS, Kos, October 1999, pp. 83–92.

110 Schlaffer, A. and Nossek, J. (1999) *Register design for adiabatic circuits*. Proceedings of the 9th International Workshop PATMOS, Kos, October 1999, pp. 103–111.

111 De Vos, A. and Desoete, B. (1999) Optimal thermodynamic processes in finite time, in *Advanced Finite-Time Thermodynamics* (ed. C. Wu), Nova Science Publishing, Middletown, pp. 249–272.

112 Elgerd, O. (1967) *Control System Theory*, McGraw–Hill Book Company, New York, pp. 446–456.

113 Paul, S. (1997) *Optimal charging capacitors*. Proceedings of the European Conference on Circuit Theory and Design, Budapest, September 1997, pp. 918–922.

114 Athas, W., Svensson, L., Koller, J., Tzartzanis, N., and Chou, E. (1994) Low-power digital systems based on adiabatic-switching principles. *IEEE Transactions on VLSI Systems*, **2**, 398–407.

115 Meindl, J. (1995) Low power micro-electronics: retrospect and prospect. *Proceedings of the IEEE*, **83**, 619–635.

116 Van Rentergem, Y. and De Vos, A. (2005) *Reversible full adders applying Fredkin gates*. Proceedings of the 12th International Conference on Mixed Design of Integrated Circuits and Systems, Kraków, June 2005, pp. 179–184.

117 Athas, W., Tzartzanis, N., Svensson, L., and Peterson, L. (1997) A low-power microprocessor based on resonant energy. *IEEE Journal of Solid-State Circuits*, **32**, 1693–1701.

118 Critchlow, D. (1999) MOSFET scaling – the driver of VLSI technology, *Proceedings of the IEEE*, **87**, 659–667.

119 Mead, C. (2002) Scaling of MOS technology to submicron feature sizes, in *Analog VLSI: Circuits and Principles* (eds. Liu, S., Kramer, J., Bergemont, G., Delbrück, T., and Douglas, R.), MIT Press, Cambridge, pp. 385–406.

120 Jackson, A. (1960) *Analog Computation*, McGraw–Hill Book Company, New York.

121 Mead, C. (1989) *Analog VLSI and Neural Systems*, Addison–Wesley Publishing, Reading.

122 Mead, C. and Ismail, M. (1989) *Analog VLSI Implementation of Neural Systems*, Kluwer, Boston.

123 Gilmore, R. (1974) *Lie Groups, Lie Algebras and Some of Their Applications*, John Wiley & Sons, Inc., New York.

124 Bullock, S. and Markov, I. (2003) An arbitrary two-qubit computation in 23 elementary gates. *Physical Review A*, **68**, 12318–12325.

125 Cybenko, G. (2001) Reducing quantum computations to elementary unitary operations. *Computing in Science & Engineering*, **3**, 27–32.

126 Geiger, R. and Schuller, G. (2002) *Integer low delay and MDCT filter banks*. 36th Asilomar Conference on Signals, Systems, and Computers, Pacific Grove, November 2002, pp. 811–815.

127 Geiger, R., Yokotani, Y., and Schuller, G. (2003) *Improved integer transforms for lossless audio coding*. 37th Asilomar Conference on Signals, Systems, and Computers, Pacific Grove, November 2003, pp. 2119–2123.

128 Oraintara, S., Chen, Y., and Nguyen, T. (2002) Integer fast Fourier transform. *IEEE Transactions on Signal Processing*, **50**, 607–618.

129 Daubechies, I. and Sweldens, W. (1997) Factoring wavelet transforms into lifting steps. *Journal of Fourier Analysis and Applications*, **4**, 247–269.

130 Buneman, O. (1973) Inversion of the Helmholtz (or Laplace–Poisson) operator for slab geometry. *Journal of Computational Physics*, **12**, 124–130.

131 Wikimedia Foundation (2010) CIE 1931 color space. http://en.wikipedia.org/wiki/CIE_1931_color_space.

132 Adams, M., Kossentini, F., and Ward, R. (2002) Generalized S transform. *IEEE Transactions on Signal Processing*, **50**, 2831–2842.

133 Li, J. (2004) *Reversible FFT and MDCT via matrix lifting*. Proceedings of the IEEE International Conference on Acoustics, Speech, and Signal Processing, Montreal, May 2004, pp. IV173–IV176.

134 Axelsen, H., Glück, R., and Yokoyama, T. (2007) Reversible machine code and its abstract processor architecture, in *Computer Science – Theory and Application*, Vol. 4649 (eds. Diekert, V., Volkov, M., and Voronkov, A.), Springer Verlag, Berlin, pp. 56–69.

135 Nussbaumer, H. (1981) *Fast Fourier Transform and Convolution Algorithms*, Springer Verlag, Berlin, pp. 81–111.

136 Wikimedia Foundation (2010) Discrete Fourier transform. http://en.wikipedia.org/wiki/Discrete_Fourier_transform.

137 Vargas-Rubio, J. and Santhanam, B. (2005) On the multiangle centered discrete fractional Fourier transform. *IEEE Signal Processing Letters*, **12**, 273–276.

138 Penrose, R. (2004) *The Road to Reality – A Complete Guide to the Laws of the Universe*, Vintage Books, London, pp. 378–380.

139 Malvar, H., Hallapuro, A., Karczewicz, M., and Kerofsky, L. (2003) Low-complexity transform and quantization in H.264/AVC. *IEEE Transactions on Circuits and Systems for Video Technology*, **13**, 598–603.

140 Wien, M. (2003) Variable block-size transforms for H.264/AVC. *IEEE Transactions on Circuits and Systems for Video Technology*, **13**, 604–613.

141 Fan, C. and Su, G. (2009) Efficient fast 1-D 8 × 8 inverse integer transform for VC-1 application. *IEEE Transactions on Circuits and Systems for Video Technology*, **19**, 584–590.

142 Fan, C. and Su, G. (2009) Fast algorithm and low-cost hardware-sharing design of multiple integer transforms for VC-1. *IEEE Transactions on Circuits and Systems – II: Express Briefs*, **56**, 788–792.

143 Bartee, T. (1960) *Digital Computer Fundamentals*, McGraw–Hill Book Company, New York, pp. 166–170.

144 Steane, A. (1998) Quantum error correction, in *Introduction to Quantum Computation and Information* (eds. Lo, H., Popescu, S., and Spiller, T.), World Scientific, Singapore, pp. 184–212.

145 Preskill, J. (1998) Fault-tolerant quantum computation, in *Introduction to Quantum Computation and Information* (eds. Lo, H., Popescu, S., and Spiller, T.), World Scientific, Singapore, pp. 213–269.

146 Berman, G., Doolen, G., Mainieri, R., and Tsifrinovich, V. (1998) *Introduction to Quantum Computers*, World Scientific, Singapore.

147 Yanofsky, N. and Mannucci, M. (2008) *Quantum Computing for Computer Scientists*, Cambridge University Press, Cambridge.

148 Stolze, J. and Suter, D. (2008) *Quantum Computing*, Wiley-VCH, Berlin.

149 McMahon, D. (2008) *Quantum Computing Explained*, John Wiley & Sons, Inc., New York.

150 Nielsen, M. and Chuang, I. (2000) *Quantum Computations and Quantum Information*, Cambridge University Press, Cambridge.

151 De Vos, A., Boes, M., and De Baerdemacker, S. (2010) *Reversible computation, quantum computation, and computer architectures in between*. Proceedings of the 2nd Workshop on Reversible Computation, Bremen, July 2010, pp. 75–81.

152 Brualdi, R. (1988) Some applications of doubly stochastic matrices. *Linear Algebra and its Applications*, **107**, 77–100.

153 de Groot, S. and Mazur, P. (1984) *Non-equilibrium Thermodynamics*, Dover Publications, New York, pp. 213–221.

154 Prigogine, I. (1980) *From Being to Becoming: Time and Complexity in Physical Sciences*, Freeman, San Francisco, p. 135.

155 Everett, C. and Stein, P. (1971) The asymptotic number of integer stochastic matrices. *Discrete Mathematics*, **1**, 55–72.

156 Barenco, A., Bennett, C., Cleve, R., DiVincenzo, D., Margolus, N., Shor, S., Sleator, T., Smolin, J., and Weinfurter, H. (1995) Elementary gates for quantum computing. *Physical Review C*, **52**, 3457–3467.

157 Wille, R., Saeedi, M., and Drechsler, R. (2009) *Synthesis of reversible functions beyond gate count and quantum cost*. Proceedings of the 18th International Workshop on Logic and Synthesis, Berkeley, July 2009, pp. 43–49.

158 Kamara, S. (2001) Quantum information theory. http://research.microsoft.com/en-us/um/people/senyk/pubs/qit.pdf.

159 Fowler, M. (2007) The density matrix. http://galileo.phys.virginia.edu/classes/752.mf1i.spring03/DensityMatrix.htm.

160 Kak, S. (2007) Quantum information and entropy. *International Journal of Theoretical Physics*, **46**, 860–876.

161 Möttönen, M., Vartiainen, J., Bergholm, V., and Salomaa, M. (2004) Quantum circuits for general multi-qubit gates. *Physical Review Letters*, **93**, 130502.

162 Bergholm, V., Vartiainen, J., Möttönen, M., and Salomaa, M. (2005) Quantum circuits with uniformly controlled one-qubit gates. *Physical Review A*, **71**, 052330.

163 Bhatia, R. (1997) *Matrix Analysis*, Springer, New York.

164 Khan, F. and Perkowski, M. (2005) *Synthesis of ternary quantum logic circuits by decomposition*. Proceedings of the 7th International Symposium on Representations and Methodology of Future Computing Technologies, Tokyo, September 2005, pp. 114–118.

165 Shende, V., Bullock, S., and Markov, I. (2006) Synthesis of quantum-logic circuits. *IEEE Transactions on Computer-Aided Design of Integrated Circuits and Systems*, **25**, 1000–1010.

166 Deutsch, D. (1992) Quantum computation. *Physics World*, **5**, 57–61.

167 Deutsch, D., Ekert, A., and Lupacchini, R. (2000) Machines, logic and quantum physics. *The Bulletin of Symbolic Logic*, **3**, 265–283.

168 Galindo, A. and Martín-Delgado, M. (2002) Information and computation: classical and quantum aspects. *Review of Modern Physics*, **74**, 347–423.

169 Miller, D. (2008) *Decision diagram techniques for reversible and quantum circuits.* Proceedings of the 8th International Workshop on Boolean Problems, Freiberg, September 2008, pp. 1–15.

170 De Vos, A., De Beule, J., and Storme, L. (2009) Computing with the square root of NOT. *Serdica Journal of Computing*, **3**, 359–370.

171 Conway, J., Dietrich, H., and O'Brien, E. (2008) Counting groups: gnus, moas, and other exotica. *The Mathematical Intelligencer*, **30**, 6–15.

172 Barenco, A. (1998) Quantum computation: an introduction, in *Introduction to Quantum Computation and Information* (eds. Lo, H., Popescu, S., and Spiller, T.), World Scientific, Singapore, pp. 143–183.

173 Vedral, V. (2006) *Introduction to Quantum Information Science*, Oxford University Press, Oxford, pp. 142–144.

174 Moore, C. and Nilsson, M. (1998) Some notes on parallel quantum computation. arXiv:quant-ph/9804034v2.

175 Tucci, R. (2005) Replacing two controlled-U's with two CNOTs. arXiv: quant-ph/0509111v1.

176 Ashenhurst, R. (1965) On reversible subroutines and computers that run backwards. *Communications of the ASM*, **8**, 557–558 and 578.

177 Lutz, C. and Derby, H. (1982) Janus: a time-reversible language (unpublished report). California Institute of Technology, Pasadena.

178 Yokoyama, T., Axelsen, H., and Glück, R. (2008) Reversible flowchart languages and the structured reversible program theorem, in *Automata, Languages and Programming* (eds. Aceto, L., Damgård, I., Goldberg, L., Halldórssen, M., Ingólfsdóttir, A., and Walukiewicz, I.). *Lecture Notes in Computer Science*, Vol. 5126, Springer Verlag, Berlin, pp. 258–270.

179 Yokoyama, T. (2009) *Reversible computation and reversible programming languages.* Proceedings of the Workshop on Reversible Computation, York, March 2009, p. 17.

180 Stoddart, B., Lynas, R., and Zeyda, F. (2009) *A reversible virtual machine.* Proceedings of the Workshop on Reversible Computation, York, March 2009, pp. 18–32.

181 Glushkov, V. (1966) *Introduction to Cybernetics*, Academic Press, New York, pp. 39–66.

182 Mukhopadhyay, A. (1971) Complete sets of logic primitives, in *Recent Developments in Switching Theory* (ed. Mukhopadhyay, A.), Academic Press, New York, pp. 1–26.

183 Even, S., Kohavi, I., and Paz, A. (1967) On minimal modulo 2 sums of products for switching functions. *IEEE Transactions on Electronic Computers*, **16**, 671–674.

184 Yong, A. (2007) What is …a Young tableau? *Notices of the AMS*, **54**, 240–241.

185 Birkhoff, G. (1946) Tres observaciones sobre el algebra lineal. *Universidad Nacional de Tucuman: Revista Matematicas y Fisica Teorica*, **5**, 147–151.

186 Borgersen, R. (2004) Equivalence of seven major theorems in combinatorics. http://robertborgersen.info/Presentations/GS-05R-1.pdf.

187 de Werra, D. (2005) Path coloring in bipartite graphs. *European Journal of Operational Research*, **164**, 575–584.

188 Comtet, L. (1974) *Advanced Combinatorics*, Reidel Publishing Company, Dordrecht, pp. 124–125.

189 Carpinelli, J. and Oruç, A. (1993) A non-backtracking matrix decomposition algorithm for routing on Clos networks. *IEEE Transactions on Communications*, **41**, 1245–1251.

190 Cole, R., Ost, K., and Schirra, S. (2001) Edge-coloring bipartite multigraphs in $O(E \log D)$ time. *Combinatoria*, **21**, 5–12.

191 Paredes, S. and Hall, T. (2005) Flexible bandwidth provision and scheduling in a packet switch with an optical core. *OSA Journal of Optical Networking*, **4**, 260–270.

192 Peng, C., Bochmann, G., and Hall, T. (2006) *Quick Birkhoff–von Neumann decomposition algorithm for agile all-photonic network cores.* Proceedings of the 2006 IEEE International Conference on Communications, Istanbul, June 2006.

193 Landsberg, P. (1978) *Thermodynamics and Statistical Mechanics*, Oxford University Press, Oxford, pp. 146–147.

194 Ebeling, W. and Volkenstein, M. (1990) Entropy and the evolution of biological information. *Physica A*, **163**, 398–402.

195 Ebeling, W. (1992) On the relation between various entropy concepts and the valoric interpretation. *Physica A*, **182**, 108–120.

196 Ebeling, W. (1993) Entropy and information in processes of self-organization: uncertainty and predictability. *Physica A*, **194**, 563–575.

197 Shannon, C. (1948) A mathematical theory of communication. *Bell Systems Technical Journal*, **27**, 379–423.

198 Elgerd, O. (1967) *Control Systems Theory*, McGraw–Hill Book Company, New York, pp. 384–411.

199 Jahnel, J. (2004) When is the (co)sine of a rational angle equal to a rational number? http://www.uni-math.gwdg.de/jahnel/linkstopapers.html.

200 Calcut, J. (2008) Rationality and the tangent function. http://www.ma.utexas.edu/users/jack/tanpap.pdf.

Solutions to the Exercises

Solutions for Chapter 1

Exercise 1.1

Each of these six functions are symmetric with respect to their two arguments. Therefore, if they are injective in their first argument, they are also injective in their second argument; if they are noninjective in their first argument, they are also noninjective in their second argument.

Exercise 1.2

Only the functions $f_3(A, B) = A$ and $f_{12}(A, B) = \overline{A}$ are simultaneously injective in A and noninjective in B. Indeed,

- $f_3(A, 0) = f_3(A', 0)$ implies $A = A'$,
- $f_3(A, 1) = f_3(A', 1)$ implies $A = A'$,
- $f_3(0, B) = f_3(0, B')$ does not imply $B = B'$, and
- $f_3(1, B) = f_3(1, B')$ does not imply $B = B'$

and analogously,

- $f_{12}(A, 0) = f_{12}(A', 0)$ implies $A = A'$,
- $f_{12}(A, 1) = f_{12}(A', 1)$ implies $A = A'$,
- $f_{12}(0, B) = f_{12}(0, B')$ does not imply $B = B'$, and
- $f_{12}(1, B) = f_{12}(1, B')$ does not imply $B = B'$.

The functions f_0, f_1, f_2, f_4, f_5, f_7, f_8, f_{10}, f_{11}, f_{13}, f_{14}, and f_{15} are not injective in A. The functions f_6 and f_9 are injective in A as well as in B.

Exercise 1.3

In general, we have $X + Y = X \oplus Y \oplus XY$. If both X and Y are minterms, then $XY = 0$ and thus $X + Y = X \oplus Y$.

Reversible Computing. Alexis De Vos
Copyright © 2010 WILEY-VCH Verlag GmbH & Co. KGaA, Weinheim
ISBN: 978-3-527-40992-1

Exercise 1.4

$$f(A, B, C) = \overline{A}\,\overline{B}C + \overline{A}B\overline{C} + A\overline{B}\,\overline{C} + AB\overline{C}$$
$$= \overline{A}\,\overline{B}C \oplus \overline{A}B\overline{C} \oplus A\overline{B}\,\overline{C} \oplus AB\overline{C} \quad \text{(see previous exercise)}$$
$$= (1 \oplus A)(1 \oplus B)C \oplus (1 \oplus A)B(1 \oplus C) \oplus A(1 \oplus B)(1 \oplus C)$$
$$\oplus\, AB(1 \oplus C)$$
$$= (C \oplus BC \oplus AC \oplus ABC) \oplus (B \oplus BC \oplus AB \oplus ABC)$$
$$\oplus\, (A \oplus AC \oplus AB \oplus ABC) \oplus (AB \oplus ABC)$$
$$= C \oplus BC \oplus AC \oplus ABC \oplus B \oplus BC \oplus AB \oplus ABC$$
$$\oplus\, A \oplus AC \oplus AB \oplus ABC \oplus AB \oplus ABC$$
$$= A \oplus B \oplus C \oplus AB\,.$$

Exercise 1.5

$$X \odot Y \odot (X + Y) = (X \odot Y) \odot (X + Y)$$
$$= 1 \oplus (X \odot Y) \oplus (X + Y)$$
$$= 1 \oplus (1 \oplus X \oplus Y) \oplus (X \oplus Y \oplus XY)$$
$$= 1 \oplus 1 \oplus X \oplus Y \oplus X \oplus Y \oplus XY$$
$$= XY\,.$$

Exercise 1.6

Let us assume that the number of 1s in the truth table of f equals φ, and that the number of 1s in the truth table of g equals γ. The number of 1s in the truth table of $f \oplus g$ then equals $\varphi + \gamma - 2\delta$. Here δ denotes the number of rows in the truth tables where both f and g have a 1. In other words, δ is the number of common minterms in the minterm expansions of f and g. We now find that

- If both φ and γ are even, then $\varphi + \gamma - 2\delta$ is also even;
- If both φ and γ are odd, then $\varphi + \gamma - 2\delta$ is even;
- If φ is even and γ is odd, then $\varphi + \gamma - 2\delta$ is odd.

Exercise 1.7

Any Reed–Muller monomial with a degree smaller than n (i.e., $A_1, A_2, \ldots$, and $A_2 A_3 \ldots A_n$) has a truth table with an even number of 1s, and is thus an even function. Only the piterm $A_1 A_2 \ldots A_n$ displays an odd number (i.e., $2^n - 1$) of 0s and an odd number (i.e., 1) of 1s, and is thus an odd function.

Because of the previous exercise, we can conclude that

- A function with a Reed–Muller expansion lacking the piterm $A_1 A_2 \ldots A_n$ is even;
- A function with a Reed–Muller expansion containing the piterm $A_1 A_2 \ldots A_n$ is odd.

Because a balanced function is a special type of even function, it lacks the piterm $A_1 A_2 \ldots A_n$.

As an illustration: the balanced functions in Table 1.2 have the following minterm expansions and Reed–Muller expansions:

$$f_3 = A\overline{B} \oplus AB = A$$
$$f_5 = \overline{A}B \oplus AB = B$$
$$f_6 = \overline{A}B \oplus A\overline{B} = A \oplus B$$
$$f_9 = \overline{A}\,\overline{B} \oplus AB = 1 \oplus A \oplus B$$
$$f_{10} = \overline{A}\,\overline{B} \oplus A\overline{B} = 1 \oplus B$$
$$f_{12} = \overline{A}\,\overline{B} \oplus \overline{A}B = 1 \oplus A \ .$$

They do indeed all lack the term AB in the Reed–Muller expansion.

The following functions $f(A, B)$ lack the Reed–Muller term AB but are not balanced:

$$f_0 = 0$$
$$f_{15} = 1 \ .$$

Exercise 1.8

$$f_2(A, B) = A\overline{B}$$
$$= (\overline{A} + \overline{B})(\overline{A} + B)(A + B)$$
$$= A \oplus AB$$
$$= A\overline{B} \ .$$

Exercise 1.9

$$f = f'\overline{A}_j + f''A_j$$
$$= f'\overline{A}_j \oplus f''A_j$$
$$= f'(1 \oplus A_j) \oplus f''A_j$$
$$= f' \oplus f'A_j \oplus f''A_j$$
$$= f' \oplus (f' \oplus f'')A_j \ .$$

Solutions for Chapter 2

Exercise 2.1

Because $a \, \Omega \, i_1 = a$ is valid for all a, it is in particular valid for i_2:

$$i_2 \, \Omega \, i_1 = i_2 \, .$$

Because $i_2 \, \Omega \, a = a$ is valid for all a, it is in particular valid for i_1:

$$i_2 \, \Omega \, i_1 = i_1 \, .$$

Combining these two results, we find that $i_2 = i_1$.

Exercise 2.2

Because $a \, \Omega \, i_1 = a$ is valid for all a, it is in particular valid for i_2:

$$i_2 \, \Omega \, i_1 = i_2 \, .$$

Because $a \, \Omega \, i_2 = a$ is valid for all a, it is in particular valid for i_1:

$$i_1 \, \Omega \, i_2 = i_1 \, .$$

Because of Exercise 2.1, we have $i_2 \, \Omega \, i_1 = i_1 \, \Omega \, i_2$. Combining the three results together yields $i_2 = i_1$.

Exercise 2.3

If $a \, \Omega \, (a^{-1})_1 = i$ and $(a^{-1})_2 \, \Omega \, a = i$, then, by multiplying the latter equation by $(a^{-1})_1$ to the right, we find that

$$(a^{-1})_2 \, \Omega \, a \, \Omega \, (a^{-1})_1 = (a^{-1})_1 \, .$$

Now we apply the former equation in order to simplify the left-hand side of this result, yielding $(a^{-1})_2 = (a^{-1})_1$.

Exercise 2.4

We assume both $a \, \Omega \, (a^{-1})_1 = i$ and $a \, \Omega \, (a^{-1})_2 = i$. We multiply the former assumption by $(a^{-1})_2$ to the left and find that

$$(a^{-1})_2 \, \Omega \, a \, \Omega \, (a^{-1})_1 = (a^{-1})_2 \, . \tag{J1}$$

Because of Exercise 2.3, the latter assumption yields $(a^{-1})_2 \, \Omega \, a = i$. Therefore, result (J1) simplifies to

$$(a^{-1})_1 = (a^{-1})_2 \, .$$

Exercise 2.5

$$()^{-1} = ()$$
$$(1,2)^{-1} = (1,2)$$
$$(1,3)^{-1} = (1,3)$$
$$(2,3)^{-1} = (2,3)$$
$$(1,2,3)^{-1} = (1,3,2) \quad \text{and}$$
$$(1,3,2)^{-1} = (1,2,3) \ .$$

$$\begin{pmatrix} 1 & 0 \\ 0 & 1 \end{pmatrix}^{-1} = \begin{pmatrix} 1 & 0 \\ 0 & 1 \end{pmatrix}$$

$$\begin{pmatrix} 1/2 & -\sqrt{3}/2 \\ -\sqrt{3}/2 & -1/2 \end{pmatrix}^{-1} = \begin{pmatrix} 1/2 & -\sqrt{3}/2 \\ -\sqrt{3}/2 & -1/2 \end{pmatrix}$$

$$\begin{pmatrix} 1/2 & \sqrt{3}/2 \\ \sqrt{3}/2 & -1/2 \end{pmatrix}^{-1} = \begin{pmatrix} 1/2 & \sqrt{3}/2 \\ \sqrt{3}/2 & -1/2 \end{pmatrix}$$

$$\begin{pmatrix} -1 & 0 \\ 0 & 1 \end{pmatrix}^{-1} = \begin{pmatrix} -1 & 0 \\ 0 & 1 \end{pmatrix}$$

$$\begin{pmatrix} -1/2 & -\sqrt{3}/2 \\ \sqrt{3}/2 & -1/2 \end{pmatrix}^{-1} = \begin{pmatrix} -1/2 & \sqrt{3}/2 \\ -\sqrt{3}/2 & -1/2 \end{pmatrix} \quad \text{and}$$

$$\begin{pmatrix} -1/2 & \sqrt{3}/2 \\ -\sqrt{3}/2 & -1/2 \end{pmatrix}^{-1} = \begin{pmatrix} -1/2 & -\sqrt{3}/2 \\ \sqrt{3}/2 & -1/2 \end{pmatrix} \ .$$

$$\begin{pmatrix} 1 & 0 & 0 \\ 0 & 1 & 0 \\ 0 & 0 & 1 \end{pmatrix}^{-1} = \begin{pmatrix} 1 & 0 & 0 \\ 0 & 1 & 0 \\ 0 & 0 & 1 \end{pmatrix}$$

$$\begin{pmatrix} 0 & 1 & 0 \\ 1 & 0 & 0 \\ 0 & 0 & 1 \end{pmatrix}^{-1} = \begin{pmatrix} 0 & 1 & 0 \\ 1 & 0 & 0 \\ 0 & 0 & 1 \end{pmatrix}$$

$$\begin{pmatrix} 0 & 0 & 1 \\ 0 & 1 & 0 \\ 1 & 0 & 0 \end{pmatrix}^{-1} = \begin{pmatrix} 0 & 0 & 1 \\ 0 & 1 & 0 \\ 1 & 0 & 0 \end{pmatrix}$$

$$\begin{pmatrix} 1 & 0 & 0 \\ 0 & 0 & 1 \\ 0 & 1 & 0 \end{pmatrix}^{-1} = \begin{pmatrix} 1 & 0 & 0 \\ 0 & 0 & 1 \\ 0 & 1 & 0 \end{pmatrix}$$

$$\begin{pmatrix} 0 & 1 & 0 \\ 0 & 0 & 1 \\ 1 & 0 & 0 \end{pmatrix}^{-1} = \begin{pmatrix} 0 & 0 & 1 \\ 1 & 0 & 0 \\ 0 & 1 & 0 \end{pmatrix} \quad \text{and}$$

$$\begin{pmatrix} 0 & 0 & 1 \\ 1 & 0 & 0 \\ 0 & 1 & 0 \end{pmatrix}^{-1} = \begin{pmatrix} 0 & 1 & 0 \\ 0 & 0 & 1 \\ 1 & 0 & 0 \end{pmatrix} \ .$$

Exercise 2.6

$$\text{Order}(()) = 1$$
$$\text{Order}((1,2)) = 2$$
$$\text{Order}((1,3)) = 2$$
$$\text{Order}((2,3)) = 2$$
$$\text{Order}((1,2,3)) = 3 \quad \text{and}$$
$$\text{Order}((1,3,2)) = 3 \ .$$

Exercise 2.7

It is sufficient to observe that there is no identity element within the set of derangements.

Exercise 2.8

$(1,2)*(2,3)=(1,3,2)$, whereas $(2,3)*(1,2)=(1,2,3)$.

Solutions for Chapter 3

Exercise 3.1

$$\begin{pmatrix} 0 & 1 & 0 \\ 1 & 0 & 0 \\ 0 & 0 & 1 \end{pmatrix} \left[\begin{pmatrix} 1 \\ 0 \\ 0 \end{pmatrix} \oplus \begin{pmatrix} A \\ B \\ C \end{pmatrix} \right] = \begin{pmatrix} 0 & 1 & 0 \\ 1 & 0 & 0 \\ 0 & 0 & 1 \end{pmatrix} \begin{pmatrix} 1 \\ 0 \\ 0 \end{pmatrix} \oplus \begin{pmatrix} 0 & 1 & 0 \\ 1 & 0 & 0 \\ 0 & 0 & 1 \end{pmatrix} \begin{pmatrix} A \\ B \\ C \end{pmatrix}$$

$$= \begin{pmatrix} 0 \\ 1 \\ 0 \end{pmatrix} \oplus \begin{pmatrix} 0 & 1 & 0 \\ 1 & 0 & 0 \\ 0 & 0 & 1 \end{pmatrix} \begin{pmatrix} A \\ B \\ C \end{pmatrix} \ .$$

Exercise 3.2

A TOFFOLI gate is conservative but not linear.

A FREDKIN gate is conservative but not linear.

Exercise 3.3

$\text{Order}(\mathbf{A}) = 2^w$

$$
\begin{array}{c}
\textbf{L} \\
\supset \qquad \supset \\
\textbf{R} \quad \supset \quad \textbf{AL} \qquad\qquad \textbf{E} \\
\supset \qquad \supset \qquad \supset \\
\textbf{AE} \qquad\qquad \textbf{I} \\
\supset \qquad \supset \\
\textbf{A}
\end{array}
$$

Exercise 3.4

No. Consider an example. We choose $n = 3$ and thus consider $\mathbf{S}_3$. Exercise 2.8 provides an example: $(1,2)*(2,3)=(1,3,2)$, where both $(1,2)$ and $(2,3)$ are involutions, but $(1,3,2)$ is not.

Exercise 3.5

The TOFFOLI gates do *not* form a subgroup of the group of controlled NOTs. In order to demonstrate this, let's take a closer look at, for example, two TOFFOLI gates of width 5, both of which have the fifth wire as a controlled wire. The former gate has the control function $f_1(A_1, A_2, A_3, A_4) = A_1 A_2$ and the latter gate has the control function $f_2(A_1, A_2, A_3, A_4) = A_3 \overline{A_4}$. The cascade of these two gates is a controlled NOT with the control function $f_1 \oplus f_2 = A_3 \oplus A_1 A_2 \oplus A_3 A_4$. This function is *not* an AND function. Thus, the cascade of two TOFFOLIs is not necessarily a TOFFOLI. Therefore, the TOFFOLI gates do not form a group. They may be regarded as generators of a group. Indeed, they generate the group of controlled NOTs.

Exercise 3.6

$\text{Index} = \frac{2^{2^w}-1}{2^{2^{w-1}}} = 2^{2^w - 2^{w-1} - 1} = 2^{2^{w-1}-1}.$

Exercise 3.7

$$
\begin{pmatrix} 1 & 0 & 0 & 0 \\ 0 & 0 & 0 & 1 \\ 0 & 0 & 1 & 0 \\ 0 & 1 & 0 & 0 \end{pmatrix}
\begin{pmatrix} 1 & 0 & 0 & 0 \\ 0 & 1 & 0 & 0 \\ 0 & 0 & 0 & 1 \\ 0 & 0 & 1 & 0 \end{pmatrix}
\begin{pmatrix} 1 & 0 & 0 & 0 \\ 0 & 0 & 0 & 1 \\ 0 & 0 & 1 & 0 \\ 0 & 1 & 0 & 0 \end{pmatrix}
=
\begin{pmatrix} 1 & 0 & 0 & 0 \\ 0 & 0 & 1 & 0 \\ 0 & 1 & 0 & 0 \\ 0 & 0 & 0 & 1 \end{pmatrix}.
$$

Exercise 3.8

Assume that g is an arbitrary element of **G**. The left coset of g is all of the elements that can be written $h_1 g$ with h_1 in **H**; the right coset of g is all of the elements that can be written $g h_2$ with h_2 in **H**. Because of the Abelian character of **G**, we have $g h_2 = h_2 g$, and so there is a one-to-one relationship between the two sets: $h_2 = h_1$.

The double coset of g is all of the elements that can be written $h_3 g h_4$ with both h_3 and h_4 in **H**. Because **G** is Abelian, we have $h_3 g h_4 = g h_3 h_4$. Because **H** is a group, we have that $h_3 h_4$ is some element h_5 of **H**. Thus, $h_3 g h_4 = g h_5$ belongs to the right coset. Conversely, an element of the right coset, in other words $g h_2$, belongs to the double coset, as $g h_2$ equals $i g h_2$ and the identity obeys $i \in$ **H**.

Exercise 3.9

–

Exercise 3.10

–

Exercise 3.11

Just like the V-configuration, the Λ-configuration consists of three FEYNMAN gates:

$$
\begin{pmatrix} 1 & 0 & 0 & 0 \\ 0 & 1 & 0 & 0 \\ 0 & 0 & 0 & 1 \\ 0 & 0 & 1 & 0 \end{pmatrix}
\begin{pmatrix} 1 & 0 & 0 & 0 \\ 0 & 0 & 0 & 1 \\ 0 & 0 & 1 & 0 \\ 0 & 1 & 0 & 0 \end{pmatrix}
\begin{pmatrix} 1 & 0 & 0 & 0 \\ 0 & 1 & 0 & 0 \\ 0 & 0 & 0 & 1 \\ 0 & 0 & 1 & 0 \end{pmatrix}
=
\begin{pmatrix} 1 & 0 & 0 & 0 \\ 0 & 0 & 1 & 0 \\ 0 & 1 & 0 & 0 \\ 0 & 0 & 0 & 1 \end{pmatrix}.
$$

Exercise 3.12

$\text{Order}(\mathbf{S}_4 \times \mathbf{S}_4) = 4! \times 4! = 24^2 = 576.$

Solutions for Chapter 4

Exercise 4.1

According to Section 3.21, we have two control functions:

$$
f_4(C, B, A) = C B \oplus B A \oplus A C
$$
$$
f_3(C, B) = C \oplus B .
$$

To hardwire, we need a combination of parallel and series connections, and thus a combination of ORs and ANDs. Rewriting the lower equation with ORs and ANDs is a straightforward task:

$$f_3(C, B) = C\overline{B} + B\overline{C} .$$

This expression contains four literals and thus leads to $4 \times 4 = 16$ switches. Rewriting the upper equation with ORs and ANDs gives, for example, the minterm expansion

$$f_3(C, B) = \overline{A}BC + A\overline{B}C + AB\overline{C} + ABC$$

with 12 literals. This suggests $12 \times 4 = 48$ switches. We can, however, do better and cheaper than this by checking that the following Boolean function:

$$A(B + C) + AB \tag{J2}$$

is identical to f_3. Only five literals leads to only $5 \times 4 = 20$ switches, and thus a total of $16 + 20 = 36$. Note that (J2) is neither a POS nor a SOP.

Exercise 4.2

Output G_1 is the result of a FEYNMAN gate. According to (3.12), we have:

$$G_1 = A \oplus B .$$

Output G_2 is the result of a FREDKIN gate. According to (3.13), we have:

$$G_2 = (A \oplus B)(B \oplus C_i) \oplus C_i$$
$$= B \oplus C_i \oplus AB \oplus AC_i \oplus BC_i .$$

Exercise 4.3

If ϵ is constant, then

$$Q \sim LW t^{-1} V_t^2$$

and so

a) Q is divided by $\kappa^1 \kappa^1 \kappa^{-1} \kappa^0 = \kappa^1$,
b) Q is divided by $\kappa^1 \kappa^1 \kappa^{-1} \kappa^2 = \kappa^3$, and
c) Q is divided by $\kappa^1 \kappa^1 \kappa^{-0.77} \kappa^{0.46} = \kappa^{1.69}$.

Exercise 4.4

From the first to second generations:

$$\kappa = 2.4\,\mu\text{m}/0.8\,\mu\text{m} = 3$$

As $38\,\text{fF}/2.0\,\text{fF} = 19 = \kappa^n$, we have $n = \log(19)/\log(3) = 2.7$.

From the second to third generations:

$$\kappa = 0.8\,\mu m/0.35\,\mu m = 16/7$$

As $2.0\,\text{fF}/0.30\,\text{fF} = 20/3 = \kappa^n$, we have $n = \log(20/3)/\log(16/7) = 2.3$. Thus, $n \approx 2.5$, so we are between model (b) and model (c).

Exercise 4.5

From (4.11), we obtain

$$Q\tau = (C V_{dd})^2 R = q^2 \frac{h}{q^2} = h\,.$$

We thus recover the Heisenberg uncertainty limit.

Solutions for Chapter 5

Exercise 5.1

$$\begin{pmatrix} M_{11} & M_{12} \\ M_{21} & M_{22} \end{pmatrix} = \begin{pmatrix} 1 + L_2 L_3 & L_2 \\ S L_1 + S L_3 + S L_1 L_2 L_3 & S + S L_1 L_2 \end{pmatrix}\,.$$

Thus

$$M_{11} = 1 + L_2 L_3 \tag{J3}$$

$$M_{12} = L_2 \tag{J4}$$

$$M_{21} = S L_1 + S L_3 + S L_1 L_2 L_3 \tag{J5}$$

$$M_{22} = S + S L_1 L_2\,. \tag{J6}$$

From (J4), we obtain $L_2 = M_{12}$. Substitution of this result into (J3) yields $L_3 = (M_{11} - 1)/M_{12}$. Rewriting the nonlinear set (J5)–(J6):

$$(S L_1) M_{11} + S(M_{11} - 1)/M_{12} = M_{21}$$
$$(S L_1) M_{12} + S = M_{22}$$

yields a linear set in two unknowns $S L_1$ and S with the solution

$$S L_1 = [M_{22} - (M_{11} M_{22} - M_{12} M_{21})]/M_{12}$$
$$S = M_{11} M_{22} - M_{12} M_{21}\,.$$

Dividing the last two results finally yields

$$L_1 = [M_{22}/(M_{11} M_{22} - M_{12} M_{21}) - 1]/M_{12}\,.$$

Exercise 5.2

If $M_{12} = 0$, then we replace (5.6) by another decomposition:

$$\begin{pmatrix} M_{11} & M_{12} \\ M_{21} & M_{22} \end{pmatrix} = \begin{pmatrix} S & 0 \\ 0 & 1 \end{pmatrix} \begin{pmatrix} 1 & L_1 \\ 0 & 1 \end{pmatrix} \begin{pmatrix} 1 & 0 \\ L_2 & 1 \end{pmatrix} \begin{pmatrix} 1 & L_3 \\ 0 & 1 \end{pmatrix},$$

leading to

$$\begin{pmatrix} M_{11} & M_{12} \\ M_{21} & M_{22} \end{pmatrix} = \begin{pmatrix} S + S L_1 L_2 & S L_1 + S L_3 + S L_1 L_2 L_3 \\ L_2 & 1 + L_2 L_3 \end{pmatrix}$$

and thus

$$M_{11} = S + S L_1 L_2$$
$$M_{12} = S L_1 + S L_3 + S L_1 L_2 L_3$$
$$M_{21} = L_2$$
$$M_{22} = 1 + L_2 L_3 \,.$$

Proceeding in the same way as in the previous exercise, we now find that

$$S = M_{11} M_{22} - M_{12} M_{21}$$
$$L_1 = [M_{11}/(M_{11} M_{22} - M_{12} M_{21}) - 1]/M_{21}$$
$$L_2 = M_{21}$$
$$L_3 = (M_{22} - 1)/M_{21} \,.$$

When $M_{12} = 0$, this simplifies to

$$S = M_{11} M_{22}$$
$$L_1 = (1/M_{22} - 1)/M_{21}$$
$$L_2 = M_{21}$$
$$L_3 = (M_{22} - 1)/M_{21} \,.$$

Because the new decomposition fails when M_{21} equals 0, we still have to find a procedure if $M_{12} = M_{21} = 0$. In that case, we cannot avoid a SWAP gate:

$$\begin{pmatrix} M_{11} & 0 \\ 0 & M_{22} \end{pmatrix} = \begin{pmatrix} 0 & 1 \\ 1 & 0 \end{pmatrix} \begin{pmatrix} 0 & M_{22} \\ M_{11} & 0 \end{pmatrix}.$$

We now can apply (5.6 and 5.7) to the last matrix on the right-hand side, and find the decomposition

$$\begin{pmatrix} 0 & 1 \\ 1 & 0 \end{pmatrix} \begin{pmatrix} 1 & 0 \\ 0 & -M_{11} M_{22} \end{pmatrix} \begin{pmatrix} 1 & 0 \\ -1/M_{22} & 1 \end{pmatrix} \begin{pmatrix} 1 & M_{22} \\ 0 & 1 \end{pmatrix} \begin{pmatrix} 1 & 0 \\ -1/M_{22} & 1 \end{pmatrix}.$$

Exercise 5.3

$$\det(1) = 1$$

$$\det\begin{pmatrix} 1 & 1 \\ 1 & \Omega \end{pmatrix} = \Omega - 1 = -2 \quad (\text{as} \quad \Omega = -1)$$

$$\det\begin{pmatrix} 1 & 1 & 1 \\ 1 & \Omega & \Omega^2 \\ 1 & \Omega^2 & \Omega \end{pmatrix} = 3\Omega(\Omega - 1) = -3\sqrt{3}i \quad \left(\text{as} \quad \Omega = -\frac{1}{2} + i\frac{\sqrt{3}}{2}\right)$$

$$\det\begin{pmatrix} 1 & 1 & 1 & 1 \\ 1 & \Omega & \Omega^2 & \Omega^3 \\ 1 & \Omega^2 & 1 & \Omega^2 \\ 1 & \Omega^3 & \Omega^2 & \Omega \end{pmatrix} = 8\,\Omega(\Omega^2 - 1) = -16i \quad (\text{as} \quad \Omega = i)$$

$\lambda(1) = 1$

$\lambda(2) = -1$

$\lambda(3) = -i$

$\lambda(4) = -i$

Exercise 5.4

The first row sum and the first column sum both equal w. All other line sums equal 0.

Solutions for Chapter 6

Exercise 6.1

The control gate with control function A_0 OR A_1 OR $\ldots$ OR A_{k-1} needs $4k$ switches. The whole circuit thus needs $4 + 8 + \ldots + 4(w - 1) = 4\frac{w(w-1)}{2} = 2w(w - 1)$ switches.

Solutions for Chapter 7

Exercise 7.1

$$\begin{pmatrix} 1 & 0 & 0 & 0 & 0 & 0 & 0 & 0 \\ 0 & 1 & 0 & 0 & 0 & 0 & 0 & 0 \\ 0 & 0 & 1 & 0 & 0 & 0 & 0 & 0 \\ 0 & 0 & 0 & 1 & 0 & 0 & 0 & 0 \\ 0 & 0 & 0 & 0 & \omega & \bar{\omega} & 0 & 0 \\ 0 & 0 & 0 & 0 & \bar{\omega} & \omega & 0 & 0 \\ 0 & 0 & 0 & 0 & 0 & 0 & \omega & \bar{\omega} \\ 0 & 0 & 0 & 0 & 0 & 0 & \bar{\omega} & \omega \end{pmatrix} \begin{pmatrix} 1 & 0 & 0 & 0 & 0 & 0 & 0 & 0 \\ 0 & 1 & 0 & 0 & 0 & 0 & 0 & 0 \\ 0 & 0 & 1 & 0 & 0 & 0 & 0 & 0 \\ 0 & 0 & 0 & 1 & 0 & 0 & 0 & 0 \\ 0 & 0 & 0 & 0 & 0 & 0 & 1 & 0 \\ 0 & 0 & 0 & 0 & 0 & 0 & 0 & 1 \\ 0 & 0 & 0 & 0 & 1 & 0 & 0 & 0 \\ 0 & 0 & 0 & 0 & 0 & 1 & 0 & 0 \end{pmatrix}$$

$$\begin{pmatrix} 1 & 0 & 0 & 0 & 0 & 0 & 0 & 0 \\ 0 & 1 & 0 & 0 & 0 & 0 & 0 & 0 \\ 0 & 0 & \bar{\omega} & \omega & 0 & 0 & 0 & 0 \\ 0 & 0 & \omega & \bar{\omega} & 0 & 0 & 0 & 0 \\ 0 & 0 & 0 & 0 & 1 & 0 & 0 & 0 \\ 0 & 0 & 0 & 0 & 0 & 1 & 0 & 0 \\ 0 & 0 & 0 & 0 & 0 & 0 & \bar{\omega} & \omega \\ 0 & 0 & 0 & 0 & 0 & 0 & \omega & \bar{\omega} \end{pmatrix} \begin{pmatrix} 1 & 0 & 0 & 0 & 0 & 0 & 0 & 0 \\ 0 & 1 & 0 & 0 & 0 & 0 & 0 & 0 \\ 0 & 0 & 1 & 0 & 0 & 0 & 0 & 0 \\ 0 & 0 & 0 & 1 & 0 & 0 & 0 & 0 \\ 0 & 0 & 0 & 0 & 0 & 0 & 1 & 0 \\ 0 & 0 & 0 & 0 & 0 & 0 & 0 & 1 \\ 0 & 0 & 0 & 0 & 1 & 0 & 0 & 0 \\ 0 & 0 & 0 & 0 & 0 & 1 & 0 & 0 \end{pmatrix}$$

$$\begin{pmatrix} 1 & 0 & 0 & 0 & 0 & 0 & 0 & 0 \\ 0 & 1 & 0 & 0 & 0 & 0 & 0 & 0 \\ 0 & 0 & \omega & \bar{\omega} & 0 & 0 & 0 & 0 \\ 0 & 0 & \bar{\omega} & \omega & 0 & 0 & 0 & 0 \\ 0 & 0 & 0 & 0 & 1 & 0 & 0 & 0 \\ 0 & 0 & 0 & 0 & 0 & 1 & 0 & 0 \\ 0 & 0 & 0 & 0 & 0 & 0 & \omega & \bar{\omega} \\ 0 & 0 & 0 & 0 & 0 & 0 & \bar{\omega} & \omega \end{pmatrix} = \begin{pmatrix} 1 & 0 & 0 & 0 & 0 & 0 & 0 & 0 \\ 0 & 1 & 0 & 0 & 0 & 0 & 0 & 0 \\ 0 & 0 & 1 & 0 & 0 & 0 & 0 & 0 \\ 0 & 0 & 0 & 1 & 0 & 0 & 0 & 0 \\ 0 & 0 & 0 & 0 & 1 & 0 & 0 & 0 \\ 0 & 0 & 0 & 0 & 0 & 1 & 0 & 0 \\ 0 & 0 & 0 & 0 & 0 & 0 & 0 & 1 \\ 0 & 0 & 0 & 0 & 0 & 0 & 1 & 0 \end{pmatrix} .$$

Exercise 7.2

From

$$a_1 = b_1 c_1$$
$$a_2 = b_1 c_2$$
$$a_3 = b_2 c_1$$
$$a_4 = b_2 c_2 ,$$

we deduce (by dividing the first equation by the third equation) that

$$\frac{a_1}{a_3} = \frac{b_1}{b_2}$$

and (by dividing the second equation by the fourth equation) that

$$\frac{a_2}{a_4} = \frac{b_1}{b_2} .$$

Therefore, we need

$$\frac{a_1}{a_3} = \frac{a_2}{a_4} ,$$

and thus $a_1 a_4 - a_3 a_2 = 0$.

The condition $a_1 a_4 - a_3 a_2 = 0$ (that is, $a_4 = a_2 a_3 / a_1$) is sufficient, as the set of four equations

$$b_1 c_1 = a_1$$
$$b_1 c_2 = a_2$$
$$b_2 c_1 = a_3$$
$$b_2 c_2 = a_2 a_3 / a_1$$

has the following solution:

$$b_1 = \text{arbitrary}$$
$$b_2 = a_3 b_1 / a_1$$
$$c_1 = a_1 / b_1$$
$$c_2 = a_2 / b_1$$

with properties

$$b_1 \bar{b}_1 + b_2 \bar{b}_2 = \left(1 + \frac{a_3 \bar{a}_3}{a_1 \bar{a}_1}\right) b_1 \bar{b}_1$$
$$c_1 \bar{c}_1 + c_2 \bar{c}_2 = (a_1 \bar{a}_1 + a_2 \bar{a}_2) / b_1 \bar{b}_1 ,$$

such that it is necessary and sufficient that b_1 satisfies both

$$b_1 \bar{b}_1 = a_1 \bar{a}_1 / (a_1 \bar{a}_1 + a_3 \bar{a}_3)$$
$$b_1 \bar{b}_1 = a_1 \bar{a}_1 + a_2 \bar{a}_2 ,$$

meaning that it is necessary and sufficient that

$$(a_1 \bar{a}_1 + a_2 \bar{a}_2)(a_1 \bar{a}_1 + a_3 \bar{a}_3) = a_1 \bar{a}_1 .$$

This condition is fulfilled because

$$a_1 \bar{a}_1 + a_2 \bar{a}_2 + a_3 \bar{a}_3 + \frac{a_3 a_2}{a_1} \frac{\bar{a}_3 \bar{a}_2}{\bar{a}_1} = 1 .$$

Exercise 7.3

The unitarity condition, that is,

$$\begin{pmatrix} a \exp(i\alpha) & b \exp(i\beta) \\ c \exp(i\gamma) & d \exp(i\delta) \end{pmatrix} \begin{pmatrix} a \exp(-i\alpha) & c \exp(-i\gamma) \\ b \exp(-i\beta) & d \exp(-i\delta) \end{pmatrix} = \begin{pmatrix} 1 & 0 \\ 0 & 1 \end{pmatrix} ,$$

leads to

$$a^2 + b^2 = 1 \tag{J7}$$

$$ac \exp(i\alpha - i\gamma) + bd \exp(i\beta - i\delta) = 0 \tag{J8}$$

$$ac \exp(-i\alpha + i\gamma) + bd \exp(-i\beta + i\delta) = 0 \tag{J9}$$

$$c^2 + d^2 = 1 \,, \tag{J10}$$

where we may disregard (J9) as it simply is the complex conjugate of (J8). Equation (J8) leads to $\delta = -\alpha + \beta + \gamma$ and to $ac = bd$. The latter leads to either

- $a = b = 0$, which is forbidden because of (J7), or
- $a = d = 0$, thus yielding $b = c = 1$, or
- $c = bd/a$, which, by substitution into (J10), yields $(a^2 + b^2)d^2 = a^2$, and so (taking into account (J7)) $d^2 = a^2$ and thus $d = a$.

Straightforward computation gives

$$\det \begin{pmatrix} \cos(\theta) \exp(i\alpha) & \sin(\theta) \exp(i\beta) \\ -\sin(\theta) \exp(i\gamma) & \cos(\theta) \exp(-i\alpha + i\beta + i\gamma) \end{pmatrix} = \exp(i\beta + i\gamma) \,.$$

We obtain $\begin{pmatrix} 1 & 0 \\ 0 & 1 \end{pmatrix}$ by imposing $\theta = 0$, $\alpha = 0$, and $\beta + \gamma = 0$;

we obtain $\begin{pmatrix} 0 & 1 \\ 1 & 0 \end{pmatrix}$ by imposing $\theta = \pi/2$, $\beta = 0$, and $\gamma = \pi$.

Exercise 7.4

We apply the decomposition

$$\begin{pmatrix} L_{11} & 0 \\ 0 & L_{22} \end{pmatrix} \begin{pmatrix} \cos(\theta_1) & \sin(\theta_1) \\ -\sin(\theta_1) & \cos(\theta_1) \end{pmatrix} \begin{pmatrix} R_{11} & 0 \\ 0 & R_{22} \end{pmatrix} \,.$$

Straightforward multiplication of these three matrices leads to

$$L_{11} R_{11} \cos(\theta_1) = \cos(\theta) \exp(i\alpha)$$
$$L_{11} R_{22} \sin(\theta_1) = \sin(\theta) \exp(i\beta)$$
$$L_{22} R_{11} \sin(\theta_1) = \sin(\theta) \exp(i\gamma)$$
$$L_{22} R_{22} \cos(\theta_1) = \cos(\theta) \exp(-i\alpha + i\beta + i\gamma) \,.$$

We try $\theta_1 = \theta$:

$$L_{11} R_{11} = \exp(i\alpha)$$
$$L_{11} R_{22} = \exp(i\beta)$$
$$L_{22} R_{11} = \exp(i\gamma)$$
$$L_{22} R_{22} = \exp(-i\alpha + i\beta + i\gamma) \,,$$

leading to

$$L_{11} = \exp(i\alpha)/R_{11}$$
$$L_{22} = \exp(i\gamma)/R_{11}$$
$$R_{22} = \exp(-i\alpha + i\beta)R_{11} ,$$

with R_{11} arbitrary. Choosing R_{11} equal to $\exp\left[\frac{1}{2}i(\alpha - \beta)\right]$ leads to

$$\begin{pmatrix} \exp\left[\frac{1}{2}i(\alpha + \beta)\right] & 0 \\ 0 & \exp\left[\frac{1}{2}i(-\alpha + \beta + 2\gamma)\right] \end{pmatrix}$$
$$\begin{pmatrix} \cos(\theta) & \sin(\theta) \\ -\sin(\theta) & \cos(\theta) \end{pmatrix} \begin{pmatrix} \exp\left[\frac{1}{2}i(\alpha - \beta)\right] & 0 \\ 0 & \exp\left[\frac{1}{2}i(-\alpha + \beta)\right] \end{pmatrix} .$$

Further decomposition of the first matrix, in other words

$$\begin{pmatrix} \exp\left[\frac{1}{2}i(\beta + \gamma)\right] & 0 \\ 0 & \exp\left[\frac{1}{2}i(\beta + \gamma)\right] \end{pmatrix} \begin{pmatrix} \exp\left[\frac{1}{2}i(\alpha - \gamma)\right] & 0 \\ 0 & \exp\left[-\frac{1}{2}i(\alpha - \gamma)\right] \end{pmatrix}$$
$$\begin{pmatrix} \cos(\theta) & \sin(\theta) \\ -\sin(\theta) & \cos(\theta) \end{pmatrix} \begin{pmatrix} \exp\left[\frac{1}{2}i(\alpha - \beta)\right] & 0 \\ 0 & \exp\left[-\frac{1}{2}i(\alpha - \beta)\right] \end{pmatrix} ,$$

leads to a bonus: the standard decomposition of $U(2)$:

$$\begin{pmatrix} \exp(i\omega) & 0 \\ 0 & \exp(i\omega) \end{pmatrix}$$
$$\begin{pmatrix} \exp(i\phi) & 0 \\ 0 & \exp(-i\phi) \end{pmatrix} \begin{pmatrix} \cos(\theta) & \sin(\theta) \\ -\sin(\theta) & \cos(\theta) \end{pmatrix} \begin{pmatrix} \exp(i\psi) & 0 \\ 0 & \exp(-i\psi) \end{pmatrix} ,$$

where – by the way – the last three matrices form the standard decomposition of $SU(2)$.

Exercise 7.5

$$\begin{pmatrix} a & b \\ c & d \end{pmatrix}^2 = \begin{pmatrix} 0 & 1 \\ 1 & 0 \end{pmatrix}$$

leads to

- $b(a + d) = 1$ and $c(a + d) = 1$ and therefore to $c = b$ and $a + d \neq 0$.
- $a^2 + bc = 0$ and $d^2 + bc = 0$, and thus (taking the previous two results into account) $a = d = \pm ib$.

Substituting the last result in the first equation gives $\pm 2ib^2 = 1$ or $b^2 = \pm i/2$, leading to $b = \pm\frac{1}{\sqrt{2}}\frac{1 \pm i}{\sqrt{2}} = \frac{1}{2}(\pm 1 \pm i)$.
Thus there are four different square roots:

$$\pm\frac{1}{2}\begin{pmatrix} 1 + i & 1 - i \\ 1 - i & 1 + i \end{pmatrix} \quad \text{and} \quad \pm\frac{1}{2}\begin{pmatrix} 1 - i & 1 + i \\ 1 + i & 1 - i \end{pmatrix} .$$

All are unitary. All have determinants equal to $\pm i$.

Exercise 7.6

$$\begin{pmatrix} a & b \\ c & d \end{pmatrix}^2 = \begin{pmatrix} 1 & 0 \\ 0 & 1 \end{pmatrix}$$

leads to

- $a^2 + bc = 1$ and $d^2 + bc = 1$ and thus $a^2 = d^2$; that is, $a = \pm d$.
- $b(a + d) = 0$ and $c(a + d) = 0$, and therefore to either $c = b = 0$ or $d = -a$.

The set of square roots therefore consists of:

- The set of two matrices

$$\pm \begin{pmatrix} 1 & 0 \\ 0 & 1 \end{pmatrix},$$

both with determinants equal to 1, and
- The four-dimensional space of matrices

$$\begin{pmatrix} a & b \\ (1 - a^2)/b & -a \end{pmatrix},$$

all with determinants equal to -1.

The set of unitary square roots consists of:

- The set of two matrices

$$\pm \begin{pmatrix} 1 & 0 \\ 0 & 1 \end{pmatrix},$$

both with determinants equal to 1, and
- The two-dimensional space of matrices

$$\begin{pmatrix} \cos(\theta) & \sin(\theta)\exp(i\alpha) \\ \sin(\theta)\exp(-i\alpha) & -\cos(\theta) \end{pmatrix},$$

all with determinants equal to -1.

Exercise 7.7

$$p_1\bar{p}_1 + p_2\bar{p}_2 = \omega\bar{\omega} + \bar{\omega}\omega = 2\frac{1+i}{2}\frac{1-i}{2} = \tfrac{1}{2}(1+i)(1-i) = \tfrac{1}{2}2 = 1.$$

Exercise 7.8

$$\begin{pmatrix} 1 & 0 & 0 & 0 \\ 0 & 0 & 1 & 0 \\ 0 & 1 & 0 & 0 \\ 0 & 0 & 0 & 1 \end{pmatrix}^{1/2} = \begin{pmatrix} 1 & 0 & 0 & 0 \\ 0 & \omega & \bar{\omega} & 0 \\ 0 & \bar{\omega} & \omega & 0 \\ 0 & 0 & 0 & 1 \end{pmatrix}.$$

Exercise 7.9

The group consists of $\pm\varphi$, $\pm i\varphi$, $\pm\nu$, $\pm i\nu$, $\pm\gamma$, $\pm i\gamma$, $\pm z$, and $\pm iz$. Thus the order is 16.

Solutions for Chapter 8

Exercise 8.1

```
if (x < 1000) then x := 0.1*x
                else if (x < 10000) then x := 0.3*x - 200
                                    else x := 0.5*x - 2200
                fi (x < 2800)
fi (x < 100)
```

Solutions for Appendix C

Exercise C.1

$$f = (A_3 \text{ NAND } A_1) \text{ NAND}[(A_1 \text{ NAND } 1) \text{ NAND } A_2]$$
$$= \overline{\overline{A_3 A_1} \, \overline{[\overline{A_1} A_2]}}$$
$$= \overline{\overline{A_3 A_1}} + \overline{\overline{[\overline{A_1} A_2]}}$$
$$= A_3 A_1 + \overline{A_1} A_2 .$$

If we denote the third output of the first TOFFOLI block by X, then

$$X = (1 \text{ AND } A_3) \text{ XOR } A_2 = A_3 \oplus A_2 .$$

If we denote the third output of the second TOFFOLI block by Y, then

$$Y = (A_1 \text{ AND } X) \text{ XOR } A_3 = A_1 X \oplus A_3 = A_1(A_2 \oplus A_3) \oplus A_3$$
$$= A_1 A_2 \oplus A_1 A_3 \oplus A_3 .$$

We finally obtain the third output of the third TOFFOLI block:

$$f = (1 \text{ AND } Y) \text{ XOR } X = Y \oplus X = (A_2 \oplus A_3) \oplus (A_1 A_2 \oplus A_1 A_3 \oplus A_3)$$
$$= A_2 \oplus A_1 A_2 \oplus A_1 A_3$$
$$= (1 \oplus A_1) A_2 \oplus A_1 A_3$$
$$= \overline{A_1} A_2 \oplus A_1 A_3$$
$$= \overline{A_1} A_2 + A_1 A_3 .$$

Solutions for Appendix D

Exercise D.1

$$N = w!$$
$$B = w(w-1)/2$$
$$L = \frac{\log(N)}{\log(B)} = \frac{\log(w!)}{\log[w(w-1)/2]} \approx \frac{\left(w+\frac{1}{2}\right)\log(w) - w}{\log(w) + \log(w-1) - \log(2)}$$
$$\approx \frac{w\log(w)}{2\log(w)} = \frac{w}{2} \; .$$

Solutions for Appendix E

Exercise E.1

If matrix A has a constant column sum a, and matrix B has a constant column sum b, then matrix $C = AB$ has a constant column sum $c = ab$. Indeed,

$$\sum_{i=1}^{n} C_{ij} = \sum_{i=1}^{n}\sum_{k=1}^{n} A_{ik} B_{kj} = \sum_{k=1}^{n}\sum_{i=1}^{n} A_{ik} B_{kj} = \sum_{k=1}^{n} B_{kj} \sum_{i=1}^{n} A_{ik}$$
$$= \sum_{k=1}^{n} B_{kj} a = a \sum_{k=1}^{n} B_{kj} = ab \; .$$

The situation is analogous for the row sums $\sum_{j=1}^{n} C_{ij}$.

Exercise E.2

We decompose the flow matrix F into two permutation matrices:

$$F = P + Q \; .$$

A possible algorithm is as follows:

- If $F_{ij} = 0$, then $P_{ij} = Q_{ij} = 0$.
- If $F_{ij} = 2$, then $P_{ij} = Q_{ij} = 1$.
- If $F_{ij} = 1$, then either $P_{ij} = 0$ and $Q_{ij} = 1$ or $P_{ij} = 1$ and $Q_{ij} = 0$.

The choice in the last case happens as follows. Entries F_{ij} that are equal to 1 are necessarily located on closed paths with right angles. In our example there are two such paths:

$$
\begin{pmatrix}
1 & 1 & & & \\
1 & & 1 & & \\
 & & & & \\
 & & & & \\
 & 1 & 1 & & \\
 & & & & \\
 & & & &
\end{pmatrix}
\quad \text{and} \quad
\begin{pmatrix}
 & & & & \\
 & & & & \\
 & 1 & & 1 & \\
 & & & & \\
 & 1 & & 1 &
\end{pmatrix}.
$$

We then follow each path, alternately choosing $P_{ij} = 0, Q_{ij} = 1$ and $P_{ij} = 1$, $Q_{ij} = 0$. If we start each path in its upper left corner, the latter choice leads to

$$
\begin{pmatrix}
1 & 0 & 1 & 0 & 0 & 0 & 0 \\
1 & 0 & 0 & 1 & 0 & 0 & 0 \\
0 & 0 & 0 & 0 & 0 & 2 & 0 \\
0 & 0 & 0 & 0 & 1 & 0 & 1 \\
0 & 2 & 0 & 0 & 0 & 0 & 0 \\
0 & 0 & 1 & 1 & 0 & 0 & 0 \\
0 & 0 & 0 & 0 & 1 & 0 & 1
\end{pmatrix}
=
\begin{pmatrix}
1 & 0 & 0 & 0 & 0 & 0 & 0 \\
0 & 0 & 0 & 1 & 0 & 0 & 0 \\
0 & 0 & 0 & 0 & 0 & 1 & 0 \\
0 & 0 & 0 & 0 & 1 & 0 & 0 \\
0 & 1 & 0 & 0 & 0 & 0 & 0 \\
0 & 0 & 1 & 0 & 0 & 0 & 0 \\
0 & 0 & 0 & 0 & 0 & 0 & 1
\end{pmatrix}
$$

$$
+
\begin{pmatrix}
0 & 0 & 1 & 0 & 0 & 0 & 0 \\
1 & 0 & 0 & 0 & 0 & 0 & 0 \\
0 & 0 & 0 & 0 & 0 & 1 & 0 \\
0 & 0 & 0 & 0 & 0 & 0 & 1 \\
0 & 1 & 0 & 0 & 0 & 0 & 0 \\
0 & 0 & 0 & 1 & 0 & 0 & 0 \\
0 & 0 & 0 & 0 & 1 & 0 & 0
\end{pmatrix}.
$$

Exercise E.3

Because, for each path, there are two possible choices for the upper left corner, we have four possible solutions to the previous exercise.

Exercise E.4

Any 2×2 matrix with all of its line sums equal to p takes the form

$$
\begin{pmatrix}
a & p - a \\
p - a & a
\end{pmatrix}.
$$

Trivial and unique decomposition into p permutation matrices yields:

$$
a \begin{pmatrix} 1 & 0 \\ 0 & 1 \end{pmatrix} + (p - a) \begin{pmatrix} 0 & 1 \\ 1 & 0 \end{pmatrix}.
$$

Exercise E.5

Any 3×3 matrix with all of its line sums equal to p takes the form

$$
\begin{pmatrix}
a & b & p - a - b \\
c & d & p - c - d \\
p - a - c & p - b - d & a + b + c + d - p
\end{pmatrix}.
$$

One of these nine numbers is the smallest, for example d. We apply

$$
\begin{pmatrix}
a & b & p - a - b \\
c & d & p - c - d \\
p - a - c & p - b - d & a + b + c + d - p
\end{pmatrix} =
$$

$$
d \begin{pmatrix}
1 & 0 & 0 \\
0 & 1 & 0 \\
0 & 0 & 1
\end{pmatrix} +
\begin{pmatrix}
a - d & b & p - a - b \\
c & 0 & p - c - d \\
p - a - c & p - b - d & a + b + c - p
\end{pmatrix}.
$$

The last matrix can be decomposed as

$$
(a - d) \begin{pmatrix}
1 & 0 & 0 \\
0 & 0 & 1 \\
0 & 1 & 0
\end{pmatrix} + (p - a - b) \begin{pmatrix}
0 & 0 & 1 \\
1 & 0 & 0 \\
0 & 0 & 1
\end{pmatrix}
$$

$$
+ (p - a - c) \begin{pmatrix}
0 & 1 & 0 \\
0 & 0 & 1 \\
1 & 0 & 0
\end{pmatrix} + (a + b + c - p) \begin{pmatrix}
0 & 1 & 0 \\
1 & 0 & 0 \\
0 & 0 & 1
\end{pmatrix}.
$$

The latter step is unique, but the former is not.

When the smallest matrix entry is not in the $(2, 2)$ position, decomposition is completely analogous.

Exercise E.6

We take one of the Birkhoff decompositions of the flow matrix:

$$
\begin{pmatrix}
0 & 2 & 3 \\
2 & 2 & 1 \\
3 & 1 & 1
\end{pmatrix} =
\begin{pmatrix}
0 & 0 & 1 \\
1 & 0 & 0 \\
0 & 1 & 0
\end{pmatrix} +
\begin{pmatrix}
0 & 0 & 1 \\
0 & 1 & 0 \\
1 & 0 & 0
\end{pmatrix}
$$

$$
+ \begin{pmatrix}
0 & 1 & 0 \\
1 & 0 & 0 \\
0 & 0 & 1
\end{pmatrix} +
\begin{pmatrix}
0 & 0 & 1 \\
0 & 1 & 0 \\
1 & 0 & 0
\end{pmatrix} +
\begin{pmatrix}
0 & 1 & 0 \\
0 & 0 & 1 \\
1 & 0 & 0
\end{pmatrix}.
$$

The first (horizontal) step is the difficult step: we must ensure that each of the five columns ends up containing exactly one heart, one spade, and one diamond. To achieve this, each permutation matrix tells us the suit order of the corresponding column. For example, the first permutation matrix tells us that the first column needs a diamond at the top, a heart in the middle, and a spade at the bottom:

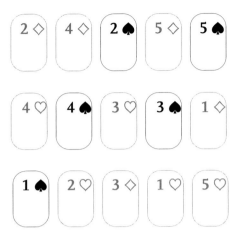

In the second (vertical) step, we ensure that, in each of the five columns, the cards arrive in the proper order: heart at the top, spade in the middle, and diamond at the bottom:

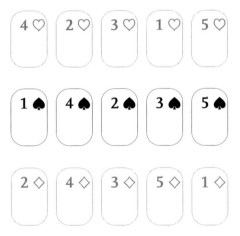

The third step is trivial: arranging each of the three rows in the proper horizontal order: 1 , 2 , 3 , 4 , and 5 .

Exercise E.7

In the first 'horizontal permutation', you are allowed to leave the upper row untouched. In the lower row, you permute the cards such that each gray card comes under a black card, for example:

K	K	2	7	6	5	2	4	4	9	3	8	3
7	1	Q	J	8	9	10	5	Q	10	J	6	1

In the 'vertical permutation', make sure that the gray cards arrive in the upper row and the black cards in the lower row:

7	K	2	J	6	5	10	4	Q	9	3	8	1
K	1	Q	7	8	9	2	5	4	10	J	6	3

As usual, the final 'horizontal permutation' is trivial: arranging each of the two rows in the proper increasing order.

Exercise E.8

–

Solutions for Appendix F

Exercise F.1

Here, for convenience, we will immediately divide by $k \log(2)$, such that all results are automatically expressed in bits:

$$\sigma = \frac{1}{\log(2)} \sum_{m=1}^{18} -p_m \log(p_m) \approx 3.36$$

$$s = \frac{1}{\log(2)} \left[q_1 \sum_{j=1}^{4} -\frac{p_{1j}}{q_1} \log\left(\frac{p_{1j}}{q_1}\right) + q_2 \sum_{j=1}^{6} -\frac{p_{2j}}{q_2} \log\left(\frac{p_{2j}}{q_2}\right) + \right.$$

$$\left. q_3 \sum_{j=1}^{4} -\frac{p_{3j}}{q_3} \log\left(\frac{p_{3j}}{q_3}\right) + q_4 \sum_{j=1}^{4} -\frac{p_{4j}}{q_4} \log\left(\frac{p_{4j}}{q_4}\right) \right]$$

$$\approx 1.96$$

where

$$q_1 = p_1 + p_2 + p_3 + p_4 = 0.10$$
$$q_2 = p_5 + p_6 + p_7 + p_8 + p_9 + p_{10} = 0.19$$
$$q_3 = p_{11} + p_{12} + p_{13} + p_{14} = 0.05$$
$$q_4 = p_{15} + p_{16} + p_{17} + p_{18} = 0.66$$

$$S = \frac{1}{\log(2)} \sum_{i=1}^{4} -q_i \log(q_i) \approx 1.40 \ .$$

Thus,

$$S + s \approx 1.40 + 1.96 = 3.36 \approx \sigma \,.$$

Exercise F.2

We proceed in an analogous manner to the previous exercise, although we take into account

$$\lim_{x \to 0} x \log(x) = 0 \,.$$

We obtain

$$S + s \approx 1.40 + 1.93 = 3.33 \approx \sigma \,.$$

Solutions for Appendix G

Exercise G.1

$$\det \begin{pmatrix} \cos(\theta) - z & \sin(\theta) \\ -\sin(\theta) & \cos(\theta) - z \end{pmatrix} = z^2 - 2\cos(\theta)z + 1$$

$$\det \begin{pmatrix} 1 - z & 0 \\ 0 & 1 - z \end{pmatrix} = (z - 1)^2$$

$$\det \begin{pmatrix} \omega - z & \overline{\omega} \\ \overline{\omega} & \omega - z \end{pmatrix} = z^2 - 2\omega z + i = (z - 1)(z - i)$$

$$\det \begin{pmatrix} -z & 1 \\ 1 & -z \end{pmatrix} = z^2 - 1 = (z - 1)(z + 1)$$

$$\det \begin{pmatrix} \overline{\omega} - z & \omega \\ \omega & \overline{\omega} - z \end{pmatrix} = z^2 - 2\overline{\omega}z - i = (z - 1)(z + i)$$

$$\det \begin{pmatrix} \tfrac{1}{2} + \tfrac{1}{2}\exp(i\theta) - z & \tfrac{1}{2} - \tfrac{1}{2}\exp(i\theta) \\ \tfrac{1}{2} - \tfrac{1}{2}\exp(i\theta) & \tfrac{1}{2} + \tfrac{1}{2}\exp(i\theta) - z \end{pmatrix}$$
$$= z^2 - (1 + \exp(i\theta))z + \exp(i\theta) = (z - 1)(z - \exp(i\theta))$$

$$\det \begin{pmatrix} \tfrac{1}{\sqrt{2}} - z & \tfrac{1}{\sqrt{2}} \\ \tfrac{1}{\sqrt{2}} & -\tfrac{1}{\sqrt{2}} - z \end{pmatrix} = z^2 - 1 = (z - 1)(z + 1) \,.$$

Index

Reversible Computing. Alexis De Vos
Copyright © 2010 WILEY-VCH Verlag GmbH & Co. KGaA, Weinheim
ISBN: 978-3-527-40992-1